M000248450

Monk's Music

Monk's Music

THELONIOUS MONK AND JAZZ HISTORY IN THE MAKING

Gabriel Solis

UNIVERSITY OF CALIFORNIA PRESS

BERKELEY LOS ANGELES LONDON

University of California Press, one of the most distinguished
university presses in the United States, enriches lives around
the world by advancing scholarship in the humanities, social sciences, and natural sciences. Its activities are supported by the UC Press Foundation and by philanthropic
contributions from individuals and institutions. For more
information, visit www.ucpress.edu.

University of California Press
Berkeley and Los Angeles, California

University of California Press, Ltd.
London, England

An earlier version of chapter 2 appeared in *The Musical
Quarterly* 86, no. 1 (Spring 2002): 82–116, published by Oxford University Press, copyright © 2002 by Oxford University Press. Reprinted by permission.

Library of Congress Cataloging-in-Publication Data

Solis, Gabriel, 1972– .
    Monk's music : Thelonious Monk and jazz history in the
making / Gabriel Solis.
        p.   cm. — (Roth Family Foundation Music in
America imprint)
    Includes bibliographical references and index.
    ISBN 978–0-520–25200–4 (cloth : alk. paper)
    ISBN 978–0-520–25201–1 (pbk. : alk. paper)
    1. Monk, Thelonious—Criticism and interpretation.
2. Monk, Thelonious—Influence.   3. Jazz—History and
criticism.   I. Title.

ML417.M846S55   2008
786.2165092—dc22   2006102231
[B]

Manufactured in the United States of America

17   16   15   14   13   12   11   10   09   08
10   9   8   7   6   5   4   3   2   1

This book is printed on Cascades Enviro 100, a 100% post-
consumer-waste, recycled, de-inked fiber. FSC recycled certified and processed chlorine free. It is acid-free, Ecologo
certified, and manufactured by BioGas energy.

FOR ELLEN, COLEMAN, AND ISABELLA,
WHO GIVE ME REASONS TO WORK AND
REASONS TO PLAY

CONTENTS

ACKNOWLEDGMENTS

AT THE END OF WRITING A BOOK LIKE THIS—or any book, I suspect—one feels that it represents not just a bit of research and interpretation, but in some way the whole of one's life for a period of years. All the influences on one's life are in some way responsible for the final shape the book takes. To say that the book couldn't have been written without the help of others, then, hardly seems up to the task of acknowledging one's debts. There are specific people I want to thank, but first I want to include a word of gratitude to those I have missed for one reason or another. Although throughout this book I have cited the authors on whom I draw most directly, I cannot say that I have recognized every aspect of this work that owes something to the influence of others. To do so would be impossible because in many instances those influences have become too much a part of me for me even to recognize them. Mikhail Bakhtin's statement that "the word in language is half someone else's" is a theme of sorts in this book. I should note its centrality in another way as well: this book, as an "utterance" (in the sense Bakhtin uses the term), is at least half others'. I have taken words and ideas from a multitude of sources, including, but not limited to, published works, and attempted to "populate them with my own intentions"—hopefully not in contradiction to their authors' intentions, but undoubtedly in ways those people may not have expected.

First I would like to recognize the thanks I owe the musicians who participated in this project. Andrew Bemkey, Kenny Drew Jr., Steve Lacy, Joe Lovano, Jim Leff, Chip McNeill, T.S. Monk, Fred Hersch, Danilo Perez, Bob Porcelli, Ben Reilly, Roswell Rudd, Don Sickler, Michael Weiss, Jessica Williams, and Randy Weston all took significant time out of their schedules to talk with me about Monk, and many others shared their thoughts in passing. In a sense this whole book should be read as an acknowledgment of them—of their music, their knowledge, and their help. Without their candor and willingness to consider the issues I asked about in interviews and informal conversations—and occasionally their readiness to tell me when they thought I was on the wrong track—I could not have begun, much less completed, the following work.

I am grateful to the Wenner-Gren Foundation for giving me a Richard C. Hunt Fellowship, which provided me a crucial semester's leave during the process of revising the manuscript. I am also grateful to the University of Illinois, which provided a number of small grants to support research assistance and travel, without which completing this book would have been much harder.

I have been immensely fortunate to have had the support, encouragement, and critical eye of many, many scholars in the process of writing this book. Their help has impacted the book in ways that citations really cannot begin to account for. Ingrid Monson, my advisor as a Ph.D. student at Washington University, has remained a primary influence on my thinking and listening; her help in all aspects of academic life has been indispensable. Travis Jackson, Scott DeVeaux, Sherrie Tucker, Robin D. G. Kelley, Susan Oehler, and Albin Zak all provided commentary and advice as I wrote the book and presented bits of it at conferences. I appreciate Zak's manifesto: "If you have a good idea, say it as plainly as you can so people can get it; if you don't have a good idea, no amount of academic jargon will cover it up." I have tried to take his words to heart. I am thankful to Guthrie Ramsey Jr., Gary Tomlinson, Crystal Judd, Carol Muller, and the cohort of graduate students at the University of Pennsylvania who made my life interesting and gave me a chance as I began thinking about how to put this book together. I am immensely grateful to my colleagues in musicology at the University of Illinois, Charlie Capwell, Donna Buchanan, Tom Turino, Bruno Nettl, Isabel Wong, John Hill, William Kinderman, Gayle Magee, Jeff Magee, Tom Ward, Christina Bashford, and Katherine Syer, who have provided constant, often surprising guidance along the way. I am in debt to the African American Studies and Research Program at the University of

Illinois for providing me with a second home in the university and for creating a reading group that supported me through many revisions of the book. I am particularly grateful to Cynthia Oliver, who read chapter drafts and gave incisive suggestions. I thank the graduate students in musicology at the University of Illinois, who have pushed my thinking in a variety of interesting ways, and who won't allow me to be intellectually lazy. I am particularly grateful to my research assistants over the years, Sylvia Bruinders, Molly Cryderman, and Jenny Fraser.

The editorial team at the University of California Press who worked on this project have earned my thanks over and over again: Mary Francis, for seeing the value in the clunky original manuscript, and for shepherding it through the process of review and publication; the four readers whose comments were thoughtful, critical, and supportive; Kalicia Pivirotto, who made sure I's were dotted and T's crossed; and Lynn Meinhardt, who cast a keen eye on words and music. Without their help this book would never have been completed.

Finally, I would like to thank the many friends and relations whose support, interest, and encouragement provided me with sustenance through good and bad. My wife and children, Ellen, Coleman, and Isabella Solis; my family, George Osner, Elise Osner, Myrtle Osner, Jeremy Osner, Miriam Osner, Blythe Sawyer, Ellen Kahaner, Craig Sawyer, Fikisha Cumbo, and Malik Cumbo; and The Friends: Kelly Ramirez, Xlc Joloronde, Chris Banks, Nathan Stinus Fredenberg, Kathy Stinus Fredenberg, Nicole Leibon, Greg Leibon, Melissa Medeiros, Erika Adams, Chris Adams, Jenny Ortman, Chris Hansen, Glenn Mejia, Jason Berg, and Patrick Vargas. I also reserve a special thank you for Kristin Tennant, who endured and even appeared to enjoy my incessant questions about semantics—this in spite of the fact that I can not accept an answer without further argumentation, even when she is (as she seems always to be) entirely right the first time.

Introduction

Perhaps the enjoyment of music is always suffused with past experience; for me at least, this is true.

. . . In the swift change of American society in which the meanings of one's origin are so quickly lost, one of the chief values of living with music lies in its power to give us an orientation in time. In doing so, it gives significance to all those indefinable aspects of experience which nevertheless make us what we are.

RALPH ELLISON
"Living with Music"

WHEN THELONIOUS MONK BEGAN RECORDING with Alfred Lion and Francis Wolff for the Blue Note record label in 1947, he had already made a permanent impression on the sound of jazz and the course it had taken to that point. As house pianist for jam sessions at the Harlem nightspot Minton's Playhouse, he had shared with other musicians a very personal sense of time, approach to harmony, and understanding of what the music could be. Though his own style was never like that of the bop pioneers, his ideas permeated their playing, and on that basis he can reasonably be said to have directly or indirectly affected every jazz musician who has played since. Nevertheless, at the end of the 1940s, despite recognition by many of his peers, Monk was still relatively obscure as a cultural figure. The Blue Note recordings were his first as a leader, he had been almost completely ignored by the jazz press, and it looked as though he might never be known as widely as his contemporaries Dizzy Gillespie and Charlie Parker. A decade and a half later, Monk had recorded numerous albums on four labels, the last of which, Columbia, was a major recording company with the budget, economic networks, and will to mass market his music in the United States and abroad. Still, he was a controversial figure. Though he was the second African American jazz musician to grace the cover of *Time* magazine (after Duke Ellington), and the third jazz musician so honored, he was still vulnerable to negative polemics by critics who were not fond of his music. With his retreat into seclusion and acoustic jazz's waning fortunes in the 1970s, it was not clear whether he would even be remembered by the next generation of Americans.

Today, three decades later, there is no question that Monk has become an icon of jazz history and American culture in general. This is made abundantly clear by a glance at the LexisNexis database of English-language newspapers. A search of the database for Monk's name in the 1990s, the period for which the database is most complete, returns thousands of citations. What is interesting about these references is that few—less than 5 percent, by my informal count—are from articles about Monk or his music. There was, of course, little new to report about Monk in the 1990s, given that Monk had been deceased for eight years by 1990 and most of the major reissues of his recordings had already been released. Rather than dealing with Monk himself, then, the references are overwhelmingly of the "X is the Thelonious Monk of Y" type, with "X" being a musician, or, less commonly, some other sort of artist, and "Y" being the genre in which that artist works. The slipperiness and imprecision in this sort of reference demonstrates Monk's position. His name is invoked as a vague but mutually understood referent to confer some cultural or artistic authority, and often to suggest countercultural hipness or noncomformism. Moreover, and equally (if not more) importantly, Monk is now commonly noted as an influence by jazz musicians from across the spectrum of the music's styles and communities.

This book explores Monk's legacy, looking at how and why musicians from successive generations have reacted and responded to that legacy. In a sense, then, it is a book of reception history, but of a particular sort. There is a place for the consideration of critical reception—the work of jazz critics, historians, and so forth—in constructing Monk's legacy, but the primary focus of this book is instead on performers and performance. Monk's legacy is central to this book, but it also stands as a case study for larger questions about influence in jazz and the concept's significance for jazz historiography. Because of the particular nature of jazz, the realm of performance has always been a space for the exercise of collective memory, of historical imagination. The music is an oral tradition based on thousands of hours of interactive, collective creation and intergenerational learning, but it is one that came into being along with and has been nurtured by recordings and the U.S. music industry. As a result, it has a long and specifically historical memory, at times nostalgic, at times celebratory, at times critical, but always concerned with maintaining the tradition.

Work on this book began with my observation that the common practice of naming those who have influenced individual jazz musicians, especially those that obtain between musicians of two different generations, often fall short in making sense of my experience of listening to those musicians. While it clearly explains something about the influenced musician's style, I always end up with more questions than answers by contemplating the nature of influence. This led me to consider what it might mean to think of musical influence in a way that captures more of my listening experience and that bears in mind the details of musicians' understanding of that influence. In a sense, I intended to examine the process through which jazz musicians learn from prior generations, explore the traces this process leaves on their own music, and investigate the ways this learning gets translated into the language of influence. The issues Ralph Ellison suggested in "Living with Music" (1995) frame this investigation: that the interpenetration of past and present is fundamental to the power of musical experience, and that it is in this experience of time that we become ourselves.

Monk's Music, as I conceived it, builds directly on Paul Berliner's and Ingrid Monson's work, extending themes central to *Thinking in Jazz* (Berliner 1994) and *Saying Something* (Monson 1996). I wanted to further refine some of the fundamental ideas these writers had about jazz as sound and social practice by considering the place of history in this music through an ethnographic orientation.[1] Thelonious Monk and the influence other musicians have cultivated through listening to and playing his music serves as a case study for the larger questions because of his ubiquity in the 1980s and 1990s. Ultimately, the project has destabilized my impression of influence and has allowed me to engage in ongoing discussions about the production of history in everyday life and the understanding of culture as a process, as well as about jazz and its place in American society.

Centrally, this book is an attempt to answer the question of how Thelonious Monk—once an enigmatic and controversial figure on the fringes of the jazz world, and now lauded as one of the greatest members of the music's canon—has become part of jazz history. The question is not precisely how was the movement from periphery to center effected. That process happened largely during Monk's lifetime and is best addressed in a biography, of which there are a number and more in progress.

The main biographical works on Monk currently in print are Thomas Fitterling's *Thelonious Monk: His Life and Music,* Leslie Gourse's *Straight,*

No Chaser: The Life and Genius of Thelonious Monk, and Laurent De Wilde's *Monk.* Fitterling's book, originally published in German, was the first of the three and is altogether straightforward. The biographical portion is brief, and to judge from the bibliography (there are no citations in the text), it is based entirely on profiles, interviews, and other materials published about Monk while he was alive. More time and energy appear to have been spent on the second and third parts of the book, which consist of Fitterling's often-insightful analyses of Monk's style as a composer and pianist and an annotated, selective Monk discography. Gourse's book is a more thorough attempt at a detailed biography. To the extent that Monk's music is discussed, the analysis comes from other sources, as Gourse herself admits (Gourse 1997, x). Gourse augments her printed sources with many interviews, noted in a general way at the end of each chapter. De Wilde's is the most peculiar of the three, generally the most poetic, and the least useful from an academic standpoint. It is characterized by passages such as the following: "From the beginning, Monk dwelt with death. It perched on his shoulder, like Socrates' demon, and urged him to cast farther the nets of his spirit. Death overwhelmed him and obsessed him. He saw it at work all around him, cutting down the great musical minds of the time" (De Wilde 1997, 210). As evocative as the language is, any attempt to parse its meaning is ultimately frustrated. Nonetheless, perhaps because De Wilde is a respectable pianist, there are lovely passages of musical description in this book that Monk fans may enjoy. Robin D. G. Kelley is currently finishing a biography of Monk that, given the rigor and brilliance of his previous work, and given his unprecedented access to Nellie Monk and Monk's papers, promises to replace all three prior works.[2] In addition to these, Chris Sheridan's *Brilliant Corners: A Bio-Discography of Thelonious Monk* offers a brief biography, comprehensive discography, and a day-by-day listing of Monk's performances and studio engagements.

This book, by contrast, focuses more on the question of how Monk became historical, that is, on understanding the process whereby Monk has survived as a presence in the music. Answering that question, if only partially and for the moment, has required drawing on diverse sources and resources. An ethnographic engagement with the jazz "scene"—with its musicians, audiences, promoters, and others—is the most important primary source for the concepts and analyses in this work. Thus, my research consisted of attendance at live performances, formal interviews, and less formal conversations with musicians and others in the scene. I have also drawn heavily on the various writings that are an important part of that world, including liner notes, published interviews, memoirs, and critical and scholarly texts devoted to the musicians and their recordings. Finally, I have used this material in a dialogue with theories and models from a number of scholarly disciplines, most notably ethnomusicology, anthropology, African American cultural studies, and historiography. I describe this as a dialogue because my understanding of those theories and models has functioned as a lens through which to understand the primary material, while at the same time I have allowed the primary material to guide my developing understanding and at times suggest a critique of the theoretical materials.

Mikhail Bakhtin, writing on the fundamentally relational quality of linguistic expression, writes, "The word in language is half someone else's. It becomes 'one's own' only when the speaker populates it with his own intention, his own accent, when he appropriates the word, adapting it to his own semantic and expressive intention" (Bakhtin 1981, 293). Henry Louis Gates Jr. picks up on this conceptual thread in his seminal work *The Signifying Monkey* (1988), constructing a theory of African American literature around the theme of appropriation and revision found in black vernacular language use and its expression in literature. Ingrid Monson, building on both of these scholars' works, opens a space in jazz scholarship for the consideration of the ways aesthetic and sociocultural issues are creatively addressed by musicians on the bandstand and in the recording studio (Monson 1995, 1999).

In *What Is This Thing Called Jazz?* Eric Porter makes an interesting intervention, complicating studies of jazz that take "signifyin(g)" as their primary metacommunicative mode by positing that jazz musicians have been important not only as producers of music, but also as commentators and theorists about music and its place in social life. Porter suggests that the incorporation of Gates's ideas from *The Signifying Monkey* into jazz studies has its limitations, claiming that "even astute, politically committed scholars working in African American or black intellectual and cultural history, some of whom describe black music as an intellectual activity, seldom devote much attention to musicians' ideas, even when analyzing the meaning and significance of their music" (Porter 2002, xvii).

It is into this ongoing conversation about expressivity in human life (and, in particular, in jazz in contemporary America) that I wish to insert this work. This book presents a case study of how jazz musicians exercise what I think of as a "historical imagination" as a fundamental part of discourse and musical practice. Jazz is a multifaceted practice for musicians. It involves integrating considerations of solo expression within a group dynamic, creative improvisation within numerous parameters, including the given harmonies of a piece of music, the generic style of the performing group, the ongoing microinteraction between soloist and rhythm section, and the exigencies of the performance venue. Within and in addition to all of these concerns, the music is "suffused with past experience," and both playing and listening involve constructing an "orientation in time," as Ralph Ellison has described (Ellison 1995, 197, 198). In order to explore this issue, I have focused on contemporary jazz musicians' experiences of Monk as both listeners and performers, looking at the ways their discussions of his performances and their own performances of his music express a way of integrating past and present in their music and their lives.

What does it mean to say that these performances and the talk surrounding them are "historical"? In a limited sense it means that by improvising, versioning, troping, and signifyin(g) on Monk's music, jazz musicians are in a sense reflecting and constructing a history of their music. This is a personal history in the sense that it is a subjective interpretation of the music of the past and what it might be in the present (and through that interpretation, a construction of how the performer might fit into that musical history). That this view of jazz performance owes much to Gates's work should be no surprise; it is interesting to note that it is also remarkably similar to the novelist Milan Kundera's assertion that "every novelist's work contains an implicit vision of the history of the novel, an idea of what the novel is" (Kundera 1988, iii).

In a more expansive sense, hearing this material as historical means crafting an analysis that moves between levels of meaning, seeing musicians' interactions not only with a music history, but with a social history as well—that is, with the functioning of power in social and cultural contexts over time. While these personal histories are not bound by the same standards of proof as is academic history, their intentions are remarkably similar. Kundera, again discussing literature (this time an interpretation of Ernest Hemingway's story "Hills Like White Elephants"), argues that such a historical interpretation of creative work is bound to reduce the work, to misrepresent it by viewing it as univocally historical, by missing its aesthetic dimensions and its inherent polyvocality and ambiguity (Kundera 1995, 142–46). Perhaps this is true all too often, but it is neither necessarily nor uniformly true. An analysis of jazz that ignores either the aesthetics or the social implications of the music is bound to tell only half the story. It should be borne in mind in this regard that the two categories feed each other, help give one another voice, at least in the context of this music. While any number of socially motivated performances have been attempted and many recorded, only those that speak to the jazz audience's aesthetic sensibilities, like Max Roach's *Freedom Now Suite,* have registered on a significant level.

That said, in the American context of racial and gendered interaction, any jazz performance of aesthetic merit is potentially political at some level. Over the years, for instance, jazz has often contested the logic of white supremacy with an image of African American humanity. Even when white musicians play for white audiences, race is often present in the background, as most Americans generally think of jazz as a music with its roots in African American culture. Also, as Eric Porter and Sherrie Tucker have eloquently argued recently, performances, especially those by female musicians, may also carry some baggage from—and may be heard in terms of—a history in which women have been marginalized in jazz, despite their presence since the very earliest days of the music, primarily as singers but also as instrumentalists (Tucker 2000; Porter 2002). These potential politics are not always active or even recognized, but often they are. As recent studies by Eric Lott and Ingrid Monson, among others, have shown, jazz musicians often conceive of their music as political in this broad way (Lott 1995, 246–49; Monson forthcoming).

Considering this music as I do in this book—thinking of jazz musicians' engagement with Thelonious Monk through the lenses of historiography and social theory—suggests a number of fundamental questions. Perhaps the most interesting ones revolve around the dialectic of historical materialism and poststructuralist idealism. This amounts to asking, What kind of truth claim can a work such as this, which posits the construction of Monk's historicity as largely subjective and contingent, hope to make?

Ultimately, I will be writing not about what Monk *is* or *was,* but what he *has been.* In a simple sense, Jean Baudrillard's theory of simulation and the "simulacra" seems applicable. In light of this, the "Monk" I am proposing here is admittedly "hyperreal"; for most of us, including most of the musicians I spoke with while researching this book, he is a collection of recordings, video footage, and stories—increasingly formalized stories, at that—that are told and retold. The materialist argument that such an analytical position is dehumanizing, and that obviously Monk did exist as a real person, although compelling, is insufficient; and yet the method of explaining Monk through the common metaphor of "the text" is insufficient as well. I am drawn to Antonio Gramsci's praxis-based theory of historiography, and the work of a number of historical anthropologists who build more or less explicitly on his theory, to find a way out of this conundrum. Gramsci argues that the notions of "truth" and "reality" that sit at the center of the materialist/idealist dialectic can be bracketed by an understanding of "objective truth" as meaning "historically subjective truth." That is, he argues that all culture (and in this he includes the notion of history) is necessarily subjective, and that the job of the social theorist is to understand the practices whereby that historical subjectivity comes about (Gramsci 1971: 445–48).

In the present case Gramsci's theory is particularly useful, because it allows for a humanization of an otherwise problematic idealist historiography without recourse to a crude materialism. I will argue that while Monk as a historical figure is a construction, and moreover one based in subjective engagements with a collection of texts, Baudrillard's theory of simulation is, as it turns out, insufficient to explain the process, precisely because the theory mistakes subjective truth for the absence of any sort of truth (Baudrillard 1983: 3–4, 11). The distinction is a fine one, but it is important nonetheless. Baudrillard writes of simulacra as "signs which dissimulate that there is nothing" (12). While this may adequately describe the sense that Monk as a historical figure is not quite the same as Monk the actual person, it fails to capture the extent to which the many acts of signification through which contemporary musicians create this historical image of Monk are real in some firsthand way. That is, it describes the Monk understood through a collection of stories, performances, recordings, interviews and so forth, but not the experiences of the many people now engaging Monk's legacy. This is the primary value of this book's ethnographic orientation: it requires an analysis that sees the many texts that comprise Monk as a historical figure—the recordings, interviews, stories, pictures, films, and so on—not as floating in a world of pure textuality, but as they circulate among individuals within a social context, being appropriated, interpreted, and applied.[3]

Increasingly, writers dealing with questions of unofficial, unconventional, or simply vernacular relationships people cultivate with history have come to think in terms of memory—both personal memory and collective, social, or cultural memory. The concept of social memory goes back at least to the 1930s and the work of French sociologist Maurice Halbwachs, who explained what he called the "social framework of memory," the idea that somehow all memory, though inherently internal, nonetheless derives much of its meaning from being held in a social frame, and that the construction of that framework is one of society's most important tasks (Halbwachs 1992). More recently Pierre Nora, in his monumental collection *Realms of Memory*, has explored the ways celebrations, memorials, pop culture, and official history, among other things, can be sites where "memory crystallizes and secretes itself," making possible the investigation of at least the tangible, lasting evidence of cultural memory (Nora 1996–98). Scores of historians, anthropologists, cultural theorists, and, recently, musicologists of various stripes have picked up on this work (among others, see Anderson 2001; Boym 2001; Confino 1997; Connerton 1989; Floyd 1995; Hutton 1993; LeGoff 1992; Fabre and O'Meally 1994; Ramsey 2003; Rosenberg 2003; Treitler 1989; Waxer 2002).

This book, following the work of Paul Connerton, Guthrie Ramsey, Robert O'Meally, and others, explores not only those traces, but also the process of remembering in jazz. What I describe is common in African American arts more broadly, and might be added to the list of contributions to American culture by African Americans, a people who "cannot not remember," to borrow a phrase. The practices of memory embedded in African American art and literature have been explored extensively in Geneviève Fabre and Robert O'Meally's collection *History and Memory in African-American Culture*, but, surprisingly, those practices in music—perhaps more obscure, and certainly less clearly semantic than the other arts—have not (Fabre and O'Meally 1994). Music's temporal quality, its unfolding over time, and particularly jazz's improvisatory character, which makes almost every performance also a composition, gives it a distinctive historicity, allowing it to be both in the moment, reflective on the moment, and in dialogue with a body of pasts.

If this sort of historicity is common to all, or at least many, jazz performances (or, even more broadly, is a part of expressivity across various media, as my reference to Kundera's ideas on the novel suggests), then the question "Why Monk?" must be asked. Why focus on Monk? Why not on some other figure? Why not on some specific practices regardless of their historical object? Indeed, precisely this question came up in one of the first conversations I had with a jazz musician while preparing to do the research for this book. I was in New York to do some preliminary research at the Institute for Jazz Studies archive at Rutgers University in Newark and to begin to contact musicians I thought might become part of this study. On my first night there I went to Sweet Basil, a Greenwich Village jazz club, to hear pianist Michael Weiss, who was playing as a sideman with Art Farmer. I had become interested in Weiss because of his reputation as an interpreter of Monk's more obscure pieces and as an excellent, if underappreciated, player. I had contacted Weiss earlier, and he was expecting me at the show. When I approached him during the break he expressed interest in the project and asked me to tell him more about what I was doing. I began a spiel about my interest in tracing Monk's influence, his legacy for the contemporary jazz world, but he stopped me short. "Why Monk?" he asked. He wanted to know why I was focusing on Monk, particularly in comparison with John Coltrane, whom he saw as exerting a greater influence on the sound of jazz today.

I was surprised by Weiss's question and had to improvise an answer, searching to put into words exactly what it was that had suggested the project to me in the first place. I continued to think about it afterwards, as I researched and wrote this book, spurred on by similar questions from musicians and friends. In answering "Why Monk?" I should first reiterate that this is a case study. Monk is by no means the only figure in jazz history for whom such a study would be appropriate, and jazz is not the only art for which one might conduct such a study. Undoubtedly, an approach to jazz historicity focused on specific processes—kinds of reference, for instance— would have the benefit of being less susceptible to lapsing into "great man" tropes. Nonetheless Monk's place in jazz makes him a good starting point for addressing these questions. His compositions and his performances of them are widely known, having made a major contribution to the backbone of the "modern" jazz repertoire, and he stands as one of the best-known figures of jazz since the 1950s. Along with this recognition, and feeding it, is the fact that it is nearly as common for a musician to claim Monk as a predecessor as to record his music. It is my contention that the project undertaken here, the careful examination of both the contemporary performances of Monk's music and the narratives in which jazz musicians situate themselves vis-à-vis Monk, will help develop an understanding of history as a dimension of expressivity in jazz that will be applicable to other cases. As for the danger of writing a hagiography that arises when dealing with a figure such as Monk, it is my hope that a study such as this comes close to capturing an insider perspective on the problem. By explaining the construction of Monk's historicity as dialogic I hope to destabilize a less reflective approach to placing him in history while maintaining a recognition of the respect jazz musicians today accord him.

The other fundamental question that this book suggests is methodological: Why follow this approach to understanding Monk? Interestingly, this was not a question that I heard from the musicians who participated in this study. They seemed to take at face value the notion that investigating Monk meant considering how he has influenced jazz in the present. I take this tacit support of my approach as the result of the fact that for each of these musicians understanding Monk has been an important project in his or her own musical development, a sort of experience and activity this is very much oriented toward the present. It is entirely through learning to play his music for themselves that these musicians have come to hear and understand him. Nevertheless, the question remains a valid one, particularly given the absence of a standard volume on the life and works of Monk or a scholarly biography.

While a more orthodox approach to writing about Monk's place in jazz history would undoubtedly throw new light onto some vexing questions about jazz in the middle of the twentieth century, the approach I have taken here illuminates other issues. It allows for a synthesis of ethnographic and historical concerns, both synchronic and diachronic aspects in the understanding of jazz; it brings new focus to one of the fundamental issues in jazz practice, the negotiation of authorship in musicians' engagement with repertoire; and it speaks to some of the most interesting contemporary questions in the humanities and social sciences, including the place of power and agency in the making of history and the functioning of the historical imagination in the making of culture. This work is therefore relevant to the present moment, rather than simply about the 1950s or 1960s.

There is a basic historical question that this book cannot answer but that is of genuine interest. Is the fundamental importance placed upon history in the jazz world today indicative of something transhistorical, or is it primarily a thing of the present moment? There is evidence that jazz has been interested in its own history for some time: early jazz concerts often took the form of a historical review, generally supporting a progressive or evolutionary narrative; and Ellington took seriously the charge of representing black history in his long-form works, especially *Black, Brown and Beige*. Nonetheless, the preponderance of self-conscious backward glances—the Ken Burns documentary, the repertory movement, the interest in repertory projects even among such progressive musicians as the World Saxophone Quartet, and the flourishing catalogue of tribute albums and jazz memorial projects—all suggest that something changed at some point in the 1980s. A full accounting of this change awaits another book, but it is worth noting here.

Although my focus is not necessarily on aspects of the music that constitute the center of musical-analytical concerns as they have been conceived within the fields of historical musicology and music theory (and, indeed, I am critical of such musical analysis as an end in itself), I do spend significant portions of this book arguing from close analysis of music.[4] The approach I generally take, looking for formal and relational production of meaning within and between specific musical performances, has significant precedent in ethnomusicology, and most significantly for this project in the work of Ingrid Monson (1994, 1996, 1999, forthcoming), Paul Berliner (1994), Travis Jackson (1998), and Christopher Small (1987). Small may not think of himself as an ethnomusicologist, but his work is "ethnomusicological" in the best sense of the term insofar as it involves a genuine attempt to understand a music culture unfamiliar to him on its own terms. This approach also has a precedent in historical musicology, particularly the branch known in the 1990s as the "new musicology," though in such scholarship, particularly when it deals with music from the Western classical tradition, meaning is usually found in musical works in the abstract rather than in specific musical performances (see, for example, Kramer 1990, 2001; McClary 1991; Tomlinson 1993, 1999). To this end I have included a number of transcriptions and extended analyses of particular recordings. These may appear forbidding to readers unfamiliar with the technical language of music theory. Nonetheless, it is indispensable to engage in close analysis of music's sonic forms if a case is to be made that music really matters.

Christopher Small's work provides a particularly relevant starting point for my close analysis of music. Although I eschew the use of his neologism "musicking" as unnecessarily jargony, the reasoning behind its coinage is unassailable. As he says, "music is not primarily a thing or a collection of things, but an activity in which we engage. . . . It is not properly a noun at all, but a verb" (Small 1987, 50). With Small, I am convinced that the most important questions about music all have to be answered with respect to specific instances of musical activity—performance and listening. I am less convinced that a single term, "musicking," is better than a set of terms, "listening," "performing," "playing," "singing," "improvising," "composing," and so on; that is, I don't think we are lacking in language to describe music as an activity, only that musicologists, and to a great degree Westerners in general, have been conditioned to think of it as a thing first and an activity second. In any case, Small's injunction to ask "not, 'What does this composition mean?' but, 'What does it mean when this performance takes place at this time, in this place, with these musicians, before this audience?'" (51–52) is at the heart of *Monk's Music*. This is the essential basis of much ethnomusicology, but Small formulates it clearly and neatly. This does not mean that one should ignore musical works—things, as it were, rather than activities—but instead one should recognize that the meaning of the musical work is always to some degree contingent upon the circumstances of its performance.

Monson takes the position, in *Saying Something,* that ethnography is "the only ethical point of departure for work in jazz studies and ethnomusicology," even in the context of a serious engagement with poststructuralist critiques of ethnographic representation and knowledge (Monson 1996, 6). Such a strong position, particularly given its moral basis, requires some consideration. It seems overstated—surely there are any number of ethical points of departure for a scholarly appreciation of jazz—but the caution that jazz musicians' perspectives on the music should be taken seriously (which is most certainly not to say uncritically) is salutary. As noted above, it is my experience that the ethnographic component of the present work is indispensable in that it has forced me to recognize the interaction of texts and people in the making of Monk's legacy. In an equally significant way, my interaction with musicians for this project served as conclusive evidence of the extent of knowledge the musicians have about this music. Such a banal claim should really go without saying; it amounts to little more than the equivalent of saying that physicists know a great deal about physics. Thankfully, the canard that jazz musicians play the music "intuitively," without understanding it—that they engage the music physically, but not intellectually—has disappeared from the scholarly literature. Sadly, it appears to persist in less formal understandings of jazz and its culture, as attested by offhand comments I heard from people while working on this book. It is my conviction that because of the legacy of racist thinking on which such an idea is based, setting the record straight on this count is one of the most important jobs that can be accomplished by critically documenting "insider" perspectives on jazz.

Nevertheless, the ethnographic study of music is not the *mere* documentation of insider perspectives, however close or far a music tradition is from the author's experience. Indeed, the relationship between insider and outsider perspectives in ethnomusicology amounts to a dialogue, or a coming to terms between the scholar, who comes to any music and culture with his or her own set of perceptions, analytical tools, and questions, and the subjects and objects of study. Such a relationship—and its fundamental importance in developing knowledge in general—was nicely described by Mikhail Bakhtin in his "Response to a Question from *Novy Mir,*" published in the collection *Speech Genres,* in which he was asked to discuss the state of literary criticism at the time. Discussing the importance of transcultural and transhistorical literary criticism, he says, "a certain entry as a living being into a foreign culture, the possibility of seeing the world through its eyes, is a necessary part of the process of understanding it; but if this were the only aspect of this understanding, it would merely be duplication and would not entail anything new or enriching. . . . In the realm of culture, outsideness is a most powerful factor in understanding. . . . We raise new questions for a foreign culture, ones that it did not raise itself" (Bakhtin 1986, 7).[5]

This book consists of three main parts: chapters 1 and 2, which focus on Monk's performances of his own music; chapters 3 and 4, which focus on small-scale aspects of the musical response to Monk's influence; and chapters 5 through 8, which consider larger-scale considerations of Monk's legacy and historicity.

Chapter 1 presents some notes on Monk's life and career as a first step in understanding his legacy for the contemporary jazz scene. I cannot pretend to have undertaken an exhaustive study of Monk's life story. As noted previously, there are a number of biographies of Monk currently available, each of which has its strengths and weaknesses. Still, it is useful to begin with a brief outline of Monk's life, focusing on those aspects of it that musicians have found noteworthy. The jazz community has traditionally been fairly small, and musicians have tended to know one another personally or with only one or two degrees of separation. In this context, the personal becomes a significant way of interpreting the music. Music making is a social act, and, as in the rest of American culture, individualism is an important paradigm. As a result, knowing Monk (or knowing about Monk) as an individual person with a biography—that is, a life story—is a prerequisite for many jazz musicians and listeners to knowing his music.

In chapter 2 I explore how an ethnographic engagement with jazz musicians can be useful in setting a course for analyzing Monk's music in the present. This involves listening to musicians speak as listeners of—and often as fans of—Monk's music. A number of significant themes arise in this process, most notably that those aspects of Monk's music that strike the musicians as particularly noteworthy are distinct from those that have occupied other analysts of his music (though some of them are themes that have been important in more colloquial conversations about him for some time). Five principal themes arose in the analysis as central to understanding Monk as a musician: Monk and time; the relationship of Monk's music to other African American musical styles through the importance of riff-based melodic unity; the pairing of linear, developmental thinking with cyclical, repetitive practices in Monk's improvisation; the idea that Monk's music in toto represents its own "world"; and, finally, the place of humor in Monk's approach to jazz. It was particularly interesting that, given the opportunity to talk about what in Monk's music has affected them most, the musicians who participated in this study focused on these large-scale concerns rather than on the small-scale markers of Monk's style on which they depend—his particular approach to chord voicings, for example, or the specifics of his use of "space." This provides a first point of interest in the process of thinking through musicians' engagement with repertoire and the construction of history: the issues that came out in these discussions of Monk are precisely those that are most conducive to a dialogic interaction. Rather than focusing on those aspects of Monk's musicality that are strong markers of his musical voice and are hard to assimilate into another's voice, these discussions focused on aspects of his playing and composing that are more readily generalized and incorporated into one's own playing.

Chapter 3 considers musicians' descriptions of the process of integrating Monk's music into their own working repertoires. In doing so this chapter addresses a central problem common to musicians from across the spectrum of jazz's subgenres: the need to somehow integrate Monk's musical voice with the performer's own. I discuss this in terms of a dialogic negotiation of authorship in the creation of a jazz performance. Chapter 4 analyzes the work of three pianists—Danilo Perez, Fred Hersch, and Jessica Williams— in greater detail. In these analyses it becomes clear that the musicians I spoke with felt that their own expressive practice was conspicuously involved in the production of a kind of history. While the analyses in the following chapters focuses on the musicians' constructions of the larger context of jazz history, those in chapters 3 and 4 address the personal experience of jazz musicians of making a place within those constructions. It is clear that this dialogue, while important, and perhaps necessary, for making a place for oneself within the jazz world, is a difficult one, and one that often involves a long process of development and maturation for the musicians involved.

In chapters 5 and 6 I focus on the creation of a mainstream, "classicizing" understanding of Monk's place in history. Classicization is a partially integrated collection of discourses and practices that, deployed in whole or in part by musicians and writers, constitutes an institutionally sanctioned view of who Monk was and is in the context of the jazz tradition—itself a construct of similar processes—and how his music should be played now. Mainstream classicization generally represents Monk as part of a lineage now understood as a "mainstream," extending from Louis Armstrong through Duke Ellington, Dizzy Gillespie, Charlie Parker, and Monk to Wynton Marsalis and the "Young Lions" of the 1990s. This "mainstream" has consolidated its cultural position in contemporary American culture through a number of institutions, notably Jazz at Lincoln Center and the

Thelonious Monk Institute. The canon-building practices on which this consolidation rests involve an attempt to construct authoritative texts of Monk's music, to think of Monk's music as "works" in a sense close to that of Western classical music. In the process it has involved the development of a theory of performance practice for the music in which a putative fidelity to the work is expected in contemporary performance.

A number of countermainstream interventions in the construction of Monk's musical legacy are discussed in chapters 7 and 8. These include two modernist claims on Monk's legacy, one from the jazz avant-garde and the other in line with a "high modernism," both of which place Monk in a line leading away from the mainstream; an Africentrist claim; and a construction that situates Monk as the instigator of a much broader pop avant-gardism. Although these constructions of Monk's place in jazz history and approaches to playing his music in the present are by no means unified in discourse or practice, I discuss them together because they share the quality of contesting one or another of the so-called mainstream's constructions, most notably the idea of a fidelity to canonic texts, a duty to play Monk's music as he did.

An element of self-production through a creative engagement with the past is at the heart of my contention that jazz history emerges in a dialogue between musicians and music. The notion that individuals, through the practices of collective memory, are involved in the production of history resonates with current historiographic theories, and I believe a sustained look at jazz as a locus for the practices of memory and history will add something to that discussion. Michael Kammen, in a review of a recent study of memory and history in everyday American life by Roy Rosenzweig and David Thelen, asks the question, "Is everyone really a historian?" His response is to remind us, in the face of a celebration of a purported democratization of historical sensibility and the power of "the people" in the making of history in contemporary America, that "knowledge and understanding are simply not the same as nostalgia and enthusiasm" (Kammen 2000). I think this distinction is important precisely because there is something significant and out of the ordinary in jazz musicians' involvement in the construction of history. I would argue that the particular creative engagement with a past becoming a history distinguishes jazz as an improvisational practice, and that jazz musicians have participated as actors, agents, subjects, and narrators in their own history in both musical practice and metamusical discourse.

PART ONE

Monk and His Music

ONE

A Biographical Sketch

THELONIOUS SPHERE MONK. It is a name like no other, ripe with allusions, as if ready-made for a man who would be mythologized in his lifetime and beatified after his death.

Much is known of Monk's life. His comings and goings, his business dealings and friendships, and his work and to some extent his play were chronicled in the pages of trade journals, in film, and in biographical writings, like those of any public figure of the twentieth century. Still, there is something about Monk's life and art that resists complete knowledge. As much as we know about the events of his life, there remains at the heart of the story a basic inscrutability. On one level he is "Mysterious Thelonious," as the title of a children's book by Chris Raschka puts it. Even to musicians who knew him well, Monk was always a little enigmatic. Like his music, he was not always predictable, and this made him engaging and occasionally difficult, but always worth spending time with. In addition to being basically inscrutable, Monk doggedly refused to compromise, either personally or artistically. His story also mirrors that of many jazz musicians of his generation: he moved from a small town in the south to the urban north, aspired to social and economic mobility, and was deeply involved with music from many spheres.

Thelonious Sphere Monk was born on October 10, 1917, in Rocky Mount, North Carolina. His birth certificate actually reads "Monk, Thelious, Jr."

(Gourse 1997, 2). His parents, Thelonious (or perhaps Thelious) Monk Sr. and Barbara Batts, were in some ways typical of their generation of African Americans. Thelonious senior was a laborer; Barbara stayed at home but took in such work as she could. When Monk was three, Thelonious senior and Barbara moved the family, including Monk's sister, Marion, and brother, Thomas, to the San Juan Hill neighborhood on Manhattan's Upper West Side. The Monks were like many African American immigrants from the south to the north, looking for a better life, for opportunities that were not available to them in a small, rural community. Not long after moving to New York, Thelonious senior returned to North Carolina, seeing the kids again only sporadically thereafter on occasional visits to New York (Farrell 1964, 85).

Throughout his childhood Monk was surrounded by music. Until he moved back to North Carolina, Thelonious senior played music in the home regularly (Gourse 1997, 7). What kind of music he played—what repertoire, in what style, and how well—is not altogether clear. Monk remembered his father playing swing-style music on the piano and dabbling on the ukulele. What he played on the uke is hard to say, but it would most likely have included an assortment of pop songs, novelty items, and perhaps blues or fiddle tunes that were the common stock of rural southern music in the early twentieth century. In addition to whatever repertoire Monk became familiar with at home, Monk would have heard a wide variety of music in his neighborhood. San Juan Hill was so named because it was home to many immigrants from the Spanish Caribbean, particularly Cuba and Puerto Rico. In such an environment Monk probably would have heard traditional and popular music from that area as well as opera and light classical music, both of which were quite popular throughout the Caribbean (in this he was more like New Orleanian musicians than many of his compatriots). Finally, Monk lived relatively near a number of great pianists of the stride tradition, and he described having listened to their music often. As he noted later, James P. Johnson was a particular favorite (Gourse 1997, 13).

In addition to all of this relatively informal exposure to music from across a wide spectrum, Monk also had some contact with formal music education. The Monk family did not initially provide for his musical training but did give his sister, Marion, piano lessons as part of the basic education of any young girl with aspirations for upward mobility. She was apparently no great talent, but young Monk stood by the piano and watched her lessons carefully. By age twelve Monk had developed some skill on the instrument, and the piano teacher suggested to his parents that his talent should be cultivated (Hentoff 1960, 134–35, and 1956, 15; Gourse 1997, 6–7). These lessons would of course have focused on developing technique (fingering, articulation, fluent music reading, and so on), but they would have done so within the framework of the Western classical tradition, thus introducing Monk to the canon of that music.

Monk also distinguished himself in his youth as a scholar and an athlete. His academic accomplishments were enough to earn him a spot at the prestigious Stuyvesant High School. However, Monk was disappointed by the apparently racist policies of the school, which allowed him to attend but ironically did not allow him to participate in the school's music program. At some point Monk's preference for music over other activities pushed him to dedicate himself to playing piano, and in his sophomore year Monk dropped out in order to pursue music full-time.

After leaving school Monk came of age musically in the parallel worlds of sacred and secular black vernacular music making. He had played publicly on occasion by his early teens, for rent parties and as an organist at Union Baptist Church, but he truly became acquainted with the rigors of life as a professional musician working as an accompanist for a barnstorming evangelist from 1935 to 1937 (Gourse 1997, 10–11; Hentoff 1956, 15; Lapham 1964, 73). There is no record of what Monk played for the preacher, but some things can be reasonably surmised. Playing for a preacher on a circuit that would have included diverse African American audiences around the country would have required flexibility in musical interaction, much as would the modern jazz performances Monk engaged in soon after. It would have required sensitivity to the vibe of an audience, and the ability to extend or contract pieces in response to that vibe. It also would have involved mastering the codes of "soulful" playing and required the ability to participate in call-and-response forms seamlessly.

At this time Monk was listening to, and appears to have been profoundly affected by, music from Tin Pan Alley. Later in life Monk recorded many standards, in quartet, trio, and solo piano versions. What is striking is that none of the pop songs he played regularly come from after 1945, and by far the majority of them were first published between 1925 and 1935—that is, during Monk's teens. As Scott DeVeaux has argued, Monk's predilection for this repertoire and the remarkably straightforward way he played it, always keeping the melody present or at least very near by, should be seen as an acknowledgment of his fondness for the music of his youth and of the debt he owed it in developing his own particular style (DeVeaux 1999a, 170, 183).

The next stage in Monk's career is one of the most enigmatic: it did not follow the trajectory it might have been expected to, and there is very little evidence as to why. Returning to New York after playing in the medicine show, Monk did not become a member of a touring band, and he did not work in any particularly high-profile contexts. He took jobs playing as opportunities presented themselves, playing where and when he could in the New York area. In 1941 he was hired by drummer Kenny Clarke to be the house pianist for Minton's, a club in Harlem famous for its after-hours jam sessions and that would become one of the sites for the development of bebop. Perhaps because of this regular showcase, Monk composed prolifically at this time, penning all of his best-known pieces, including " 'Round Midnight," "Straight, No Chaser," and "Epistrophy," all of which would quickly become modern jazz standards.

Oddly, unlike his compatriots at Minton's—including, most famously, Dizzy Gillespie and Charlie Parker—Monk did not translate his position at the forefront of the new music into recording contracts, tours, and the other trappings of musical fame. Although by the mid-1940s bop was the hip music par excellence, Monk was really not on the radar outside the small world of his fellow musicians. It is hard to be certain how to account for this, but some plausible reasons are related to the way that Monk has been seen since then as an uncompromising individualist and a quintessential outsider. The most compelling reason that Monk might not have found the same fame as others is that he wasn't playing bop. By this time Monk had clearly developed the distinctive, idiosyncratic approach to harmony that he would use for the rest of his life, and this approach had in fact been central to the development of bebop. He did not, however, adopt a melodic approach that was at all similar to that of Parker or Gillespie, opting instead to focus on careful and unusual interpretations and elaborations in his spacious, angular melodic voice. Perhaps most importantly, he did not engage in the kind of virtuoso display that was so key to the music of nearly all of his contemporaries. While many were playing faster and more densely than ever before, playing a game of musical one-upmanship, Monk played fewer and fewer notes, letting the silence speak. Opting out of musical gamesmanship may well have been a sound artistic goal, but it requires audiences to pay close attention and dig deep to hear what makes the music good.

It was during this time that Monk met and married Nellie Smith. She was important to Monk in a number of ways; she often earned the family living when Monk was unable, but perhaps most significantly she supported him emotionally and physically during periods when he was under psychological strain. The home life that Thelonious and Nellie Monk cultivated was remarkable in that it contradicted cherished stereotypes about jazz musicians. The two were devoted to one another and their two children. Both Thelonious and Nellie were essentially homebodies, more interested in cultivating family life than being "on the scene." In the end, this disinterest in touring and public life could well have contributed to the difficulty Monk had developing his career.

It was not until 1947 that Monk got a chance to record as a leader, with the Blue Note label. Those recordings, released as singles and on an album under the title *Genius of Modern Music,* were far from ideal, but they still sound bracing today. The fidelity is not great, and Monk's sidemen are a mixed bag: Art Blakey is not at his most sensitive, and the horn players do not always seem to know quite what to do with Monk's tunes. Still, there is an excitement and a clarity in Monk's playing that prefigure his best recordings that would be released later. The recording of "Thelonious," the fourth track on the original LP release, is exemplary. This version begins with Monk playing the A section—with its repeated one-note melody— solo, as was to become his standard opening. If this were not stark enough, he is then joined by Blakey on the hi-hat. By the time the horns come in (Idrees Sulieman, tp; Danny Quebec West, as; and Billy Smith, ts), we are already deep in a world of sound that is totally Monk. The horns weave a dense counterpoint around the tolling single-note melody, broadcasting a roughness and energy that is enhanced by edgy timbres and a "wide" approach to intonation. The solos are unremarkable until Monk comes in with a little gem. He keeps the single-note melody in sight throughout the A sections, building a brilliant stride accompaniment around it noteworthy for its insistence. Here Monk is most in his own world and absolutely uninvolved with musical fashions of the time.

As brilliant as these recordings sound now, it is hard to imagine audiences embracing them at the time. Most of the singles were released with little or no notice from the jazz press, and those that were reviewed came in for little praise and much criticism. A *Down Beat* review of "Misterioso" and "Humph" from 1949 seems prejudiced from the outset: "Two more sides by the pianist who did *NOT* invent bop, and generally plays bad, but interesting piano." The reviewer is put off by what he hears as Monk's technical and creative shortcomings. "Monk fingers around trying to get over the technical inadequacies of his own playing, plus getting lost in one arpeggio cliché variation . . . that takes him fifteen seconds to get out of. . . . This is veritably faking a rather large order and only [Milt] Jackson and John

Simmons' bassing redeem it" (Levin 1949). In 1951, George Hoefer finds equally little to like in a single that has Monk playing the standards "Nice Work If You Can Get It" and "April in Paris." As Chris Sheridan notes, Monk is "damned if he does and damned if he doesn't" (Sheridan 2001, 20). People found Monk's own music hard to understand, but Hoefer is certainly not interested in hearing Monk as an interpreter: "Monk's forte is originality and he doesn't get much of it in these two versions of standard melodies" (Hoefer 1951). *Metronome* published an equally tepid review in 1951. A few years later, in 1953, *Down Beat* finally included a review of Monk that was quite complimentary, though mystifyingly brief. Of a single including Monk's songs "Let's Cool One" and "Skippy," the reviewer says, "Tasty dishes of cucumber and peanut butter, served by a svelte sextet." Aside from noting Monk's bandmates and giving the songs four and three out of five stars, respectively, that is the whole review.

Monk's relationship with Blue Note continued for a few years, into 1952, and his career moved steadily forward, despite major personal and professional troubles. In 1951 Monk was arrested and convicted on narcotics charges. The legal trouble and its aftermath could have been devastating, but Monk persevered, and the event became one of the most important in defining his image for succeeding generations. The arrest was not groundless—Monk was in possession of narcotics, for whatever reason—but the matter was probably treated more severely than it might have been had Monk not been black, defiant, and a jazz musician. Because Monk was uncooperative he spent time in jail for the charges, an experience that was apparently psychologically damaging. Monk, after all, was by no means a hardened underworld figure. Worse than the experience of imprisonment, however, was the loss of his cabaret card, a license to perform in New York City taverns and nightclubs. Whether or not Monk was framed on the narcotics charges, as has been suggested, the punitive withdrawal of his livelihood was clearly unjust, and a glaring example of the ways in which the New York police arbitrarily used the card system to punish and control musicians.

In spite of his inability to perform in Manhattan (the cabaret card regulations did not apply to clubs in the Bronx, Brooklyn, and Queens) and his disinclination to travel, the period from 1952 to 1957 saw the gradual emergence of Monk as a public figure. In 1952 Monk signed with Prestige Records, which was building its reputation for modern jazz. Monk was unhappy at Prestige, despite the opportunity to work with a number of notable colleagues, including Miles Davis and Sonny Rollins. Three years later, in 1955, Monk's contract with Prestige was bought out by Orrin Keepnews at Riverside Records, at which point began arguably the most fruitful period of Monk's whole career.

Keepnews was an interesting figure, a jazz fan who stepped in at just the right moment and produced a staggering body of recordings. His work with Monk was particularly inspired, leading to many of the most interesting albums in his oeuvre. The first two albums Keepnews produced with Monk were, respectively, an album of standards and an album of Duke Ellington tunes. All of the work was reimagined in Monk's inimitable style, showing Monk as an interpreter of the highest caliber. The idea behind these albums was to give listeners something familiar to hang on to while absorbing Monk's unique approach. Monk was quick to point out in an interview with Ira Gitler some years later that he himself had wanted to do the recordings because they were all songs he liked (Gitler 1957, 20). In any case, the recordings do involve familiar material, but at least as noteworthy is the way they highlight just how distinctive Monk's approach is; there is no mistaking this for Art Tatum or Nat "King" Cole or Teddy Williams or Bud Powell, even though this is a repertoire that any of them might have played. Keepnews continued to present Monk in the best possible light, producing the recording *Monk's Music,* which includes Monk playing with Coleman Hawkins and John Coltrane, respectively, on two versions of "Ruby, My Dear"; recording Monk live with Johnny Griffin and later John Coltrane on tenor; and teaming Monk with composer Hall Overton in order to present Monk's music in a large group format without simply adopting a standard big band orchestration.

In 1957 Monk's fortunes took a turn for the better when, with the help of his friend and sometime patron, the Baroness Pannonica de Koenigswarter, he secured the return of his cabaret card (Farrell 1964, 86). His first major public appearance following this was an extended engagement at the Five Spot, a Greenwich Village tavern that was to become a central spot in the hipster culture of the late 1950s and early 1960s. In 1959 Monk was arrested on drug charges a second time, again under questionable circumstances, and again he lost his cabaret card. After a time, however, he secured its return with the help of the Baroness de Koenigswarter (Farrell 1964, 87). In 1962 Monk signed with Columbia Records, a major label with the ability to promote him quite broadly. Throughout the 1960s Monk appeared regularly in the United States and abroad, at nightclubs, concert halls, and jazz festivals, with a fairly stable quartet, and in 1964 he became only the third jazz musician to have his portrait on the cover of *Time* magazine, after Duke Ellington and Dave Brubeck.

The 1960s were a period of mixed fortunes for Monk. He played throughout the decade with Charlie Rouse, who had come into the quartet in the late 1950s. His performances were more lucrative, and Monk had the opportunity to play in Europe and Asia for wildly appreciative audiences that seemed finally to have caught up with his musical ideas. Monk's recordings for Columbia benefited from top-of-the-line studios, the sensitive producer Teo Macero, and extensive promotion and distribution networks, but they were not as consistently interesting as his work from the 1940s and 1950s. Monk was no longer composing prolifically, and the few tunes he composed in this period, such as "Stuffy Turkey," are not among his best. This was also a time of deteriorating health for Monk, and he suffered alarming periods of dissociation that became more serious and more frequent over the years (Gourse 1997, 200, 204–6, 225). Tragically, Monk's downturn in mental health was exacerbated by inept care (Gourse 1997, 277–78). That said, throughout the decade Monk and Rouse were able to find compelling material in the tunes they had been playing for years. The 1964 recording made live at the It Club in Los Angeles is among the best of Monk's recordings, and the 1968 recording *Underground,* Monk's last for Columbia, is outstanding.

It is difficult to know anything about the last decade and a half of Monk's life except in vague terms. Monk's contract with Columbia ended in 1968, signaling the beginning of the end of his career. He continued to perform regularly, albeit sporadically, until 1974, and recorded some of his finest trio and solo performances for the Black Lion label in 1971. By the end of 1972, however, he had begun a process of general withdrawal. He moved to the Baroness de Koenigswarter's residence in Weehawken, New Jersey, and by 1975 he had become almost totally reclusive. Monk described himself as simply being tired, and his illness was never satisfactorily diagnosed or treated (Gourse 1997, 289–96; Lacy, personal communication). On February 5, 1982, Monk died from an aneurysm in Weehawken.

Monk died just as his legacy, which the rest of this book examines in detail, was becoming clear. In the early 1980s jazz musicians were becoming more interested in acoustic, post-bop-influenced sounds, after a decade in which the highest-profile music was electric and engaged with rock, soul, and funk. When more bop-influenced music rose to the fore again, it did so with a self-awareness and an explicitly "traditional" sense that it had not had before. Jazz was newly minted as "America's classical music" and dubbed a national treasure by the U.S. Congress. In tandem with a rise in the profile and status of acoustic, post-bop jazz, this period also saw an upturn in the money to be made playing, recording, and teaching jazz. Given the expanded cultural and economic capital circulating in jazz at the time, this was also a time for increased (or at least increasingly visible) contestation over what sounds were and were not jazz.

Since his death Monk's recordings have continued to sell in significant numbers, and a number of important recordings of his have come to light and been released. At this point virtually everything he recorded in the studio is commercially available, including outtakes and alternate takes from many sessions. In addition, a number of live sessions have been released, most notably the Carnegie Hall tapes of Monk with John Coltrane, which were unearthed from the Library of Congress's collections and released in 2005. These will undoubtedly remain the primary route for both musicians and listeners to become familiar with Monk and his legacy, along with the biographies and films that document his life and work. The purpose of the rest of this book is to look into the ways those documents, as well as the memories and stories of other musicians, have been kept alive as part of the ongoing story of jazz in the years since Monk's death.

Hearing Monk

History, Memory, and the Making of a Jazz Giant

PUT A MONK RECORDING ON YOUR STEREO. Any recording will do for the moment, whether it's one of the slightly dodgy, loose-limbed, rough and perhaps not-quite-ready Blue Note recordings from the late 1940s; one of the tough, searing Riverside recordings from the 1950s, when it seemed like every month produced new musical insights of stunning originality; or even one of the polished but arguably less powerful Columbia recordings from the 1960s, when Monk was consolidating his style. Listen to Monk's performance of "Little Rootie Tootie" from a live concert at New York's Town Hall in 1959, for instance (Monk 1959). The recording is classic Monk: he plays the first section of the melody alone, and then the band joins in for one time through the head, followed by a series of solos, and the head out. Monk keeps his band hanging together through the performance's nearly nine minutes by weaving a logical thread as front man and accompanist. What is this sound coming out of the speakers? What does it mean? It is crabbed, gnomic, beautiful, peculiar, and funny, and it projects the impression of a great depth and grace. To some it may be off-putting, but to others it is immediately engaging, touching a chord in even relatively uninitiated ears. It accumulates layer upon layer of meaning and pleasure with greater attention to the music and its connections to the worlds of music and experience surrounding it. Hearing Monk take a little bit from the very end of the head, a dissonant chordal interjection used as a response to the end of the A section melody, and follow its possibilities through Charlie Rouse's solo choruses gives one sense of its musical depth; hearing a flurry of ideas and references interspersed with bits of the head's melody in Monk's solo gives another.

This chapter answers the questions posed above—what is that sound and what does it mean—by exploring the ways Monk's music has been meaningful not just to any listeners, but to other jazz musicians, a special set of listeners who are exceptionally knowledgeable and invested in the music, but not entirely unlike other fans. The pleasure experienced when listening to Monk is distinct for musicians, because for them listening is directly tied to performing. This is not to suggest that nonperformers do not have intense, pleasurable, significant experiences of listening—of course they do, and if they didn't there would be no audience for music—but that the act of performing adds an aspect to the experience of listening. Nonperforming listeners are often content to see jazz performance as a mystery (very few, for instance, know why one lick sounds good and another doesn't, even though they can certainly tell when it sounds good or doesn't); jazz musicians, for the most part, are not.

Each individual's history and listening habits are distinct, but invariably jazz musicians share a background as lovers of the music and voracious listeners. Describing a favorite recording can send musicians into a reverie as they hear the music in their minds. The signs are obvious. Sitting in a Starbucks on 111th and Broadway on a late-summer morning in 1999, Bob Porcelli described listening to Monk's "Ask Me Now" over and over again on his turntable as a younger man. "I would play it," he said, "and as soon as it was over I would back it up and play it again. I wore out that record!" As he spoke his posture changed, he smiled, and his eyes lit up as he was transported to an apartment in the Bronx decades earlier. This is what Ralph Ellison means about music locating us in time. "Ask Me Now" is a special song for Porcelli, a thread that runs through his life. It connects a teenager wearing out an LP in his parents' apartment to a young man spending every spare minute and dime soaking up bebop as it flew out of horns downtown, to a man in late middle age finally feeling like he has made it as a jazzer after years playing mostly in salsa and Latin jazz bands. When he hears the song in his head, or when he stands on stage and plays it with T.S. Monk's band, that experience of depth becomes transformative.

The task at hand, then, is to draw on the knowledge and experience embodied in musicians like Porcelli, contemporary interpreters of Monk's music, to bring a new perspective to musical analysis. What results from this approach is not so much an analysis of what Monk and his music *are,* or even *were,* but of what they *have been* to the community loosely defined as the collection of people with Monk as a common interest. Rather than a process of translation—finding the appropriate technical language to express experiential descriptions of Monk's music—this amounts to a kind of discovery through asking what it is about Monk's music that prompts these experiences. Although the question is not, strictly speaking, historical, it provides a critical perspective on two of the most important aspects of jazz history—the recordings and the people's discourse about them—ultimately making it possible to situate Monk more carefully in some narrative contexts.

Monk's music presents any number of intricate puzzles and lessons, but five aspects emerge as particularly significant for contemporary jazz musicians. These include the singularity of Monk's approach to time, his characteristic use of developmental logic in his soloing, the unified quality of his individual performances, his use of humor or playfulness, and, finally, the way in which his music in toto represents an entire self-created world. Considered individually and together, these aspects are the subject of musicians' interest in Monk's ability to integrate and satisfy modernist and vernacular aesthetics in the creation of music in the context of a distinctly African American musical world. It is significant to an understanding of the relationship between memory and history in jazz that the musicians with whom I worked on this project overwhelmingly chose to address these large-scale aspects of Monk's music (instead of smaller-scale issues as the idiosyncrasies of his use of dissonance, particular chord voicings, and personal licks) when asked open-ended questions about Monk's lasting contribution to jazz. While the technical aspects of Monk's style are easy to distill and imitate, his most important contributions to jazz are much harder to copy. It is those large-scale qualities of his work that place him in a distinct position as a pianist, as a jazz musician, and as an African American artist and intellectual at mid-century.

It is clear from even a cursory overview of Monk's life, as described in chapter 1, that many of the issues Monk faced were problems generally faced by African American musicians at the time. Race was a factor in his professional life, his treatment by the authorities, and ultimately in his psychological diagnosis and treatment or lack thereof. What might be less immediately obvious but is no less true is that listening to his music and talking about it is also inherently bound up with questions of race. Race, along with class and gender, is one of America's great historical touchstones and fault lines, in many ways the country's central problem but also one of its primary sources of community and solidarity. Inasmuch as jazz is a music that orients us in time—a music that is a space for historical action and interpretation, as Michel-Rolph Trouillot might describe it—race is always present, either in the foreground or the background (Trouillot 1995). Amiri Baraka (LeRoi Jones) most thoroughly followed the implications of this observation in *Blues People* (Baraka 2002).

Musicians' descriptions of Monk's music inexorably lead to a focus on the ways in which Monk was able to create a music that found the intersections of Western and African diasporic aesthetic canons and practices, melding relationships to vernacular expressivity and modernism, working in what Houston Baker has described as an "Afro-modernism" (Baker 1987, xiv–xv). Rather than cobbling together a European-derived melody with an African-derived rhythm, or a modernist sense of individualism and a vernacular communalism, Monk's music created a synthesis on a deeper level, and on such grounds that different listeners have often found in the same performances the expression of those aesthetics that most speak to them. It seems important, then, to highlight the points of intersection that have made this music so compelling to so many. Such a project proposes to undermine a kind of "hyper-difference" in the representation of musical Africanness and Europeanness, while avoiding the erasure of the distinctly African American qualities of the music in the construction of an "over-likeness" to Western concert music.[1]

PLAYING TIME, FEELING TIME

Time is the quality that most profoundly distinguishes music from most other arts. Unlike a painting or a building, music cannot be experienced outside of time; unlike a poem or novel, music cannot be heard at one's own pace. Music creates its own experiential frame in and through time; in this it is like film and theater. Good music alters our sense of time's flow; and though we have developed relatively little special terminology to describe the flow of music in time, differences in this flow are very important in the way we sense the distinctiveness of each kind of music. So it is not surprising that when asked about Monk, musicians who know his music well often single out his peculiar approach to time for special attention.

It is, of course, in the nature of these very individual sensations that there would be differences of interpretation. For instance, Ben Riley and T.S. Monk, both drummers who played with Monk at one time and who now make Monk's music a significant part of their performance repertoire (Riley with the group Sphere and T.S. Monk as the leader of his own sextet), have remarked on Monk's unusually solid time keeping as something that set him apart from even from many of the best jazz musicians.[2] In contrast, Don Sickler, who relies heavily on his sensitive ear for musical detail as an arranger and producer, notes that Monk's peculiar rhythmic phrasing can be disorienting, at times making it difficult to hear or infer time from his playing, particularly in a quartet or trio context. This surprising incongruity of experiences in hearing Monk points to the subtle complexity of his approach to rhythm and meter.

To see how musicians' descriptions of Monk's time can be used as a starting point for some musical analysis, it is helpful to consider the shades of meaning *time* may have in a discussion of jazz. Musicians use the word *time* in various contexts to refer to a number of interrelated facets of the temporal aspect of playing jazz. *Time* may refer, among other things, to a general sense of the underlying pulse of a piece, as in, "He has a good sense of time." In addition to this metric sense, *time* refers to the subtle ways a musician may play with the basic tempo, phrasing ahead, in the center, or behind the beat in order to create shadings of feeling. It may also, especially with respect to drummers, refer to one of a few specific rhythmic accompaniment patterns, as when a musician is said to be "playing time" (Berliner 1994, 151, 316, 318, 326, 337). The term often functions as another way of talking about the creation of a groove in collectively improvised music. Ralph Peterson underscores the importance of a musician's feeling for time when he says, "how important it is—when you're playing a solo— *rhythmically* what the notes say. [It's] almost as important, if not *as* important, as the notes themselves, because if you miss a note and the *rhythm* is logical, then the idea comes across. . . . But if you miss the time . . . if you blow the time you're more likely to do irreparable damage to that particular section of the music" (quoted in Monson 1996, 29).

Given the potential for bad time to do "irreparable damage" to a performance, it is not surprising that musicians would hold in particular esteem those who can be relied on to play with a solid feeling for time. More than an objective measurement, though, the evaluation of a musician's feeling for time is relative, happening in the moment of playing together. Solo performance offers its own challenges, and Monk, at least, solved these challenges with a very different approach to time than he used in group settings. Pianist Laurent De Wilde describes a good rhythm section making time as "a truly mystical and communal experience . . . an act of love as opposed to masturbation" (De Wilde 1997, 34). Because it is central to the fundamentally interactive process of establishing and maintaining a groove, good time involves both a solid, unwavering sense of tempo and a sensitivity to and ability to interact with band mates' collective approach to phrasing within a given tempo.

Tempo

Ben Riley sees Monk's approach to tempo in the performance of his own pieces as a marker of a deep understanding of the pieces' expressive potentials. He is particularly impressed with Monk's ability to play "in between all of the tempos"—that is, not to play everything in one of three generic tempos, fast, medium, and slow—and his ability to play pieces in different tempos from one performance to another (Riley 1999).[3] In Riley's opinion, this sense of rhythm, which is often aligned with physical, intuitive, or nonintellectual musicality, is actually a sign of Monk's great intellectual achievement as a musician because it allowed him to understand the music better, and thus take the performance to another level with great regularity. As Riley puts it, playing a piece at many different tempos "makes you become more in tune to the music, the music that you're playing. So once you're in tune, whatever tempo you play it, you hear where it's going" (Riley 1999). This would seem less striking (and less ironic) were it not for a history of mapping the mind/body distinction racially.[4]

Oddly, Riley's assertion that Monk played his own compositions in a variety of tempos sits uncomfortably with pianist and writer Laurent De Wilde's claim that "Monk's compositions have *one* specific tempo, sometimes two, but they're always the same" (De Wilde 1997, 72). De Wilde makes the unassailable point that it was not Monk but others, following Miles Davis's lead, that chose a wide variety of tempos for works like " 'Round Midnight" or "Well, You Needn't." It does not necessarily follow, however, as De Wilde suggests, that Monk himself conceived his pieces as having one and only one proper tempo. De Wilde looks to the recorded evidence for confirmation of his theory, and having checked each of Monk's recorded versions of a particular tune with a metronome, he determines that, "Aside from a few rare exceptions, the tempo doesn't budge a hair. [Monk] hears his compositions at one tempo, just like there's usually only one way to play a certain chord behind the melody. This is almost unheard-of in jazz—the ultimate protean form" (De Wilde 1997, 72).

Although it is possible to take issue with De Wilde's dismissal of tempo variations in Monk's recordings of "I Mean You," for example, as insignificant, his point remains relatively valid.[5] There certainly are pieces, such as " 'Round Midnight," that Monk recorded regularly over the course of his career at a similar tempo each time. The contradiction between Riley's and De Wilde's impressions of tempo in Monk's performances requires an explanation that somehow encompasses both experiences. In one sense this may be an object lesson in the result of a music history such as De Wilde's that relies exclusively on recordings.[6] Despite the fact that Monk recorded certain tunes repeatedly—more so, perhaps, than any of his contemporaries—the recorded versions of any given tune reflect only the tip of the proverbial iceberg compared with the number of times he performed it. In this sense someone like Riley, who played with Monk over the course of years, clearly has a more reliable position from which to say how Monk played his own pieces. He provides an otherwise unattainable glimpse of how Monk played, because he heard Monk more often than even the most avid, fanatical listener, and he was inside the performances, not just hearing the tempo, but playing in it. Moreover, because tempo variations affected the way he played a piece, Riley would have felt even the smallest variations that might seem insignificant to an audience. Nonetheless, the fact that Monk chose to record many of his compositions at the same tempos multiple times cannot be ignored. These recordings become documents and take on an importance, if only because of their permanence.[7]

Beyond the differences in the performances that constitute Monk's music for Riley and De Wilde, the difference in their interpretations of his playing also relate to the larger lesson each sees in them. Both Riley and De Wilde embed their discussions of Monk's use of tempo in larger statements about how they approach playing the compositions themselves. To Riley, understanding the many tempos in which Monk played his own compositions explains the variety of interpretive possibilities open to the group Sphere when they approach Monk's music. He suggests that the ability and freedom to play Monk's music in a variety of tempos has kept Sphere's engagement with the music dynamic and open-ended. In his words,

> We make arrangements up as they go along a lot of times. One guy decides, "Uh oh, let me try this," and the other two of us say, "Oh, okay, that's where he wants to go," and we go there. And that's from understanding and trying to understand one another, 'cause we're always listening to each other. See, this is why when you hear us play, we might play the same thing all week long, but every night it's not going to be the same,

because each night we come in with a different feeling for it, a different tempo. (Riley 1999)

De Wilde on the other hand, justifies a performance style through his description of Monk's approach to tempo, but his argument is based on an understanding of Monk's compositions as musical "works." Musicologists have spilled plenty of ink recently over what is meant by this tricky concept, the musical *"objet,"* but here it represents concrete, complete, replicable vehicles for expression, to be approached much like a classical piece. De Wilde, for example, credits the performances on *That's the Way I Feel Now,* a tribute album of Monk pieces recorded by jazz and rock musicians shortly after Monk's death, as making Monk's music sound "amazingly fresh as ever," and says that the music will continue to do so "ten centuries from now played on instruments you can hardly imagine . . . as long as [the pieces are] played exactly as he wrote [them]" (De Wilde 1997, 71). For anyone familiar with the debates about historical authenticity in the early music movement this will seem incredibly naïve. The origins and consequences of this line of thinking with regard to Monk's music are discussed in more detail in chapters 5 and 6.

Time

What Riley spoke of in terms of "tempo," T.S. Monk expanded on with a broader consideration of Monk's feeling for time. In his words,

Thelonious had the *best* time-keeping ability of any jazz musician [Ben Riley, Max Roach, Roy Haynes, or I] ever played with. Nobody, *nobody* kept better time than Thelonious. And it was magical. And it forced you, from a rhythmic standpoint, to swing the hardest you will have ever swung in your life. You can ask Roy Haynes, you can ask Max Roach, you can ask me, you can ask any of the drummers, from Leon Chancler, who played with Thelonious, to any of the cats who played a night here, a night there with him, and they'll all tell you, "Man, Thelonious was like a magic carpet, man." All of a sudden it was another rhythmic center that was coming from him and was carrying you, and you the drummer! You're supposed to be the rhythmic center. This is one of the things that I didn't realize till I played with another piano player. 'Cause you have to remember, for me, in a serious jazz context, the first piano player I ever played with was Thelonious, so that was normal. But nowadays, having really played with a lot of badasses over the last decade or so, nobody even comes close, you know, in terms of carrying me. I, I lay down a serious groove, you know. I can swing. I never feel like anybody's carrying me, like I felt with Thelonious, cause he just had a special time thing. And you'll find that all of us that have played, whether you go back to Shadow Wilson, you know, Denzil Best, all the drummers that played with Thelonious from the very beginning, anybody who's spent time with Thelonious, including Kenny Clarke, became melodic. All of a sudden they got this wide, melodic sense. Got this conversational approach to their instrument, in relation to the other instruments, as opposed to simply laying down a rhythmic foundation for everybody. (T.S. Monk 1999)

The vehemence of this statement is striking, even considering that T.S. Monk is a man who speaks in superlatives, particularly about playing with his father. Even more striking was the very real awe in his voice and on his face when he described the experience of playing with his father. He was genuinely surprised by the power of his father's rhythmic sensibility, his time feeling, to impact the performances of everyone working with him.

The creative force of Monk's feeling for time in performance is very difficult to appreciate fully from recordings alone. The experience of time is different for musicians participating in the music's creation than for listeners, particularly listeners who are not in the interactive, ritual space of a live jazz performance.[8] This difficulty is cast into relief by Don Sickler's impression that Monk's playing relies on the rhythm section to establish solid time so that he can phrase outside of it. As he says,

[Monk] requires the rhythm section. The whole secret to Monk was [that] the rhythm section always has to be real swingin'. And that gives him the basis to let him do *his thing;* . . . he's not gonna play the swing, he's not going to make it [swing], he's not like . . . a Wynton Kelley, for example, [who] really portrays the swing, I mean, [an] immaculate, exciting player in that respect. But that's not Monk, that's not his contribution. It's gotta be swinging, and he plays, he puts his stuff on top of it, and that's magic. If the rhythm section's rushing and dragging and slipping around and everything else, then it would simply destroy what he's trying to do. Then it would all sound like chaos, you know, sound like avant-garde somethin'-or-other. . . .

You know, I produce a lot of records, so, in other words, I'm in there, and all of a sudden I can push a button and, and, eliminate the bass, and push another button and eliminate the drums, you know, if I want to be able to hear what the piano player is doing, for example. Well, you can always still kinda tell where the time is and whatever else by the way they're playing, you know. With Monk there's some things, I think, where if you took out the bass and drums it could confuse a lot of people as to where the time is some of the time. A lot of the time it would be very relative, 'cause he actually knows where it is, it's just he places his stuff in a unique, very personal way, and only he's able to really do it. (Sickler 1999)

Sickler's impression that the quartet sound Monk aimed for required solid, groove-oriented playing from the bassist and drummer is completely borne out by his recordings. Although, as T.S. Monk notes, playing with Monk may have opened up new melodic, "conversational" opportunities for drummers, the conversation always took place within the framework of a solid rhythmic groove. As the testimony of musicians who played with Monk shows, however, recordings alone are not a sufficient source to understand how that groove was created. Sickler does not, of course, suggest that Monk did not, or could not, play in a way that swung. Instead he points out the way that Monk's rhythmic phrasing complicates the sense of time created by the bass and drums. Underlying this is an unspoken explanation of why Monk chose "inside," bebop-oriented rhythm players for his quartets, despite the reproaches critics aimed at Monk in the late 1960s and 1970s for not playing with more avant-garde musicians. Regardless of exactly how the groove arose in Monk's recordings, it is clearly the time feeling he wanted. Since a groove ultimately depends on interaction, as strong as Monk's time may have been, he needed to play with musicians who were sensitive to his particular time feel and could add their own voices to create a whole greater than the sum of its parts.[9]

Although a recording may not shed much light on how a performance develops a groove, it may at least provide a document of the sort of rhythmic vitality Monk nurtured in his quartets. The performance of "Eronel" on Monk's 1963 Columbia recording *Criss-Cross* shows the exemplary sound of Monk's working band, with Charlie Rouse on tenor sax, John Ore on bass, and Frankie Dunlop on drums.[10] This band played together almost daily and had developed a feel that was so unified, so integrated, that at times it became stultifying. Their recordings are exceptionally clean and tight—especially when compared, for instance, with Monk's work with various bands on Blue Note and Riverside. At best this led to good, if understated, performances. Often, though, it robbed Monk's music of the energy it might have had. At work here seems to be a potential conflict between the value of the band "locking into the pocket," that is, feeling time together just so, and the value of the dramatic tension created by what Charles Keil describes as "participatory discrepancies." At its best, though, as on this recording, the band's unity of purpose was synergistic. Monk sets a deeply solid backbeat $\frac{4}{4}$ feel in his three-measure solo introduction, so that there is no question about exactly how the time should go, and when the band enters they are right in sync with Monk's feel.

When listening it is easy to hear Ore and Dunlop as the rhythmic center for the performance, but T.S. Monk's and Ben Riley's descriptions press us to hear Monk's piano initiating and guiding the time feel. All three, then—Monk, Ore, and Dunlop—were involved in a subtle, responsive project of taking time by the shoulders, shaping and molding it for their own pleasure, and drawing an audience into the space of the recording.

DEVELOPMENTAL LOGIC, MUSICAL UNITY, CALL-AND-
RESPONSE, AND RIFF-BASED PLAYING IN MONK'S MUSIC

After noting the importance of Monk's feeling for time, musicians often remark on his penchant for creating formally integrated and compelling compositions and performances. Fred Hersch describes Monk's formal language, comparing him with Beethoven, Brahms, and neoclassical Stravinsky. An exemplar of the best in jazz, Monk's music is "musical story-telling in real time, using the subject at hand, the specifics of the piece." The experiential unity of whole performances, as Hersch elaborates, stems from the way Monk worked as a composer:

> I think every Monk tune has to be about something. It can be about a rhythm or a motive or two, or it can be about a person or a situation or a mood, but it has to be about something. It's not just . . . it's not *just* notes. There's always a point to all Monk's tunes; always some kind of musical or programmatic point. And he doesn't use that many elements in a tune. When you really get down to it, he makes a lot out of a little. And that's important; too many people think that jazz composing is, you know, you throw in the kitchen sink, and you have these long, epic sorts of things. And often in those kinds of things, you just improvise on one or two chords, because you'd never be able to work with all that stuff. (Hersch 1999)

Other musicians echo this basic pair of points, that Monk's approach to form involved a kind of linear, narrative quality, and that in both the composed pieces and his performances of them, including his improvised solos and accompaniment, Monk made economical use of materials to create unity. Not only does this inspire comparison with Beethoven and Brahms, but this quality also explains comparisons between Monk and Duke Ellington.

There are many possible routes for coming to terms with Hersch's basic point that Monk's music is "about" something. At times, as Hersch notes, Monk's songs are clearly about some extra-musical topic. Many were written for. family and friends, such as "Pannonica," written for his benefactor, the Baroness Pannonica de Koenigswarter, and "Little Rootie Tootie," named for his son T.S. "Toot" Monk (the train sounds at the beginning of the song reference a cartoon train that was a favorite of the young Monk and from which he got his nickname). Others seem to capture a mood: "Ruby, My Dear" is tender, while "Monk's Mood" (originally titled "That's the Way I Feel Now") is melancholy, or at least introspective. No doubt the songs could be heard as referring to and commenting on many of the basic tropes of contemporary American music. Certainly, as discussed later in this book, I think many of these songs have been heard in terms of tropes about high versus low art, and artistic genius (and all that goes with it). On a fundamental level, however, I think the songs and their performances are about experiences that do not translate easily into words, but that are best described in terms of tension and release, and in terms of expectation built and satisfied or denied. In this sense, Monk's music is about the experience of music—about itself; as Hersch says, it is "about a rhythm or motive or two."

This is the aspect of the music's meaning that is most closely related to form, and this is why the sense of unity in form is such a significant one. Musicologists are accustomed to speaking of musical form as something abstract, atemporal, a frame for events on the musical surface; and by habit formal sophistication, perhaps even more than harmonic elaboration, has become tied to the great achievement of the Western classical tradition. As a result there is a highly developed language for the discussion of musical form—developed in the works of major late-nineteenth- and early-twentieth-century figures such as Heinrich Schenker and Donald Tovey and in the work of academic music theorists today— that takes the Western classical tradition as its only model. Far less has been said about musical form in other traditions, in part because the dominant model of formal analysis has taken so-called linear forms—works that follow a narrative (introduction, rising tension, climax, denouement)—as the only interesting forms, while cyclical approaches that are common in many of the world's musics—pieces that work by the repetition of smaller or larger bits ("repetition with a signal difference," as it were)—have not been the object of as much focus. But form in many traditions, and certainly in jazz, generally involves some mix of linear and cyclical experience in the creation of tension and release. The reason unity in form has such significance—to jazz musicians as much as to classical composers—is that the phrase *unity in form* glosses the idea that musicians have created experiences of tension and release, expectation and its resolution, that are satisfying, to themselves and to audiences. Given this, there is room for a formal analysis of jazz that is more responsive to the experience of listening, though, and because a distinctive approach to form is so commonly noted as one of Monk's contributions to the music, it is a good place to start.

The impression that Monk brought a storyteller's sense to improvisation, creating solos that have a narrative logic, a linear thread to follow, is conveyed in many recordings. The performance of "Bags' Groove" on an all-star recording with Miles Davis and Milt Jackson from 1954, for instance, is a stunning example. The recording became famous in part for an apocryphal story about tension in the studio among these musical giants (a story that both Monk and Davis denied in later interviews), but it is really more noteworthy for the quality of the music they managed to make together (Gitler 1957, 30, 37; Szwed 2002, 115–16). Monk is particularly on point here, and in this minor blues written by Milt Jackson, Monk fills eight choruses of a nine-chorus solo with a gradual expansion of a single motive. The recording shows Monk's engagement with the African American tradition of riff-based composition and his striking integration of that aesthetic with a penchant for abstraction and understatement that is a significant area of overlap between the blues tradition and classical modernism. Monk's dogged tenacity could easily have sounded dull, and it is only by dint of his exceptional wit (and the fact that he had years of practice at precisely this kind of improvisation by 1954) that the result is light and interesting. The severity with which Monk limits his materials in "Bags' Groove" responds neatly to the head, itself a threefold repetition of a single motive over a skeletal interpretation of minor blues changes. In other instances Monk is less programmatic, but still a single motive can occupy him for multiple choruses—much longer than is typical for most jazz musicians—and he often derives subsequent motives from previous ones.

On this recording Monk takes the third solo, after Davis and Jackson, and approaches each of his nine choruses as an individual unit that he combines to build a larger musical edifice, using the choruses as bricks in a wall, so to speak. Monk begins each chorus with a characteristic riff distinguished by its texture and rhythm, each a version of a single motive, and moves through the chorus with that musical idea, generally foreshadowing the following chorus's riff in the final measures of each chorus. This can be heard as a call-and-response chain, each chorus heard as a call that is answered by the following chorus, which in turn becomes a call. He arranges these ideas in a clear pattern that creates a double-humped structure to the solo, with a line climaxing in the fourth chorus and another in the eighth.

The first line of development involves the gradual addition of pitches in tandem with a subdivision of rhythmic values. In the first chorus he focuses on the interval of an open fourth, with an eighth-note riff (ex. 1, choruses 1–9). Monk then uses triplet eighth notes in the second chorus, filling in the harmony with an arpeggiation. In measures 7–12 of the second chorus, the end of the triplet riff with which Monk is working becomes a reference to his composition "Misterioso"—a broken sixth pattern. This broken sixth becomes the basis for the third chorus's characteristic motive, now taken up a notch from the previous chorus by the transformation of the riff into sixteenth notes. Throughout the third chorus Monk gradually expands the end of the sixteenth-note riff from a single pitch (mm. 1–6), to a dyad (mm. 8–10), and finally a chord (mm. 11–12). Monk then takes up the chordal texture he built in the third chorus as the characteristic texture for the fourth chorus, a climactic "shout" chorus, with close-voiced block chord riffs reminiscent of big band arrangements. Here Monk broadens the rhythmic profile, using longer note values to give a sense of arrival to the climactic point.

The sense of climax in this chorus depends in large part on the increased volume and intensity Monk brings to the chorus, an increase that is subtly reinforced by Clarke and Heath's accompaniment. Both clearly recognized the developmental process Monk was creating and tried to bring something to it. In the first two choruses both accompanists play softly, reacting to the very sparse texture Monk creates. They swell slightly with the internal climax of the blues form in measures 9–11, but keep their playing generally understated. In the third chorus Clarke adds snare hits for the first time, reinforcing the building sense of excitement. With Monk's creation of a sense of climax in the fourth chorus Clarke and Heath both play somewhat louder, and Heath takes the energy up another notch by emphasizing ringing lower pitches, those in which the string bass has its fullest presence. This moment shows a unity of thinking among the performers, not just in Monk's improvisation. The strategies the three musicians use to build excitement serve the double ends of bringing out the individual musicians' sounds and communicating coherently together.

In choruses five through eight Monk builds a different sort of develop-

Example 1. "Bags' Groove": Thelonious Monk's solo, right hand only (Miles Davis 1987a, track 1, 6:48–9:35).

Example I *(continued)*

(continued)

Example 1 (continued)

ment, working in two-chorus groupings. He goes back to the triplet riff from chorus two and works with a layering of dissonance. In choruses five and six Monk uses the triplet riff, ending it with sharply dissonant clusters. He then extracts the clusters from their original context and uses them as the basis for a riff in chorus seven, juxtaposing them with a resolution tone. In the eighth chorus Monk abandons the dissonance for the resolution, building the entire chorus on the single resolution note, quickly shortening pitch durations throughout the chorus. This brings the entire solo to an emotional high point that is defused with the downbeat of the following chorus. It sounds almost unplanned, as though Monk expected the next soloist to enter on that downbeat, and when he didn't, Monk appended a final chorus to the balanced structure he had created in the preceding eight choruses. That said, Monk often ended his solos with a chorus or more of comping, though usually with less of a radical disjuncture between the comping and what preceded it; that is, he usually prepares the ground in the preceding choruses. This chorus, like others where Monk comps to end a solo, nicely brings the emotional level of the performance down to a point at which Davis can enter and build something on his own terms.

There is more to creating a sense of linear or narrative form, of course, than simply going through a set of logical permutations on a motive. Monk's mastery of time, tempo, and, for that matter, rhythm combine with an exceptional sense of the dramatic possibilities available to a pianist who uses the instrument "orchestrally." Narrative form can involve the sense not only that events occur in a satisfying order in time, but even more that we, the listeners, are being carried through time, that we are living in the music's flow of time. Monk achieved this often, but he was at his peak when playing solo. The recordings of Duke Ellington's piece "Everything Happens to Me" that Monk made for the Columbia album *Solo Monk* in 1965 show this beautifully. The song was one of Monk's favorites: he included it on his first Riverside recording and came back to it regularly during his career. Perhaps the black humor in the song appealed to Monk, and perhaps its fatalism took on a resonance when he reflected on all the adversity he had faced over the years. The verse, which Monk doesn't play but surely knew, captures a dark irony: "Black cats creep across my path / Until I'm almost mad / I must have raised the devil's wrath / 'Cause all my luck is bad."

In any case, as with a handful of other standards—"I'm Just a Gigolo," "I Love You Sweetheart of All My Dreams," and "(I Don't Stand) a Ghost of a Chance with You," for instance—Monk plumbs the depths of beauty hidden in the song. In all three takes of "Everything Happens to Me" that are commercially available from the 1965 recording, Monk creates an arch-like form, building intensity and then resolving it. This is less remarkable in itself than the way he accomplishes it. The version originally released has only two choruses, both of which are ornamented versions of the melody rather than new improvisations on the changes.[11] Using a gradual broadening of texture, expansion of register, and intensification of ornament, Monk builds to a climax at the end of the second A section of the second chorus, and then defuses the tension with a return to a more sparse, contracted, simple version of the melody for the final B and A sections. In the third take this same pattern holds, though Monk has more opportunity to build on it because he extends to three choruses. In both cases, though more strikingly in the third take, Monk also creates a sense of elasticity of time that is deeply effective. He subtly creates a sense of increasing momentum along with the expansion of texture and register, so that when the final bridge comes and he shifts to a much slower pacing (though not a slower tempo) and starts using a substantial rubato, time seems to come to a screeching halt. Time can then begin again, albeit with less intensity than before, to bring the song gently to its conclusion.

Monk's practice in his solo playing of crafting a complete performance in which everything relates more or less obviously to the melody of the head points to another aspect of his distinctive approach to form: the creation of whole performances (beyond just his solos) that have an integral unity. Unlike Ellington or Charles Mingus, the two musicians most commonly associated with attempts to create large-scale form in jazz, Monk virtually never experimented with unusual forms, unusual arrangements, or other "compositional" devices. Instead he worked in the standard improvisational framework to achieve the same ends. Monk's versions of his own songs and standards share with the dominant bebop and post-bop players of his time the basic "head, solo, solo, solo . . . head" form. Musicians who claim Monk as an influence often point to the fact that within this framework he developed a distinctive formal conception as he sought ways to make the performance's solos more than a series of bounded units.

As noted before, Fred Hersch points out that this musical approach flows from Monk's compositions, each of which is tightly unified. Virtually any Monk tune could serve as an example for Hersch's point that Monk composed any given piece with a limited set of resources, and that each piece seems to be "about" something musical. Monk's blues tunes do this most compellingly: "Misterioso" uses a repeated broken ascending sixth interval as the basis of the entire head; "Straight, No Chaser" is broken up into a number of short "snippets," all of which present versions of a single motive; others, like "Bolivar Ba-Lues-Are" and "Blues Five Spot," are even more traditionally riff-based tunes in which Monk uses a single motive as the basis of all three parts of a standard twelve-bar blues pattern. Even in cases in which Monk does not compose with the kinds of motivic materials that sound immediately rifflike, his approach to musical process shows an affinity for the riff-based music of his youth.

"I Mean You"

In the blues Monk found a strong precedent for motivic unity and economy. Traditional blues songs are almost always riff-based, composed from a single melodic idea, though not always from such miniscule musical kernels as are Monk's. Monk, however, brought this same aesthetic to his compositions in thirty-two-bar popular song forms as well. In the tradition of pop songwriting the precedent was not for such economy, but often for writing long, lyrical melodies. Nonetheless, Monk often infused the form with a distinctive riff-based motivic conception, creating short pieces that work with a single musical idea. The well-known piece "I Mean You" provides an excellent glimpse of how Monk accomplished this. The head is forty measures long, divided into a four-measure intro, thirty-two measure chorus, and four-measure coda. At the beginning of the first A section Monk presents a riff from which he then draws most of the melodic material for the rest of the piece through playful repetition and revision. This use of a single motivic riff with numerous permutations imbues the piece with a sense of call-and-response troping.

The effect of this piece, like that of all AABA song forms, is that of a circular path: a departure and return, with the strongest sense of closure reserved for the end of the final A section. What sets this piece, like many of Monk's songs, apart from the standard repertory is that Monk managed to create a sense of contrast in the bridge using riffs derived motivically from the A section, relying on harmonic contrast, textural changes, and changing rhythmic feels in addition to melodic transformations.

In performance Monk surrounded this song form with a four-measure statement that serves as both introduction, transition, and coda. In a way, this short statement is the most intriguing part of the entire tune, because its relationship to the head cannot be explained by traditional tonal theory, even taking into account common jazz extensions of tonality.[12] Moreover, it presents motivic material that is related only very distantly, if at all, to the riffs that suffuse the head proper, yet it sets up another level on which the piece may be heard as unified, involving a juxtaposition of $E\flat^7$ and F. The introduction begins with an $E\flat$-dominant seventh riff, emphasizing 1, 5, and flat-7. This motive is immediately repeated, shifted back a half-beat, and foreshortened by one beat, creating a new rhythmic profile. The only notable relationship between this and the riff that opens the A section is the off-beat quarter note pickup on which they both begin. Harmonically, the introduction stretches any tonal interpretation. The entire four measures project a sense of $E\flat^7$, never suggesting a move to F. When F comes as the tonic at the beginning of the A section it is not so much a consequence of what preceded it (as it might sound were it prepared by a progression from its dominant), but a departure, a new starting point, shifted a step up. The material is even more surprising when it reappears at the end. Far from rein-

forcing the sense of closure on the tonic, as is typical for a coda, ending on
E♭7 undercuts the tonic, suggesting either some further movement—that is,
pointing forward in time—or simply reveling in the dissonant, unexpected
sound of the E♭7 chord in the context of a fairly straightforward F tonality.
This second interpretation gains credence from the fact that the E♭7/F juxtaposition also occurs at the beginning of the bridge, where an E♭7 immediately follows the arrival on the tonic at the end of the second A, here used to
harmonize an F in the melody. This E♭7 is followed by another direct move
back to F two measures later, reinforcing the centrality of the juxtaposition.

Monk's use of motives from the head in his soloing and accompaniment
is one of the most commonly noted aspects of his personal style, his improvisational voice. Rather than provide what would be a gratuitous demonstration of this feature through examples, I would like to focus on a less frequently noted aspect of the way he integrates those materials from the head
in his soloing, as it surfaces in two recordings of "I Mean You," one from
1948 with Milt Jackson, and one from a live performance with John Coltrane
in 1957.[13] What seems most compelling about these examples is that they
show Monk working at something much like the synthetic "Afro-
modernism" Baker theorized, establishing a kind of unification as a set of abstract musical relationships, and at the same time establishing unification as
a way of furthering the dynamic interaction among improvising musicians.

In both of these performances of "I Mean You," Monk takes the second
solo, following Jackson and Coltrane, respectively, each a musician with a
voice that is distinct and different from his own. In performances in which
Monk took the first solo he often started with a largely unadorned statement of at least part of the head, often with little variation, before launch-
ing into other material. Following his sidemen's strong solos, however,
Monk takes time to transition from their sound worlds to his own. Instead
of immediately using materials from the head, Monk in both cases starts his
solo with new material that sounds plausible coming after the previous solo.
After these transitions Monk then begins to work within his own sound
world, introducing materials drawn from the head. In the recording with
Coltrane, Monk uses an extended solo as an opportunity to intertwine
materials from the head with new materials handled motivically. In the
earlier recording, with Jackson, the movement from Jackson's improvisation to materials drawn from the head takes the whole of Monk's sixteen-
measure solo and provides the performance as a whole with a neatly drawn
shape of departure and return.

This aspect of Monk's playing is compelling precisely because of the way it involves Monk's sensitivity to the potential of the pieces he composed as vehicles for improvisation and his sensitivity to and ability to work creatively with the other musicians in his ensembles in actualizing those potentials. This might seem ironic, given Miles Davis's famous objection to Monk's comping style, alluded to above, but is strongly supported by the loyalty of musicians in Monk's working quartets of the late 1950s and 1960s. If Davis found Monk a difficult accompanist, clearly Charlie Rouse found him sympathetic.

Although I suggested above that Monk worked within the sort of synthetic "Afro-modernism" that Baker theorized, such a synthesis would appear, at least in my analyses, to be interior to Monk and anterior to performance. That is, Monk thoroughly accomplished the synthesis of vernacular and modernist practices that Baker's "Afro-modernism" relies upon (though it seems unlikely that he would have thought of it in those terms) before the moment of performance. Moreover, this really is a synthesis and not a juxtaposition; the performance as a whole speaks to both aesthetics rather than concatenating materials that satisfy one or another aesthetic, but not both. Thus a listener with little or no knowledge of or appreciation for traditional African American aesthetic concerns can listen to Monk and appreciate him entirely as a musician working with the same issues as did modernists from the classical music world and vice versa.

MONK AND LIGHTNESS

When musicians discuss Monk's legacy, his expression of a lighthearted quality, described variously as play, fun, humor, or joyfulness, repeatedly comes to the fore. Beginning as early as the late 1940s, critics suggested this sort of hearing, as in Paul Bacon's "The High Priest of Be-bop," one of the first articles published about Monk in the jazz press (Bacon 1949). Since then Monk's playfulness has been noted in liner notes and articles, becoming a standard item of discourse. Nevertheless, this quality generally remains unexamined. Given the frequency with which this topic appears, it bears further consideration, as it is a key to understanding what is at stake with the issue and explaining the problems that have arisen in its discussion over the past half century.

Ben Riley and Steve Lacy, each of whom played with Monk (Lacy for a short time in 1960, and Riley as Monk's regular drummer from 1964 to 1967), both remarked upon humor as an important aspect of Monk's musical style (Lacy 1999a; Potter 1988, 379). Riley saw an ability to hear the lighthearted quality of Monk's music as perhaps the single most important quality a musician has to bring to the table to play it well. "We have to learn the humor," he said,

> because [Monk] had fantastic humor in his music. And this is one of them things that most people don't collect in what they're doing: that humor. See, they do everything else—note-wise and whatnot—but they forget the humor. And he was a very humorous person. If you listen to some of that phrasing you have to laugh. [You have to] say, "How did he figure that out?!" You know? These are the things that you have to bring to the table: do it your way, but don't neglect the humor. (Riley 1999)

As Steve Lacy pointed out, the fun aspects of Monk's music flowed from the musician's general sense of humor. Lacy came to know Monk well in the 1960s, and he described a humor and playfulness that pervaded their interactions.

> STEVE LACY: I used to go [to Monk's house] almost every day, and soak it up, really. Hang out with him. Take a walk. Listen to his little, you know, asides and jokes. He had a lot of humor, really, and play. Play. It was about play. The guy liked to play, you know.
>
> GABRIEL SOLIS: And the music?
>
> LACY: Very playful. And *he* was playful. Played ping-pong. He liked to play games, he liked to play jokes, he liked to play with words, with ideas, with costume, with clothing, with shoes, with hats. He was a grown-up child, really, a genius. (Lacy 1999a)

The humor and playfulness Lacy associates with Monk both hinged on doubleness, a penchant for punning and irony, a pleasure in the double meaning that can simply be clever or absurd but can also point to a much deeper reevaluation of everyday things. Lacy's favorite example of Monk's wordplay amounted to an admonition that to play jazz seriously Lacy would have to listen closely, carefully, and often to what was going on around him. He repeated Monk's words with a grin, years after he first heard them: "You got to dig it to dig it, you dig it?" (Lacy 1999a). Another fine example of Monk's playfulness with words is his often-repeated deadpan remark, "It's always night, or we wouldn't need light." Although the specific ways Monk played with words may well have little bearing on our hearing of his music, his general way of suggesting new experiences of the mundane is important, as is his delight in playing with double meaning.

Roswell Rudd, who played extensively with Lacy, both in the late 1950s and toward the end of Lacy's life, at the turn of the twenty-first century, sees an even more expansive playfulness or humor at the heart of Monk's music. He described this quality in terms of the coexistence of binary oppositions: "[Monk's music] is very well thought out, and behind this clear and graphic facade, um, there's the female component—there's the moon component, as I call it—that's subtly shifting, subtly changing, [that] peeks out and says, 'Over here,' and then disappears. And then pops up over here, you know. That's always in there, too. It's yin/yang stuff" (Rudd 1999). I asked Rudd if this was something he saw as a "fun" aspect of the music, and he replied that all jazz is fun music, but that Monk was particularly good at a kind of fun or playfulness that came from incorporating and interpreting what he heard around him. "I think Monk knew as much about convention as he did about unconvention," he told me. "[He had] the knowledge of unconvention, the knowledge of mistakes, surprise, the unpredictable, the unforeseen, you know, having an intuitive sense about all this stuff, and then having that, having taken some of that and put a frame around it" (Rudd 1999). Rudd sees Monk's knowledge of musical conventions—the banal and the transcendent, pop music and classical music, and, significantly, forms and structures that a listener might expect—as the basis of his ability to deliver the unexpected. As he sees it the humor in Monk's music comes from the interaction of these two expressive modes—the conventional and the unexpected—rather than from the use of unexpected or anomalous materials alone.

The humor and sense of play in Monk's music is generally easy enough to hear, but it is almost always hard to explain or even describe. Monk and Dizzy Gillespie, for example, are at opposite poles: Monk is the great introvert, Gillespie, the great extrovert. Monk's humor can bring a smile, a conspiratorial nod, a sense that some little moment has been shared among those in the know; Gillespie's, however, is more likely to produce a full-fledged laugh. Because of this difference it is much easier to point to unambiguously humorous moments in Gillespie's recordings. Gillespie often uses exaggerated gestures, musical "clowning," so to speak, to achieve his ends. Delivered in live performance with a grin, a missed note, a high note that cracks, or a series of exaggeratedly dissonant bebop phrases (which might have started out as a simple mistake) can all turn into broad musical jokes.

The song "Ool-Ya-Koo," recorded live with his big band in 1948, presents Gillespie, an experienced and dedicated showman, at his humorous best. Gil Fuller's composition, a little riff-based blues in the model of the territory bands of the previous decades, is dressed up with a crunchingly dissonant horn introduction. After two times through the head, with Gillespie and others singing the head to the scat syllables "Bee-ya-ba-da ool-ya, bee-ya-ba-da ool-ya-koo," Gillespie and another singer trade a series of scat choruses. Gillespie sets the tone for the whole song by starting his first chorus with a blues-inflected quote from "Twinkle Twinkle Little Star." From here on the song is a study in contrasts. One musician sings a sparse, quiet chorus and another follows with a spray of sixteenth notes at full voice; high pitches contrast with low; and a chorus in duple rhythm is followed by one devoted to triplets. Even the singers' use of scat syllables produces witty contrasts. In the sixth solo chorus, a little more than two minutes into the performance, Gillespie digs into the entertainer's bag of tricks, working the audience beautifully. After trading a series of short, rhythmically active phrases, Gillespie sings an extended falling smear on the syllable "Booo." The timing is perfect, and in the calculated silence afterward the audience responds with a laugh. Skilled in the performer's art, Gillespie picks up the cue and repeats the smear, "Booo," no doubt with a big smile.

It is hard to imagine a moment like this in one of Monk's performances, in large part because his musical language is quite different from Gillespie's, but also because he presented himself and his music quite differently. A look at Monk's album covers, for example, reveals a musician projecting an almost relentlessly serious image. When, on occasion, the imagery does vary, it produces a sly grin or a puzzled chuckle rather than the open laugh Gillespie courted. The covers for *Monk's Music* (1957) and *Thelonious Alone in San Francisco* (1960), both released by Riverside, are quirky. Rather than showing Monk's glowering visage, underlighted, backlighted, or spotlighted against a dark background, as most of his album covers do, both *Monk's Music* and *Alone* present full-color images against a light background. *Alone* shows Monk, with a big smile on his face, riding a cable car and waving—a stock tourist image that would be more at home on a Tony Bennett or Frank Sinatra album than on one of Monk's. The incongruity, a clever inside reference, produces at most a smile of recognition; it is not working the audience for a laugh. The photograph is by William Claxton and the cover design is credited to Paul Bacon. Both artists worked extensively for Riverside and had a keen understanding of how to capture a musician's sensibility in the creation of marketing images.

The cover of *Monk's Music* is more complicated but has a similar effect. The image of Monk sitting in a little red wagon wearing a suit, sunglasses, and a plaid hat is one of the most memorable in all of jazz. The photograph is credited to Paul Weller and the cover design once again to Bacon, but there is reason to believe that Monk was quite involved in the creation of this image. According to Monk, the original cover design included a photograph of himself in a cowl, standing at a pulpit and holding a glass of liquor. Monk objected to the image for reasons that are not altogether clear, and Keepnews, who was producing the session, agreed to change the cover. Monk claimed that the idea for the final image was his, although, of course, the staging, lighting, and other technical aspects of the photograph are no doubt the work of Weller (Brown 1958, 15). In any case, Monk clearly took an interest in the album cover and how it represented him. Perhaps it was a clever rejoinder to critics who had by then made a habit of describing him as childlike, the photo displaying the incongruity of a man, with nothing childish about him, sitting in a child's wagon. Perhaps it was, as Monk himself claimed, simply an image he liked that represented his intensity: he was so involved with his music that when it struck him, he could compose anywhere, even in his son's wagon (15). In either case, the effect requires far too much thought to get an immediate response like a real laugh.

Because of this understated, thoughtful quality of Monk's humor and game playing, it can be hard now to know when his constant musical puzzling was intended as humor. In most cases musical humor requires more than mere sound, relying also on bodily gestures, facial expressions, and verbal and gestural interaction between musicians to signal both its creation and appreciation. The opportunity to observe Monk's style of interaction in a live performance is limited by the small quantity of performance footage currently available on video, which includes material excerpted from Columbia Records' archive for the film *Straight, No Chaser,* the documentary *Thelonious Monk: American Composer,* and live concerts in Paris, Japan, and Norway recorded in 1959, 1965, and 1966, respectively (Seig 1991; Zwerin 1988). These few hours of footage provide a regrettably small sampling from which to analyze Monk's performance style, but they do show, above all, that Monk, despite a reputation for detachment from practical considerations, was savvy about using the total performance to achieve his aesthetic ends, both serious and playful.

The Cultural Politics of Playfulness

Relatively few musicologists dealing with the Western classical tradition have written about the humorous and playful aspects of the music they study. The exception to this rule is the work of Gretchen Wheelock and other Haydn scholars, who have had the opportunity to consider humor deeply because, as Wheelock says, "few accounts of Haydn's music, from his own day to ours, fail to mention wit and humor in connection with his instrumental works" (Wheelock 1992, ix). The lack of attention paid to humor elsewhere in historical musicology seems to be, in part, a result of the investment modernist aesthetics has made in music as a serious intellectual endeavor, and a corresponding discomfort with humor and playfulness, both of which are seen as debased modes of expression. It may also be in part a result of musicology's focus on abstracted musical texts. With the exception of a handful of works, such as Mozart's *Ein musikalischer Spass,* humor in classical music, as in jazz, arises most perceptibly in the act of performance rather than in the musical text itself. Indeed, Wheelock's exceptional work is valuable precisely because rather than trying to locate Haydn's humor in the music itself, she sees it as necessarily dialogic: "Questions of a joke's utility address not only the relation of a composer to his audience, but also the local (intra-opus) provocation of a musical jest . . . and the implications of jesting as an interactive process that engages listeners, players, and works in progress" (5). It follows, then, that since historical musicology has, until very recently, generally been more concerned with musical texts than with musical performances, humor and playfulness have remained relatively undertheorized.

In the case of jazz, and perhaps especially in the case of Monk's music, there is an added problem of cultural politics surrounding the scholarly investigation of musical humor, stemming from jazz's constant negotiation of a space between the poles of popular and classical music, and between modernism and vernacular expression. This opposition must be viewed through the filters of race and class, and not simply in formal, musical terms, if it is to be understood. Jazz scholars have been in the uncomfortable position of having to justify their subject to an academic community invested in a separation between valorized "art" and denigrated "entertainment."[14] As a result they have felt the very real need to argue for the seriousness and intellectual rigor of jazz, to demonstrate the ways it masterfully satisfies a classical aesthetic. Scott DeVeaux eloquently argues that the scholarly construction of the jazz tradition "as an artistic heritage to be held up as an exemplar of

American or African-American culture" has a potentially limiting effect on the possible historical narratives with which it can be told (DeVeaux 1991, 552). He is particularly concerned that this project reifies the jazz tradition as stable and unified, and thus smoothes over or omits altogether those details of historical particularity that do not fit what he calls the "Romantic" narrative. It also leads scholars to pay insufficient attention to aspects of the music that are less valued within the modernist aesthetic, including, among other things, playfulness. To further complicate matters, racial stereotypes inflect the meaning of these musical, aesthetic issues. There is a history, going back well into the nineteenth century, of portraying African American men as lacking seriousness—as lazy and comical, as buffoons—in literature and the media. This typology was important in the construction of race in vaudeville acts, and it made its way into the twentieth-century cinema in the archetypal figure of Stepin Fetchit (Bogle 1994, 7–8). While artists such as Richard Pryor have used the comedic tradition as a position from which to critique the dominant culture, the typology remains problematic.

The association of humor and play with childhood adds a layer to the issues involved in considering Monk's use of these types of musical expression. The tradition of seeing African American men as incapable of serious intellectual achievement has been coupled with white America's troubled stance toward their masculinity more generally. Toni Morrison captures this evocatively in her description of Cholly Breedlove in *The Bluest Eye*. In her account of Breedlove's sexualized degradation at the hands of a Southern, white power structure and his subsequent personal disintegration Morrison powerfully portrays a white fascination with black men's physical manhood and the concomitant denial of access to social and cultural masculinity, as well as the potential consequences of this relationship (Morrison 1972, 147–50). Ralph Ellison considers similar issues in *Invisible Man* (Ellison 1952).

In a less extreme way, jazz critics in the 1950s and 1960s often viewed Monk through a similar lens, taking interest in his physical transgressions of the dominant culture—his odd clothing, hats, and sunglasses and unorthodox sleeping and eating schedules—and using these and his gruff style of interaction to construct him as a "man-child." As early as 1949 Paul Bacon described him as "unmalleable, exasperating, sometimes perverse to the point of justifiable homicide," and explained this by saying that Monk sees things "very much in the manner of a child" (Bacon 1949, 9–10).[15] Later, Lewis Lapham reiterated the contention that Monk was "an emotional and intuitive man, possessing a child's vision of the world."

Despite the patently racist association of African American men with humor and fun and thereby with childishness, as well as the implicitly Eurocentric logic historically requiring that jazz be justified on terms established by classical music aesthetics in order to be accepted into the academy, a complete understanding of Monk's music requires hearing the playful side of his expressive palette. This does not, however, mean accepting the baggage that comes with it. Indeed, in an interview for this project Fred Hersch specifically singled this out as a mistake, adamantly saying that he always heard Monk's music as playful, but at the same time, "of course, very profound." When I asked him if these weren't conflicting descriptions, he responded, "No, no, no. Fun, you know, is serious. I know just how hard he worked on his themes, and the effort that he put into doing things just so, so that it sounded effortless, or sounded natural, or sounded easy, but in fact, it wasn't" (Hersch 1999).

"MONK CREATED A WORLD"

Jazz musicians use metaphors of communication, especially that of developing one's own voice, to describe their aesthetic goals. This metaphor suggests an understanding of a shared space within which a performer can use his or her voice and in time be heard. Musicians commonly refer to Monk as having a unique voice, as did Joe Lovano in an interview for this project. He described being drawn to Monk's playing in his teens because he could recognize it and hear what he describes as Monk's musical "personality" in it. Lovano found this particularly interesting because, as a horn player, he had already discovered the variety of sounds that are possible on saxophone from listening to the stars of the day, but Monk's music helped him hear such expression in other instruments as well (Lovano 1999).

In addition to this communication metaphor, some of the musicians interviewed for this volume used a spatial metaphor to describe Monk's music as inhabiting its own world. This sort of metaphor is not commonplace, and it suggests that Monk is different from other musicians by virtue of his having created more than just an individual voice, but rather an entirely separate space for discourse. Entering into conversation within this world is seen as requiring a major effort beyond that needed to converse within the broader jazz world. Alto saxophonist Bob Porcelli first suggested this metaphor as he talked about his dissatisfaction with interpretations of Monk's music that do not use the original chord changes or that alter the original melodies of the compositions.

Every time I play "Ask Me Now" I'm trying to get more and more into it, yet, I'm not taking it out, like on another kind of song you'd take it out to some other area, I'm still just *in Monk's world*. I'm trying to get into it. In fact, I'm *in an enclosed space that he created*, you know. Whereas with another kind of song I might go anywhere if I feel like it, you know, evolving the song. But I feel like his songs, when I'm evolving them, I'm only evolving it to try to learn what he made out there. (Porcelli 1999; emphasis added)

I asked Porcelli whether he found trying to inhabit this world limited his musical options, and he replied, "No! Not at all, because it's such a huge thing, you'll never get the whole thing" (Porcelli 1999). Porcelli's description of this enclosed musical world comes from specific differences between the approaches Monk and his contemporaries took to the building blocks of a voice—stylistic phonemes, so to speak—and, importantly, the kinds of intermusical connections in his playing.

In order to explore this it will be useful to consider Monk's playing in the extended recording of "Blue Monk" with Art Blakey and Percy Heath, from the 1954 Prestige recording *Thelonious Monk*.[16] At just over seven and a half minutes, the trio's recording of "Blue Monk" stands out as one of the first recordings in which Monk had the opportunity to develop an extended solo and to allow his sidemen to stretch out as accompanists. The trio takes "Blue Monk" at a very leisurely pace, using the slow tempo to highlight the steady walking character of the scalar riff from which the head is built. Monk's approach to realizing the head emphasizes the melody's riff-based structure, and he generally leaves the accompaniment to Heath and Blakey. Monk's solo is remarkable, stretching out to fourteen choruses, each one of which uses short rifflike motives that give the sense that each chorus is a new head.

While Monk's approach to form and the restraint he used in choosing the materials with which to build the solo is distinctive, one of the most significant aspects of this performance is its self-referentiality, which gives the impression that Monk's music constitutes its own world. Many of Monk's solo choruses sound generically like heads, but the second and third are remarkable in that each of them sounds like a specific head chorus. The second (ex. 2) is strongly reminiscent of "Bolivar Ba-Lues-Are," and the third (ex. 3) is the head of "Blues Five Spot." Both of these are tunes that Monk recorded only later ("Bolivar" in 1956, on the *Brilliant Corners* album, and "Five Spot" in 1958, in live performance at the Five Spot nightclub), and so they may indeed not be references at all but rather newly composed lines that Monk

Example 2. "Blue Monk": Thelonious Monk's solo, second chorus, mm. 1–4 (Thelonious Monk 1982, track 1, 0:41–0:48).

Example 3. "Blue Monk": Thelonious Monk's solo, third chorus, mm. 1–3 (Thelonious Monk 1982, track 1, 1:01–1:07).

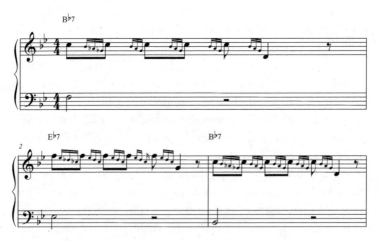

liked and used later as heads of their own.[17] Later, in measures 9–12 of his ninth solo chorus, Monk quotes the broken-sixth pattern from "Misterioso," a blues he had recorded some years previously for Blue Note.[18] Regardless of whether he is referencing previously composed tunes or composing new ones in this performance, the listener's impression is that Monk is working in his own sound world, creating a large intermusical context in which to hear all his performances of blues as part of a single pursuit of that form's meaning and musical possibility.

Monk brings this approach to intermusical reference to performances of other pieces as well, particularly his own compositions in standard song forms. This is apparent in live recordings, such as the one with John Coltrane discussed above. In the first cut, "Trinkle Tinkle," Monk quotes liberally from the melody of "In Walked Bud" in his solo.[19] Interestingly, he plays "In Walked Bud" immediately after. The liner notes for the album relate that this was the original performance order of these two tunes. Thus, a bit of intermusical reference becomes a way for Monk to achieve continuity over a long time span and to focus attention on his music as an integral project, rather than simply on the smaller units within it—individual pieces and their performances. Something similar happens in the live recording from the It Club in Los Angeles, recorded in 1964. "Blue Monk" is the first tune to be played, and Monk then refers to its melody in later songs, notably in "Rhythm-a-ning," which comes a few tracks later.

Such intermusical references can give the impression that Monk created in his musical career his own self-contained world. The spatial metaphor used by Porcelli to describe Monk's music is resonant because it expresses the sense of wonder a musician might have when exploring territory that he knows exists but is just out of sight, an experience comparable to that of a geographical explorer. That such a hearing is facilitated by the broad experience of Monk's music made possible by our position in time—we are listening to a collection of recordings long after their creation—should not be dismissed. Our point of view can lead to misinterpretations, or at least different interpretations than one might have made hearing this music as it was performed for the first time, but it is the point of view from which a legacy is constructed, and as such must be recognized as significant.

CONCLUSION

Now put that Monk recording on again—the dodgy Blue Note side, the breathtaking Riverside classic, the slightly routine Columbia, perhaps even the surprising Black Lion recording from the very end of Monk's active life—or, better yet, put on each one. What makes the music tick? Why has it held such intense fascination for so many musicians for more than thirty years? The most obvious thread running through all these recordings, connecting the 1940s with the 1970s, will be a surface detail—a whole-tone scale, an augmented chord arpeggio, a melody played with a distinctive rhythmic displacement. If this were the heart of the music, however—that most compelling, most original part that musicians couldn't ignore—the music might well have faded into obscurity along with Monk's place in jazz history, or it might have been assimilated with relatively little fuss. Think of all the fabulous, distinctive players and composers whom musicians admire and who have inspired others but have not made the leap from the lists of an individual's favorite musicians into the canon of great musicians. Tadd Dameron, Ed Thigpen, Sonny Stitt, and Leroy Vinnegar, for example, are all distinctive musicians who contributed to their own scenes and to the work of their followers. The larger jazz world, however, would not be significantly altered without their impact. Monk is different. Those sides remain vital, and have something virtually every jazz musician can learn from today.

There is a dynamic at work whereby jazz musicians create a legacy, and the following generations internalize, sustain, and even grow that legacy, that is distinctive to the jazz tradition. It would be easy, and would even have been fashionable at one time, to describe this process as a kind of pastiche, a postmodern play. Michel de Certeau's term *secondary acts of production* could be used to describe jazz musicians taking what the industrial world gives them and remaking it in a variety of ways into something more useful, more personal perhaps, but somehow unmoored. But this is too easy, and it does not really explain the power of recorded performances in the lives of the musicians and audiences involved. Rather than creating a world at the end of history, an experience in which historical time collapses into a giant atemporal simultaneity, the music involved—Monk's performances and later musicians' interpretations following Monk—and the stories, theories, and critiques that surround the music create a dense web situating people in very personal experiences of history.

The first part of this book has involved looking back at Monk and his music with jazz musicians of today and trying to ascertain who Monk was in his own time and how his recordings resonate for contemporary musicians. The rest of this book looks forward, asking what is involved in taking hold of the legacy of a musician like Monk and drawing on his influence to create new work in the present. The process is inherently one of dialogue, between a musician and his or her past, all taking place in particular circumstances.

PART TWO

Monk, Memory, and
the Moment of Performance

THREE

The Question of Voice

IN 1981 VERNA GILLIS, head of Soundscape music, produced one of the first tributes to Thelonious Monk, a concert series titled "Interpretations of Monk." The series consisted of two performances, an afternoon and an evening concert, on November 1, 1981. Each concert featured two pianists, one per set, playing solo and with an ensemble. The pianists, Barry Harris, Muhal Richard Abrams, Anthony Davis, and Mal Waldron, were stylistically distinct, but each had some connection with Monk or his music. The ensemble was largely the same for each of the four sets, including Steve Lacy on soprano saxophone, Don Cherry on pocket trumpet, Charlie Rouse on tenor saxophone, Roswell Rudd on trombone, and a rhythm section of Richard Davis on bass and Ben Riley alternating with Ed Blackwell on drums. In addition to the music, Nat Hentoff spoke about Monk and his place in jazz history, Amiri Baraka read a poem written for Monk, and there were multimedia presentations dedicated to Monk. All of the pieces on both programs were Monk's compositions, many of them pieces that virtually no musician besides Monk had attempted in public and that Monk himself had seldom recorded, such as "Gallop's Gallop," which Lacy performed solo. Despite problems finding financial backers early on, the concert series appears to have been a success, garnering laudatory reviews ("Interpretations" 1981; Jeske 1982, 57; Wilson 1981, C15). The four sets were released a short time later as a pair of recordings with the same title.

The idea of a concert featuring jazz masters interpreting Monk's compositions is hardly unusual today. It is possible to find a review of one or two such concerts for each year of the last decade in the *New York Times* alone. In addition, there are numerous recordings dedicated to his music each year. By contrast, in 1981 a concert series such as "Interpretations of Monk" was rare enough to prompt the *Times'* jazz writer, John S. Wilson, to remark that although " 'Round Midnight" was played regularly, Monk's music "[had] not received the attention that a composer of his originality deserves" (Wilson 1981). How can this change be explained, and what does it mean for Monk's position as a figure in the jazz world since his death in 1982?

The following chapters are dedicated to these questions, and to investigating the differences and the continuities in the various approaches to interpreting Monk's music. The performances of Monk's music and the creation of historical narratives about him presented in these chapters provide a case study in the uses of the past in creating and interpreting meaning in the present. I focus first on the overriding issue shared across the spectrum of performances of Monk's music, the need to develop a consistent, personal voice and to integrate it with Monk's while exploring his compositions. Then I turn to the development of views of Monk's legacy within a jazz-institutional mainstream and from various positions outside that mainstream. Together these chapters attempt to locate individuals playing music in the various social and cultural contexts they inhabit. In order to do this, it is necessary to consider the intricacies of musical sound in performance, as well as the politics of identity and identification that those sounds make audible.

A GLIMPSE OF PERFORMANCE

On a very cold night in early January 1999 I went to New York's Birdland jazz club to hear pianist Danilo Perez's trio play the second half of a double bill. Perez followed Charlie Haden, who had played the first set of the night with a large ensemble. I had missed Haden's set, arriving late to find the club sold out. Disappointed at being turned away, I walked the few blocks from Birdland to Seventh Avenue and found a cup of coffee to keep myself occupied until the next set started. After forty-five minutes or so I walked back to the club. By then the wind had picked up, making the night feel even colder. When I got to the club Haden's group was still playing, by then more than half an hour past the scheduled end of the set. The music I heard coming through the front door was cooking, and the audience seemed to be in the groove along with the musicians. Outside a line had begun to form, all of us energized (though only partially warmed) by the prospect of being transported for an hour or so by that kind of sound.

When Haden's ensemble finished and the club thinned out, those of us who were there for Perez's set were allowed into the club. I paid the cover charge and took a seat at the bar. I looked around as the stage was prepared for the smaller ensemble. The club was almost filled to capacity—unusual for New York jazz clubs, especially during the late set. Not only was the house packed, but there were also a number of musicians in the audience, including most of the members of Haden's group.

When Perez's trio took the stage the energy in the room was already crackling. With such an air of expectation, the stakes were high. I found out from Perez some time later that this was the first New York gig he had played with this working rhythm section, which included Jon Benitez on bass and Antonio Sanchez on drums (Perez, personal communication). Benitez had been on the scene as a sideman for some time, but Sanchez was far less experienced. He was a student at the New England Conservatory in Boston, where Perez teaches, and had mostly played in rock and fusion contexts. This gig was his first professional-level jazz job. In addition, because there were so many musicians in the audience and there was no extended run during which the band could get used to the club and its audiences, the pressure was on to deliver an exemplary performance.

Drawing on the energy in the room, and on the pleasure of exploring music together in a recently formed ensemble, the trio gave an absolutely transfixing performance. It was enjoyable enough for the trio that all three musicians remembered it vividly some months later when I next saw them. They locked into the pocket almost from the opening notes and stayed there for the entire set. The audience, electrified by the music, alternated between silence and roaring approval. The trio played five tunes, including two by Monk. The Monk compositions, "Bright Mississippi" and " 'Round Midnight," clearly formed the centerpiece of the performance, this despite the fact that they played three of Perez's own tunes. The energy with which the band played the Monk compositions, their placement—first and third—in the set, and their length all contributed to making them the focus of the set.

At the time I was most struck by the way the immediate concerns of the performance—the tasteful use of virtuosity in the construction of a cyclical, groove-oriented feel and in the foregrounding of linear, developmental musical thinking—were enmeshed with an attention to musical meaning deriving from the performance's relation to other music, other performances: the musicians were using the act of performance to engage Monk and a history of playing his pieces. Rather than showing a slavish devotion to the composer in an "authentically Monkish" performance, as a repertory band might, or erasing a sense of the past, creating an experience in which the pieces might be radically decontextualized, Perez, Benitez, and Sanchez managed to create a synthesis. Their voices were unmistakably present, but at the same time Monk's voice, and the voices of those who interpreted the pieces with him, shared the foreground.

CONVERSING WITH MONK IN THE JAZZ NOW

The synthesis I heard in that performance, and that one can hear in the best performances of Monk's music by other musicians today, is at the heart of musical and social practice in jazz. An exploration of this process and the resulting music goes to the heart of understanding jazz on every level—as sound, as a social and cultural practice, and as an aesthetic system—at least in the recent past. The centrality of such synthesis can be heard in the music and in the shared challenges that musicians express relating to their engagement with Monk's music on the microlevel of the actual performance. When looking at the choices jazz musicians make about how to play Monk's compositions—what sorts of arrangements to use and how to improvise on the piece, for example—as well as the choice of what pieces to play, a commonality emerges that cuts across divisions of subgenre, age, and aesthetic orientation. All of these musicians feel that working with Monk's music presents the same challenge: they need to balance the demands of the past with those of the present. Moreover, they generally agree that this challenge is different in degree, if not in kind, when performing Monk's music as compared to the other repertoire they perform. In other words, they feel compelled when playing this repertoire to engage Monk's authorial voice and precedent while simultaneously developing their own, individual voices. Later chapters will consider the variety of solutions that various jazz musicians have found for this problem and what those solutions can tell us, but for the moment it will be instructive to focus on the ways the problem itself is remarkably similar across the jazz spectrum.

Understanding what goes into playing Monk's compositions provides insight into a concern that arises repeatedly in conversations about jazz among musicians, writers, and fans. There is a tendency to see jazz both as a single, unified sphere of cultural expression, and as a balkanized genre, divided into multiple, mutually antagonistic camps, each guarding its territory and occasionally proclaiming itself the rightful center of attention. I contend that this double discourse—unity and division—is replicated in musical practice. Clearly neither unity nor division is a truer representation of jazz. Each captures an aspect of the music while potentially obscuring another.

Writers who have worked closely with jazz musicians, from Ben Sidran and Nat Hentoff to Ingrid Monson and Paul Berliner, have consistently found them to be engaging interpreters of their own work. I found the same thing. By asking musicians to talk about their experiences playing Monk's music over the course of their careers, it has become clear that this repertoire poses many challenges and rewards that go beyond the strictly formal for those who approach it seriously. The music has become an important part of their public and private selves. On one level they say that listening to Monk and learning his music has helped them "find themselves"—that is, it is important in the process of constructing a private, largely internal identity. On another level, they suggest ways in which performing his music has been a part of making a place for themselves within the jazz world— that is, it helps them develop a public identity, a social and cultural space. Because much jazz still takes place in live performance, not only the musicians' musical sound but also their stage presence is significant in the ways they craft these identities. These highly individual performances of identity gain resonance from their situation within broader webs of meaning, moving from the level of personal social contact through such overarching constructs as race, class, and gender.[1] The implication is that repertoire in general has the potential to be made to speak about musicians' identities, but Monk's music has been especially important in this way, and has produced a particularly substantial and dedicated following, for reasons outlined in the previous chapter. At least in the 1990s, Monk's legacy was one of a very few that almost all jazz musicians felt they needed to wrestle with.

A central question in all of this is the place of history in individuals' lives. Later chapters address the production of historical narratives—lineages, so to speak—but this and the following chapter ask about a more implicit, internalized history—what I call the historical imagination—and its role in the choices musicians make in the moment-to-moment activity of jazz performance. On the most widely generalizable level, this includes a further consideration of the agency of individuals in crafting their own historical narratives and those of the groups with which they identify. Of more specific significance to a history of the arts is a focus on the meaning of "influence" in historical narratives and the way it functions in jazz. Finally, in the course of moving from concrete musical events to abstractions about historicity, it is crucial to bear in mind the importance of a combination of power and pleasure. Musical studies that take on the challenge of contemporary cultural theory on the one hand and close musical-analytical studies on the other, diametrically opposed as they may appear to be, have both been criticized—often justifiably so—for missing the point by ignoring the aesthetic impulse at the heart of all music making. This is not a sectarian critique: musicologists from every part of the discipline—"old" and "new" musicologists, ethnomusicologists, and music theorists alike—have been accused of "killing the music." My interest in bringing musical pleasure into the discourse in this book stems from the important place it held in interviews with musicians and because it brings the theoretical materials into a more sustainable context.

COMPOSITIONS AS VEHICLES FOR IMPROVISATION

The choice of repertoire—that is, deciding what tunes to play in a given session, and even before that what tunes to learn—is fundamental to jazz (and other kinds of music as well, of course). It determines much of the aesthetic direction of a performance, and the particular challenges that will be set before the musicians. It also, however, impacts the economic life of the musicians and plays a prominent role in the music's cultural politics and in projections of musical identities. Given this, the place of musical repertoire in the jazz world has been relatively little studied, at least in and of itself. Studies of other improvised musical traditions—Batá drumming, rumba guaguancó, and Arabic classical music, for instance—offer few models beyond the purely technical. There is a substantial body of work relating to the technical aspects of improvising melodies over particular harmonic structures, one of the primary skills necessary for a jazz musician to interact with repertoire, and there is some ethnographic literature, most notably Paul Berliner's monumental volume *Thinking in Jazz*, that deals with how repertoire figures in the process of becoming a jazz musician.

There is, as Berliner describes it, an "eternal cycle" of relationship between precomposed materials (especially repertoire) and improvised music. One of Berliner's most striking observations on this subject is that learning a repertoire of pieces is a basic prerequisite for developing competency as a jazz musician for two reasons. First, it allows musicians to abstract theoretical principles of the music from concrete examples, and second, the shared repertoire is a basis for collective music making, and thus a port of entry into a musical community. Though Berliner does not pursue the idea, it is possible to extrapolate from his work that learning repertoire is at the core of building a sense of tradition for jazz musicians, and as such is a principle space for the creation of collective memory. The time is ripe, then, to move beyond the technical in order to see how repertoire becomes the bearer of and a key way of signaling cultural meaning, of creating collective memory.

There are a number of different ways that musicians categorize the pieces the play. They may be separated by purely technical criteria, as, for example, pieces based on "rhythm changes," blues forms, new chord progressions, a musical mode, or other less harmonically driven formats.[2] They may also be conceptualized in terms of when they were composed: they may be "early jazz" compositions, swing tunes, bebop, or post-bop pieces. Here periodization involves not only temporal criteria, but also a number of basic expectations about technical features, particularly harmonic, rhythmic, and melodic profiles. Tunes may also be categorized according to social considerations, such as on the basis of who composed them and for what purpose. Thus a piece may be a standard—a pop tune not composed with jazz performance in mind, and likely intended for performance as part of a Broadway musical—or it may be a jazz composition, a piece originally created by a jazz musician for a jazz performance.[3] Musicians further differentiate between those compositions that are their own—"originals"—and those that are not. Though other writers have not addressed this final method of differentiation, which amounts to a social history of the work, the musicians who participated in this study saw it as particularly salient, distinguishing Thelonious Monk's compositions from other ones they play regularly regardless of formal and temporal similarities they may bear to each other. Thus a blues or "rhythm changes" tune by Monk is notably different from an original one and from one drawn from the repertoire of standards or traditional tunes, regardless of the extent to which it shares technical features with those from other repertoires.

THE PRESENCE OF MANY VOICES

Jazz is unusual, if not unique, in the particular relationship that arises between the musicians and the pieces of music they play. There is always a balance between the authorial contributions of the composer and the musicians' creation of their own version of the piece (with the exception of a musician performing his or her own composition, which presents different interpretive issues). That is to say, the composer and the performer are both thought of as authoring the piece as it is played. This could well be a difference in kind rather than degree as compared to the Western classical tradition, in which the piece is a fixed composition and the performer has no authorship, or to Hindustani improvisation on a *rag*, in which the piece is quite simply a model for improvisation and that model has no composer per se.[4] The balance of authorship is shifted to one side or the other in any given jazz performance, but the multiplicity of voices is generally salient. Monson, Berliner, and others have addressed other ways in which multiple authorship works in jazz, particularly in the incorporation of licks from others' improvisations into a musician's working vocabulary and in the interaction among band members. The question of how musicians attend to both their own voice and the composer's in creating whole performances, however, particularly in the case of tunes by a composer whose voice is as strong as Monk's, has yet to be addressed in detail.

This is a particularly interesting issue because of the importance in jazz of the development of an individual voice as a part of each musician's creative growth. The jazz world places an enormous premium on individuality; not having a recognizable voice of one's own can be a source of strident criticism. I first became aware of the importance of developing a voice from a conversation in the late 1980s with Mel Williams, a musician, disc jockey, and concert promoter in northern California who played extensively in the Oakland jazz scene in the 1960s. Williams was a storehouse of knowledge about the musical and historical aspects of jazz, and I saw him as a mentor, often going to him with questions about who to listen to and why. I asked him what he thought about Wynton Marsalis, who had received a great deal of praise in the musical press by then, and he told me that despite Marsalis's prodigious "chops," or technical virtuosity, he didn't like to listen to his recordings because he didn't yet hear Marsalis's own voice in them. As he put it, "I hear Dizzy Gillespie, Louis Armstrong, Lee Morgan; but I don't hear Wynton Marsalis." Whether his judgment changed over time I don't know, because the subject never again came up in our conversations, and Williams's passing in 1999 coincided with the beginning of my work on this project.

The importance to jazz musicians of developing an individual voice is underscored in Travis Jackson's "Jazz Performance as Ritual" (2000), where he discusses what he calls musicians' "normative views of jazz performance." The musicians Jackson spoke with noted that what is important "is not so much that one should be 'innovative' or do something *novel* in terms of sound or approach, but that one should strive for something *different* and *distinctive*" (100; emphasis in the original). This applies as much to the use of preexisting materials taken from other sources as to the creation of new material. Jackson notes that "musicians who do not possess their own sounds, who seemingly mimic the sound of other musicians, are singled out for particularly harsh criticism, [and are] sometimes referred to as 'clones'" (100). It is eminently clear that the ability to make preexisting material one's own in myriad ways is a singularly important skill for the developing jazz musician. In the case of interpreting Monk's music, this act is complicated by the need musicians feel to make the music their own while still retaining the perceptible presence of Monk's voice.

It is not clear where this imperative comes from. The development of one's own sound is not a notable goal of musicians from most of the world's traditions, nor is it primary even in all African, American, or African American traditions. A particularly clear instance of the opposite position can be found in Charles Keil's book *Urban Blues*. In an interview, B. B. King, surely one of the most recognizable blues musicians in the world, explicitly downplays the importance of sounding different from others, and he seems quite happy with the fact that many blues musicians copy him (Keil 1966, 108). The desire to distinguish one's music has been very evident in the world of Western classical composition since at least the nineteenth century—even pathologically so in the twentieth century—and jazz musicians could certainly have developed this aesthetic goal as a result of being from the same general (Western, industrial) culture. In addition, having a voice may be doubly important for jazz musicians because the African American culture that jazz comes from has so often been denied a voice by the American power structure. Finally, this imperative must be conditioned at least in part by jazz's history as part of the music-industrial complex, which encourages—even requires—artists (as products for sale) to be recognizable in the marketplace.

At the risk of belaboring a mundane point, I'd like to more clearly describe what I mean by *voice*. Musicians, listeners, and scholars generally use the term unself-consciously, and as a result its meaning is a little vague. In my conversations with musicians the term was never used to mean precisely the same thing, but there was a general consensus about its core meaning. In most cases, musicians discussing Monk's voice had in mind a combination of the nuts and bolts of his idiosyncratic musical style (i.e., chord voicings, rhythmic approach, use of space, and favorite licks) and the macrolevel aspects of his approach to the music, which are singled out in chapter 2. But the term also suggests something more intangible, an interpersonal quality.

That is, people are recognizable as much for their style of musical interaction and use of musical references as for their use of a particular way of voicing an E-minor-ninth chord or the like.

CONVERSING WITH MONK

Naturally, each musician experiences and describes the process of engaging Monk and his music differently. In conversation, some musicians explicitly spoke to the issue of preserving Monk's voice in their performances of his music and the danger of obscuring their own voices in the process, while for others it came up implicitly. Yet others brought the issue up in order to downplay its importance. Each musician's answers to my questions about this said something about his or her position within the jazz world and the larger music industry, in addition to their music making per se. Although the musicians' responses were highly individual, there emerged a number of generalities with respect to both the ways the musicians characterized this issue and the ways they came to terms with it. This is as might be expected, given their engagement in a more or less shared musical world. Musicians commonly described their relationship with Monk's music as contradictory: they were originally drawn to it because they saw something in it that would give them an opportunity to express themselves more fully than did much of the other repertoire they had learned; but the process of actualizing that opportunity, of expressing themselves through or with Monk's music, was a difficult, even perilous, process. What became clear was that for all of these musicians Monk's music was dynamic, and their involvement with it and feelings about playing it changed notably over time.

It is common for musicians first to become interested in learning Monk's music in depth because they find something in his compositions and in the way that he played them that addresses specific musical concerns with which they are occupied at the time. Roswell Rudd, for instance, began playing Monk's music after experimenting with "traditional," or Dixieland, jazz in a college band at Yale University. He explained the attraction this way.

ROSWELL RUDD: Well, for me . . . I think the key word is "polyphony." Both in the rhythmic and harmonic sense. I've always had a penchant for lines, not only in the outer voices— melody, bass, and so forth—but inner lines [are] very important to me, because as a Dixieland performer that was the role that I played.

GABRIEL SOLIS: As a trombone player?

RUDD: Yeah. I played an inner line. But I was particularly curious about how Monk's polyphony worked. Where he would have very functional bass lines . . . I'm talking about root bass lines. Like real root, fundamental bass lines. No funny business there. And very clear, honed-down, graphic kind of melody. And what was going on between the melody and the bass, this is what I was really curious about: what to play as an accompaniment to melody and bass and drums in that music. (Rudd 1999)

Monk's music gave Rudd the opportunity to play idiomatic trombone parts, accompaniment lines ideally suited in range and function to what he was trying to accomplish as a musician. The fact that Monk often had intricate, sophisticated countermelodies in the range between bass and melody—both in his arrangements of the heads and in his accompaniment to his sidemen's solos—made his music uniquely interesting to Rudd. It allowed him to incorporate lessons about interactive musicality that he had learned in a Dixieland context to a modern jazz idiom in a way that felt very natural to him.

Steve Lacy described an equally personal though somewhat different reason for his growing interest in Monk's music during his formative years as a jazz performer. He was interested in many kinds of music, studying the compositions of J. S. Bach, Anton Webern, Igor Stravinsky, Duke Ellington, Kurt Weill, and Bela Bartók, for example, but, as he says, "I gave special attention to Monk's things, because, for one thing, they fit my horn. That's what attracted me in the first place, in the 1950s, was that the material was perfect for me. It was difficult, full of challenges and problems, but it wasn't too low and it wasn't too high. Nobody else was playing it, it seemed like it was made for me, or I was made for it. For my horn, the soprano, really, it was perfect" (Lacy 1999a). According to Lacy, Monk's compositions demonstrated an important combination. From a technical standpoint they worked well on his horn and provided him with the sorts of challenges he needed, but they were also ideal because other people (except, of course, Monk himself) were not playing them at the time.

For Fred Hersch, playing Monk's music is "liberating" and "fun" (Hersch 1999). Hersch plays, in his words, "about one-third stuff that I've written, and then one-third stuff that comes from the world of 'standards,' . . . and the rest . . . stuff that comes from jazz composers." Among his many recordings is an album of solo piano interpretations of Monk compositions. Monk's pieces allow Hersch to explore a very different side of his own musicality than do Tin Pan Alley songs, the repertoire for which he is best known. He described playing a Monk tune as an opportunity to work in a strictly musical frame of reference without considering song lyrics in his interpretations. In answer to a question about how he approaches Monk as compared to standards, Hersch told me, "See, with Strayhorn I have words to deal with, or almost always; with Rogers and Hammerstein, who I've also done . . . I have words to deal with. See, with Monk there are no words to deal with. So you're dealing strictly with, you know, harmony, melody, rhythm, period" (Hersch 1999). As are many musicians when they discuss their interaction with musical models, Hersch is involved in a complex web of formal questions, relationships with past performances, and the negotiation of public and private subjectivity.

These opportunities for musical learning and growth experienced when getting to know Monk's compositions are often balanced by serious difficulties. Roswell Rudd described having significant problems soloing on Monk's compositions as a younger musician, and he suggests that this is the greatest challenge of playing Monk's repertoire even now. He described the basic problem in terms of self-expression:

> Thelonious Monk and others made very wise choices about who they had in their bands, because not everybody was able to sort this stuff out and infuse [it with] their own personalities. And that's what, I think, we needed to do [with] a composer as original and distinctive as Monk. I mean, you could not take a composition of *his* and, you know, play it and then put it on the back burner and go your own way. You know, you really have to deal with the components of the composition. (Rudd 1999)

Ultimately, Rudd sees the process of "really" learning to play Monk's music as a worthwhile endeavor. In describing the ongoing project of learning the music he moved fluidly between language focused on the music itself and a consideration of personal growth.

> It'll happen that I'll be falling asleep or eating a meal, or just at an off moment, and I'll be *seized* by one of his pieces, you know, just a couple of bars of one of his things will light up in me and I realize that I'm going to have to go into that in the near future. And this never stops, these moments of his sounds and his pieces that have gotten into my body over these years, they live in there and they keep re-evoking. And the whole, the whole thing

about personal growth and personal evolution is that you have to go with these calls. You can't ignore these calls. These are about survival. About maintaining, about further growth, adding your own personality to the mix, which is inevitable *if you heed the call*. But you have to heed the call. (Rudd 1999)

The difficulty Rudd describes, the necessity of getting all the way into the pieces while also putting himself into the performance, was a real concern for Steve Lacy as well, leading him to abandon the performance of Monk's music altogether at one point. His reason for not playing Monk's music for a time mixes what might be characterized as formal and contextual, or psychological, criteria.

Oh, *yeah*. You know there's a very important point there. . . . No matter how many years I've played that music, it wasn't mine. And that's why, after a while, I got unsatisfied with the way I was playing it, and I put it on the shelf for about twelve years. I didn't touch it for a long time because I wanted to play what was mine. . . . And I, you know, I felt I was never, could never do real justice to his music 'cause it wasn't mine, no matter how much I played it. . . . I don't feel that way any more. Now I feel it's as much mine as it is anybody's. (Lacy 1999a)

Significantly, Lacy's description uses language that is not strictly musical but also refers to authorship or ownership: "I felt I . . . could never do real justice to his music 'cause it wasn't mine, no matter how much I played it." In explaining why he no longer has qualms about playing Monk's music, Lacy focused on changes in the popularity of Monk's music during that time. As he put it, "I can hear it in the supermarkets in Paris, . . . while I'm shopping, you know. So if it's gotten that far, really, it's anybody's, it's everybody's" (Lacy 1999a). Additionally, Lacy himself changed dramatically over time, maturing as a composer and bandleader, and it seems likely that this contributed to his comfortable return to Monk's music as much as the change in the music's cultural position.

Pianist Michael Weiss played Monk's music extensively as a student, learning and mastering the language of bebop and post-bop mainstream jazz, and he delved deeply into the more obscure pieces by Monk and other jazz composers in the 1980s as he developed a reputation in the New York jazz scene. He led a regular Monday night trio at Bradley's jazz club for a number of years, focusing principally on this repertoire. This facet of Weiss's work culminated in a 1990 project for the Smithsonian Institution featuring rarely performed compositions by Monk, Bud Powell, and Charlie Parker. In conversation Weiss remembered the performance with Charles McPherson and Tom Harrell fondly, but said that at this point he wouldn't be interested in doing anything similar. He explained his reasons at length, claiming that he came to feel that he couldn't express himself—couldn't fully find his own voice—in that repertoire. He described playing Monk tunes regularly at one point and feeling, "Am I really expressing myself in all the range of stuff I'd like to express? Am I getting that stuff out, playing this material, or am I having to squash a lot of that in respect for the material that I'm playing?' " (Weiss 1999). As for Lacy and Rudd, for Weiss the personal, expressive issue is inextricably intertwined with more formal musical concerns:

> I was having to do my best to do justice to the music, but it wasn't totally satisfying. [Pause] It was just confining. A lot of hard music is confining. That's why people don't play it: cause it's too . . . hard. It doesn't give you the freedom to create. Because the harmonic progression is very constricting. It's a big challenge, you know. You try and find creative ways to maneuver through a complex chord progression, like "Off Minor's," which is not too bad. It's hard, but it's written in such a way that you can weave very melodically through it, if you know how. But some tunes are not that forgiving. And after a while you ask yourself, "Why? Why am I doing this?" You know? I have to play *me*. I have to play material that I will feel satisfied and fulfilled playing, not just because it's hip and it's important and it's great. (Weiss 1999)

I was surprised at the vehemence with which Weiss expressed his current relationship to Monk's music, considering that throughout our conversation up to that point he had focused on how much value he found in the music, and how central it was to his own conception of how to play, both because of the general lessons it had taught him about accompanying and solo construction and because of the ways specific Monk pieces had affected him. His position becomes clearer in light of his own place in the jazz industry. Weiss has been a professional jazz musician for most of three decades, and has received the recognition of his peers and critics alike. Despite this, he has had great difficulty making the transition from a high-level sideman to a respected composer and leader in his own right. He sees the profusion of tribute albums in the past decade as a significant impediment to the development of a new generation of mainstream jazz composers, including himself.

Weiss noted another limit on the agency of a jazz musician, particularly a sideman: the economic and social structure of the jazz performance context. As a sideman Weiss must balance his expressive needs with the concerns of the leader for the performance. In an informal conversation he said he no longer plays Monk regularly in concert because he wants to play his own compositions as much as possible. Of course, he said, that only goes for dates on which he is the leader; when playing for someone else— Art Farmer or Johnny Griffin, for example—if they call a Monk tune, he plays it. Ultimately, the person controlling the finances has the final say regarding repertoire. Not only that, but the leader may (and often does) have specific expectations about how that material is to be played. This applies not only to the arrangement of the head, but also to the manner of accompanying the soloist. Weiss likes improvising melodic, contrapuntal accompaniments, where the comping "has its own independence and it's really . . . more like a countermelody or counterline coexisting with the soloist, rather than purely supporting the soloist," in a way similar to Monk's comping style (Weiss 1999). However, as he said, "Not all soloists are comfortable with that type of comping. I know Griffin isn't. No, it distracts him, 'cause he hears it and starts listening to it, and it takes his attention off what he's doing. So I can't comp like that with Johnny, even on Monk tunes!" (Weiss 1999). Weiss is clearly willing to adjust his playing in order to make the performance as a whole successful, and to fulfill the expectations of the band leader, because he likes playing with Griffin and because the final, musical result is worth it. Moreover, the adjustment is not outside the musical realm in which he is comfortable. His expression is not stifled by Griffin's expectations so much as channeled in a particular direction.

LIVING THE MUSIC, PLAYING THE HISTORY

The struggles and pleasures musicians describe as part of coming to terms with Monk's music resonate strongly with the theory of influence in poetry that Harold Bloom sets out in *The Anxiety of Influence*. According to Bloom, all modern poets, with the single exception of William Shakespeare, have been locked in an oedipal struggle with their immediate predecessors. For influence to be fruitful—that is, for a poet to use influence to create something other than derivative work—a poet must engage in "anxiety and self-saving caricature, [in] distortion," and in "perverse, willful revisionism" (Bloom 1973, 30).

Bloom is careful to limit his theory to the medium of poetry, but it nevertheless seems applicable to music in general, and to jazz in particular. There are two reasons for this: first, because the jazz tradition relies so heavily on interrelational, intergenerational learning, and second, because jazz performance, like poetry, is consistently understood in terms of the development and expression of the self. The way in which both poets and jazz musicians might deny their indebtedness to a precursor's model suggests a strong resonance between these two arts with respect to an anxiety about influence. Bloom quotes Wallace Stevens from a letter to the poet Richard Eberhart on this subject. Stevens says, "I sympathize with your denial of any influence on my part. This sort of thing always jars me because, in my own case, I am not conscious of having been influenced by anybody. . . . But there is a kind of critic who spends his time dissecting what he reads for echoes, imitations, influences, as if no one was ever simply himself but is always compounded of a lot of other people" (7). There is a striking similarity between this and, for example, Fred Hersch's assertion that as a young player he avoided transcribing anyone else's solos at all costs, and that although there might be similarities between his arrangement of a Monk tune and Monk's, such consistencies should be understood as stemming from formal requirements of the material itself, and not from Monk's performance of it. It should be noted, however, that for every musician who expresses some anxiety about the extent to which their approach to performing Monk's music could be understood to owe something to Monk's own performances, there are at least an equal number who are comfortable acknowledging others' influence. John Murphy (1990) underscores this in his article "Jazz Improvisation: The Joy of Influence." The words of musicians presented in this book as well strongly suggest that influence is often seen as both a joy and a struggle. The idea was expressed particularly nicely by Stan Getz in an interview published in the mid-1980s: "I never tried to imitate anybody, but when you love somebody's music, you're influenced" (Martin 1986).

Whether coming to terms with others' influence is a joy or a struggle, it is inevitable, as it is built into the process of becoming a musician. Mikhail Bakhtin's description of language alluded to in the introduction is apposite for music, as well. Bakhtin describes words as having "the 'taste' of a profession, a genre, a tendency, a party, a particular work, a particular person, a generation, an age group, the day and hour" (Bakhtin 1981, 293). It is through this taste that words become fully meaningful, reaching beyond their simplest, syntactical meanings. That these "tastes" are themselves powerful becomes clear as Bakhtin expands on the psychological ramifications of the notion of a relational understanding of language:

> As a living, socio-ideological concrete thing . . . language, for the individual consciousness, lies on the borderline between oneself and the other. The word in language is half someone else's. It becomes "one's own" only when the speaker populates it with his own intention, his own accent, when he appropriates the word, adapting it to his own semantic and expressive intention. Prior to this moment of appropriation the word does not exist in a neutral and impersonal language (it is not, after all, out of a dictionary that the speaker gets his words!), but rather it exists in other people's mouths, in other people's contexts, serving other people's intentions: it is from there that one must take the word, and make it one's own. And not all words for just anyone submit equally easily to this appropriation, to this seizure and transformation into private property: many words stubbornly resist, others remain alien, sound foreign in the mouth of the one who appropriated them and who now speaks them; they cannot be assimilated into his context and fall out of it; it is as if they put themselves in quotation marks against the will of the speaker. (293–94)

Bakhtin's recognition that some words easily come to sound as part of the speaker's own personal language while others "stubbornly resist" and "put themselves in quotation marks" is particularly resonant. Nevertheless, despite the potentially alienating quality in these musicians' interactions with Monk, all of them have ultimately found that the process of overcoming that alienation—often by learning to manage and make aesthetic value out of the quotation marks—is a thing of great value, aesthetically, socially, and psychologically.

It is this quality of utterances (musical as well as linguistic) that are carried from one's past that makes playing jazz a mode for engaging the historical imagination, as I suggested at the beginning of this chapter. In *Silencing the Past,* Michel-Rolph Trouillot (1995) adamantly argues that official history has generally misrepresented the breadth of people involved in "the field of historical production." In his words, academic historians "grossly underestimate the size, the relevance, and the complexity of the overlapping sites where history is produced, notably outside of academia" (19). Trouillot suggests three ways in which all people are, at one time or another, involved with the production of history: first, as "agents," by which he means historically effective groups (his examples include workers, slaves, and mothers); second, as "actors," by which he means the sociocultural complex of individuals existing within specific sociohistorical contexts; and third, as "subjects," his term for "actors when the historian claims access to their subjectivities as self-conscious," such as individual strikers described by the historian as actors "who *intend* to strike, and *do* strike intending to do so" (23; emphasis in the original). This final category provides the most difficulty, but at the same time the most potential for understanding how and why historical discourse is a part of everyday life. Trouillot considers individuals' potential for historical subjectivity as the process through which they become "fully historical," as they are engaged "simultaneously in the socio-historical process and in narrative constructions about that process" (24). Having said this, Trouillot opens up a broader field for understanding historical subjects than he had at first. Subjects are, on the one hand, the product of historical narrative; but all of us are also subjects each time we engage in the telling of historical narrative.

The many ways that playing Monk's music amounts to a kind of historicity will become clear in later chapters, but the subject is also important here. Because all jazz performances involve, first and foremost, the act of molding something new out of something old, it is in the struggle to deal with personal growth and evolution that Roswell Rudd described that musicians develop the sense of their own place in the music. The lineages they place themselves in then take on more and more resonance in performance and reflections on performance over time.

FOUR

Three Pianists and the Monk Legacy

Fred Hersch, Danilo Perez, and Jessica Williams

AS THE PRECEDING CHAPTER SHOWED, jazz musicians often speak eloquently about the demands of Monk's legacy and about the pitfalls they face
on the way to developing their own voices when playing Monk's music. In my
interviews, however, they spoke less explicitly about the ways they solved those
challenges in particular instances. Nonetheless, particular performances and
the degree to which they represent good solutions to those challenges are worth
considering for their own sake and for the light they may shed on more general questions about the nature of borrowing and revision in jazz. The overriding question for such an analysis is, When is the interaction of the voices—
Monk's and those of the musicians playing his music—creatively satisfying
and productive? There are plenty of dull, lifeless, derivative, or just indifferent
recordings of Monk's pieces in record label catalogues the world around, so
those gems of creative engagement where Monk's music shines in another's
hands are dear, indeed. Of course, this is highly contested ground: it is easy to
find both partisans and detractors for any performer and any performance of
Monk's music. And, as evidence of the centrality of the question just posed,
praise or criticism of any performance is often phrased in terms of the extent
to which it succeeds or fails to integrate a sense of Monk's authorial presence
while at the same time incorporating the interpreter's own voice.[1]

Naturally, for performers and audiences alike the expectations that apply
to any jazz performance must be met before the question of whether an

engagement with Monk's music succeeds in balancing authorial voices can be addressed. A fairly concise summary of factors musicians consider necessary for a performance in a club or a recording session to be successful can be found in Travis Jackson's article "Jazz Performance as Ritual." Jackson points to "the importance of having an individual voice; developing the ability to balance and play with a number of different musical parameters in performance; understanding the cultural foundations of the music; being able oneself to 'bring something to the music'; creating music that is 'open enough' to allow other musicians to bring something despite or because of what has been provided structurally or contextually; and being open for transcendence to 'the next level' of performance, the spiritual level" (Jackson 1998, 96). In this sense playing a Monk tune has an important generic similarity to playing a blues, a standard, or any other piece.

The specific criteria musicians use to decide whether a performance of Monk's music is satisfying, whether it "works" or not, are at least as elusive as the values Jackson notes. Critique commonly rests on the extent to which a performance does or does not depart from Monk's versions of the piece, and, more generally, on the extent to which interpreters borrow from or integrate Monk's style. Borrowing and integration may involve the use of specific references to Monk's harmonic, textural, and rhythmic vocabulary—for example, the use of stride-style left-hand figures, whole-tone runs, or dissonant clusters, especially those incorporating both flat and natural versions of upper chord tones—or may involve broader concerns, such as the extent to which a musician improvises using motives from the head to create a solo that has some integral unity, as Monk often did. Musicians from amateur to professional are generally divided on where to draw a line between a legitimate kind of referentiality and a derivative performance. (The description of a musician's style of playing a Monk tune as "Monkish" can seem oblique or snide, depending on tone of voice and such, but is generally critical. Any changes to the compositions, from local reharmonizations to large-scale changes in the character or feel of a piece, can be compelling or seem forced, depending in large part on whether they seem justified in some way, whether they seem "right" or not. Musicians I interviewed for this book were generally disdainful of performances in which they thought the attempt to personalize Monk's music was superficial, an overlay of novelty to hide the fact that the musician had nothing new to say.

There is some tension over aesthetic ideals here. On the one hand, there is a sense that the pieces contain within them some essence and that the best interpretations enlighten by uncovering some previously unnoticed or un-explored facet that inheres in the music rather than by bringing something altogether new to it. On the other hand, however, musicians also stress their desire to reinvent a piece by bringing something of themselves to the in-terpretation. This can lead to such apparently self-contradictory statements as the following by Travis Jackson: "The point . . . is not so much that one should be 'innovative' or do something *novel* in terms of sound or ap-proach, but that one should strive for something *different* and *distinctive*" (Jackson 2000, 38). While this may seem like semantic hairsplitting, the statement's significance cannot be overemphasized. It is conceptually con-voluted because it represents the genuine doubleness of the aesthetics gen-erating it.

In the three examples that make up the bulk of this chapter I would like to highlight the remarkable variation in the ways jazz musicians have ap-proached the shared concern of crafting interpretations of Monk's music that they feel adequately engage Monk's voice as they hear it while at the same time bringing out their individual sound. Looking at Danilo Perez, Fred Hersch, and Jessica Williams, three pianists, all active on the scene in the 1990s and today, I will consider the variety of strategies the musicians use to maintain Monk in their performances of his music. The impact of cultural politics, and particularly of race and gender, on this process emerges as significant in my analyses, as does the interrelation of formal musical language and languages of subjectivity and identity in the musi-cians' descriptions of playing the music.

DANILO PEREZ: "REFLECTIONS"

In the previous chapter I described the striking sense of rightness in Danilo Perez's live performance of Monk's music that I experienced one winter eve-ning at Birdland. That same sense also comes through in his recorded work, though, like many contemporary jazz musicians, Perez has no personal con-nection with Monk. Perez is a young musician who in the mid- to late 1990s began receiving a great deal of attention from jazz critics and established masters for his abilities as a pianist and composer. An Afro-Panamanian, he grew up in an environment that was (at least) bi-musical, listening to and participating in Panamanian traditional music and Western classical music. He was educated in classical piano in Panama, attending the National Con-servatory, and soon moved to the United States to study classical and jazz piano, attending Indiana University of Pennsylvania and, for a short time,

Berklee School of Music. After leaving school Perez worked with a number of jazz masters, most notably Paquito D'Rivera, Dizzy Gillespie, and Jon Hendricks, all of whom have been enormously important in mentoring younger musicians in the jazz community. In 1992 he began working as a bandleader, and he has recorded periodically since then to growing critical acclaim.

In Perez's eyes, working with Jon Hendricks was an important step in getting to know Monk's music. As he remembers it, playing with Hendricks "was my first professional gig playing jazz. And he had a very big repertory of [Monk tunes]. So, that was the first time I had to learn Monk tunes. I guess at that time I wasn't really ready . . . to assimilate such a different sound. I don't think I'd fallen in love yet at that time, but that was the beginning of me dealing with Monk" (Perez 1999). Perez notes that it wasn't until some years later that he began really incorporating Monk's music into his own repertoire as a soloist and leader. The experience of playing with Hendricks's band nonetheless influenced how he approached Monk's compositions as a leader. Working with a leader who had a strong connection to and affinity for Monk's music established a foundation for approaching the music later on, when he felt ready to engage it.

Perez's description of the process of bringing Monk's music into his working repertoire—of "falling in love"—is illuminating. Perez's troubles with Monk's compositions when he first played them with Hendricks stemmed not so much from strictly formal problems, such as finding ways to negotiate unusual and at times counterintuitive changes when soloing, but from not being "ready to assimilate such a different sound."[2] It was not until Perez found a compelling relationship between Monk's music and his own musical frame of reference that he was able to bring Monk's pieces into his regular repertoire. Playing Monk with Wynton Marsalis's ensemble, he began to hear what he described as a New Orleans/Caribbean groove in the music. At that point, he said it felt "very comfortable, rhythmically, playing. I felt like I didn't have to, I wasn't recalling anybody else anymore. I found, like, I found something; like I discovered [something]" (Perez 1999). Perez built on that experience. He explained:

I started *really* working on Monk, but this time I found that he had probably the closest connection to anybody in my childhood, to my musical background, than any of the other piano players I have checked out. Because he was the one that told me, that reminded me, that percussion and drums are a part of this music, very strong. And of course I grew up on the drum, on percussion, and I mean right away [there was] an unusual connection I hadn't felt before. So I started messing [around] with the music, looking for different ways to [play it].

Until that point I [was] still making that transition, how to play with the Latin thing, especially playing jazz. How to have that sensibility of jazz, but with Latin rhythms and that. And still I was going back and forth. And Monk *really* hooked it up for me. It was like, "Pam!" (Perez 1999)

I asked Perez whether he felt that when he started "working on Monk" there was a danger that Monk's voice would somehow overshadow his own, and he responded:

Oh, definitely, definitely. There's no doubt about it. . . . But it's almost like if you were born in San Francisco and somebody brings you to New York and you feel like, "Oh. This is where I belong." You see, Monk, that's what he . . . he brought me to another place And once I found it, I said, "Oh, this is it, this is my culture. This is where I belong." So right away I discovered *myself*. So it wasn't, I wasn't afraid of something. (Perez 1999)

The way that Perez moves fluidly between a discussion of his formal engagement with music making and his experience of personal musical growth is remarkably similar to the way other musicians describe getting to know Monk's music.

As Perez developed his interest in Monk's music, he found that his own sound world and that of Monk shared certain African diasporic qualities that allowed him to connect with the music more deeply. He described the process in this way:

See, I think what happened . . . the feel of harmony and melody that jazz has, well, [it would] take you many years before you really found that relation, 'cause it's almost European, actually, but jazz has a lot of connection with percussion and drums of Africa, you know, seriously, *solid*. And culturally that was something that I grew up on. So I found in jazz that element of connection. See, up until that time I didn't. I was thinking of changes and learning people's tunes, but I never thought that it was with all of this [he sings syncopated drum pattern]. I mean it was, I would do it, but I didn't think [of it that way]. In other words, that wasn't a priority.

But once I felt that it was that connection [he snaps], it allows me—see, it's almost like I found my strong point and could *move on*. That helps all the other things. (Perez 1999)

The implication in Perez's contrasting descriptions of first playing Monk's music in Hendricks's band, when he "wasn't ready to assimilate such a different sound"—a time when, as he tells it, he was deeply involved with Bill Evans's music—and later, when he was ready to "*really* work on Monk," is that learning from a particular music involves a give and take, a dialogue of sorts. Rather than describing a process of *influence*—a unidirectional process in which the musician is a sort of tabula rasa—Perez describes how he brings his own subjectivity to his engagement with others' music, drawing from the music the lessons he needs to learn at the time. This, however, is not an arbitrary process; Perez did not hear things in Monk's music that are not there. Both Perez and Monk bring something to the dialogue, and for the conversation to be productive Perez must maintain some balance between his own voice and Monk's. He has brought a set of desires and expectations to the music, but has also remained open to hearing what Monk has to say.

In 1996 Perez released *PanaMonk,* a tribute album consisting of recordings of his own compositions, works by Monk, and one standard, "Everything Happens to Me," a song from Monk's repertoire of standards (Perez 1996).[3] It was Perez's first recording for the newly revived Impulse label and may have been seen by producer Tommy LiPuma as an opportunity to introduce Perez to a wider audience. By setting Perez's new material in the context of more familiar compositions by Monk, the recording could capitalize on the recognition value of Monk while still allowing Perez to include his own work.[4]

Rather than seeing the tribute album as an impediment to making a space for himself, as Michael Weiss described (see chapter 3), Perez actively pursued the opportunity to make the recording. He described it as "something I needed to do. 'Cause . . . approaching Monk and being able to approach it *personally* will give me the diploma, the graduation, the confidence that I needed to step on my own completely, just try things, you know. And it *did;* it did for me. It just, it just gave me that spiritual thing, to play Monk without sounding *like* Monk, but having the spirit of Monk" (Perez 1999). Perez was particularly enthusiastic about establishing himself as a part of the jazz tradition by recording this album. He no longer felt like an apprentice, but now felt he had real credibility in the jazz world: he would no longer be relegated to that marked category, "Latin" jazz musician. It is interesting to note that Perez uses the language of "official," worldly culture to describe the acquisition of cultural capital; this project, when successfully completed, would confer upon him a "diploma." The project would also give him some kind of otherworldly authority, in his words, "that spiritual thing."

Perez's *PanaMonk*—with Terri Lyne Carrington on percussion, Avishai Cohen on bass, and Jeff "Tain" Watts on drums—is put together as a large-scale work with some sense of unity, as concept albums generally are. Because it is organized around a single idea (in this case, Monk's music), the concept album must be judged at least in part on how it works as a single entity. *PanaMonk* is arranged around two very short performances of Monk's evocative ballad "Monk's Mood," which are used as a frame around a succession of originals and Monk compositions. The opening track presents a single statement of the bridge of "Monk's Mood," with no A sections or solo choruses, and the final track presents what should be heard as the closing A section. The musical language in both tracks is interesting. Perez plays with a free rubato reminiscent of Monk's own solo piano recordings of his compositions, in a style that sounds eminently reminiscent of Art Tatum's *The Complete Solo Masterpieces* recordings on Pablo Records (Tatum 1991). At the same time Perez intermixes the dense harmonies and textures of mainstream jazz piano since the 1960s with some harmonic gestures derived from Monk's personal style.

Between these epigrammatic statements Perez interprets Monk's compositions using a lush, post-bop harmonic language and multifaceted references to Monk's performances of the pieces themselves—and, even more significantly, making references to Monk's style as an improviser—while recasting the pieces in Latin and even occasionally funky pop rhythmic grooves. "Reflections," the seventh track on the disc, bears closer analysis as one of the most successful performances on the CD, both in terms of the relationship between the various voices in the performance and as a virtuoso performance in its own right.

"Reflections" opens with a solo piano introduction in which Perez plays two measures out of time followed by the bridge of the piece (ex. 4). These scant ten measures provide not only a formal introduction to the performance as a whole, but also an introduction to the wealth and density of indexical relations that Perez will pursue throughout the piece. The first notes Perez plays—an introduction to the introduction, of sorts—move the listener from silence into the sound world of this music with an abstraction of Monk's harmonic and textural language. Perez strikes a series of harmonic clusters that introduce the key of the piece, A♭ major.[5] Perez's use of an idiosyncratic Monk gesture, striking chords percussively and then letting up one or more of the keys, leaving one ringing, is the most striking incorporation of Monk's sound in this opening gesture. It dramatically invokes Monk's presence through a peculiar textural or timbral complex of sound. Perez also refers to Monk through the harmonic use of dissonance—particularly the minor ninth G♭ over F in the fifth cluster. Monk also peeks through in the melodic augmented fourth relationships between C and G♭ in the upper voice from the fourth to fifth chords and in the bass moving from the fifth to sixth chords. That Perez presents this in the context of a post-Monk harmonic language is made most evident by his use of more strictly textural minor seconds in the lowest voice. In Monk's work such dissonances almost always have some harmonic significance, but as jazz has incorporated a less strictly functional harmonic language in the past forty years, the presence of seconds for their own sake, for the frisson they generate, has become more common.

The following eight measures present the bridge proper. The principal rhythmic interest in this section is Perez's alternation between a $\frac{6}{4}$ and $\frac{4}{4}$ feel, with the half note remaining roughly equivalent, a rhythmic nuance common in much Afro-Caribbean and Latin American music. The $\frac{6}{4}/\frac{4}{4}$ contrast plays out as a concurrent polyrhythm only in measure 5 of the bridge, but the sense that there are two alternating divisions of the measure imbues the entire section.

In measures 5, 7, and 8 of the bridge Perez changes harmonic style, effectively changing referential style. Here his use of more consonant, less tritone-saturated harmonies and homophonic texture is reminiscent of a gutsier, bluesier style. Here, rather than referencing Monk directly, he brings another sound into the mixture, creating a sense of connection between these musics and showing that he sees them as compatible sound worlds. Such eclecticism is typical of Perez's playing. Indeed, the ability to move deftly from one feel to another, both through rhythmic nuance and harmonic/melodic language, is one of Perez's strongest skills as a musician.

In both the introduction and the first chorus, Perez interprets the piece in a way that makes occasional reference to Monk's voicings and response figures without suggesting a significant reliance on a specific Monk recording. At no time is there the sense that Perez is attempting to re-create Monk's arrangement of the tune as a whole. In measure 4 of the bridge, for example, Perez plays a figure that responds to the principle melody of the first three measures. Monk generally played a similar response figure at this moment, with similar pitch content (this figure is relatively consistent throughout Monk's various recordings of the piece), but Perez, rather than

Example 4. "Reflections": Introduction as played by Danilo Perez (Danilo Perez 1996, track 7, 0:0–0:35).

play the figure exactly as Monk did, alters it to fit within the rhythmic language he has crafted for this performance (ex 5).

By contrast, in measure 8 of the bridge Perez omits a different sort of response figure that Monk often plays—a bass interjection of an E♭ on the second half of beat one and both eighth notes of beat two, followed by an off-beat descending arpeggiation between E♭ and A natural on beats three and four (ex. 6). This guides the ear, underscoring the harmonic and melodic similarity between this measure and measure 2 of the A section. In both

Example 5. "Reflections": Response figure, bridge, m. 4, left hand only
(a. Thelonious Monk 1986, disc 12, track 5; b. Danilo Perez 1996, track 7).

a. Thelonious Monk

b. Danilo Perez

Example 6. "Reflections": Thelonious Monk performance, first chorus,
bridge, m. 8 (Thelonious Monk 1986, disc 12, track 5, 1:12–1:15).

measures the melody moves in half notes from F to F♭, headed toward E♭
in the next measure—that is, from the fifth above a ii chord to the flat ninth
above a dominant, moving strongly toward resolution on the fifth of the
following I chord. This melodic/harmonic move is motivic in "Reflections," occurring in a somewhat elaborated form in measures 6 and 8 of the
first A section as well. Because this figure shows up in other Monk tunes
and in Monk's improvisatory language, it has weight beyond its structural
function within the composition, bringing Monk to mind through its very
presence.

   Although Perez does not use the bass-voice response Monk crafted to underscore the connection between this moment in the bridge and material
from the A sections, he does, nevertheless, mark the correspondence between sections musically. In measure 8 of the bridge Perez elaborates the F–F♭

Example 7. "Reflections": Danilo Perez performance, first chorus, A1, m. 2 (Danilo Perez 1996, track 7, 0:39–0:41).

movement with a gesture that reaches up to E♭ a seventh above and then arpeggiates down through D♭, C, and A♭ before reaching F♭. He further delays the F♭ with a passing G♭ on beat three. When he reaches measure 2 in the first A section of the chorus that follows, Perez echoes this elaboration with a simplified version that uses only the E♭, C, and A♭, and that adds a lower grace note to the F♭ (ex. 7). This constitutes yet another way Perez is able to incorporate Monk's approach to the piece—that is, to keep Monk's voice present—while making the performance his own. This is what semioticians would call an "indexical" relation, a sort of reference that is different than his use of a technique associated with Monk for the opening chords of the recording. In the first example the relationship to Monk was accomplished through a specific, nonarbitrary sonic resemblance, a relationship of "iconicity," whereas in the second the relation between the two is more abstract. In one case the relationship is created by sonic resemblance and in the other it is created by sonically divergent motives that fulfill the same musical function. Both are mediated, contingent processes; both require a listener who has a wealth of cultural information—or, more precisely, a personal musical past, an internal soundtrack that contains sounds similar to those of the performer—to complete the process by hearing Perez's playing in a referential framework and making the connection between various performances.

Perez continues to mix these various ways of keeping Monk present in the following two choruses, both of which work within the space Paul Berliner describes as moving "from interpretation to improvisation" (Berliner 1994, 171). Perez departs, at times radically, from the melody of the piece throughout these choruses, but he always returns to a fairly straightforward statement of key motives from the head at significant points. This serves as a device to punctuate his improvised statements, and as a way of giving the performance an overall sense of unity. Moreover, it helps give Monk's precomposed materials greater conceptual weight in the performance. In addition to playing a formal role, this soloing style also functions referentially. As discussed in chapter 1, Monk's ability to keep the precomposed melody alive in his improvised solo choruses is commonly noted by musicians and writers as one of his strongest stylistic markers. Perez himself noted in an interview for this project that Monk set the standard for "motivic improvisation" (Perez 1999).[6]

Perez's solo style here is particularly reminiscent of Monk's solo performances of his own compositions. Monk's performance of "Reflections" on the album *Thelonious Alone in San Francisco,* recorded for Riverside Records in 1959, serves as a good example (Monk 1986, disc 12, track 5). This performance gives the impression that each chorus is an interpretation of the melody, the first and the last chorus staying closer to the precomposed melody, those between departing from it more but never venturing into the improvisation of entirely new material. While this style is by no means peculiar to Monk, it is one he used often—perhaps more often than his contemporaries—and to great aesthetic advantage. It is not a style that Perez routinely adopts when playing his own or others' compositions, so here it clearly seems intended to refer to Monk. By using such indexical strategies that reference Monk, without, however, being limited to referencing him, Perez can create a richly textured relation to the past while remaining committed to the present performance. The result is a remarkably successful combination of voices.

This combination of voices was even more explicit in Perez's live performance in January 1999 that I described at the outset of the previous chapter. When I attended the concert, I was particularly interested in the ways he used visual cues to heighten the sense of referentiality to Monk. As Travis Jackson has noted, visual and verbal cues are helpful tools for constructing a successful jazz performance, allowing musicians to communicate their intentions and judgments of the ongoing performance with bandmates (Jackson 1998, 160–67, 178–81). Visual cues are also very important in communicating musical references. Musical reference is a tricky form of expression, because it requires a shared recognition that a cue—a particular lick, for example—somehow brings to mind something outside the immediate context. The potential for misunderstanding or incomprehension is great, so it is not surprising that musicians would use any resources at their disposal to reinforce their referential intentions. Perez, for example, in this performance provided a striking visual clue to his reference to Monk during an extended bass solo on "Bright Mississippi." Perez stopped comping in the third chorus, got up from the piano bench, and began dancing. His dance was strikingly reminiscent of Monk's own on-stage dance, as described numerous times and captured on film in Charlotte Zwerin's 1998 film *Straight,*

No Chaser (Troupe 1998, 106; Zwerin 1998). Most importantly, this dance reinforced a musical relationship, as Perez laid out while Jon Benitez soloed. On its own, laying out might not be heard as a reference to Monk (it was one of Monk's common practices but is not associated uniquely with him), but doing it during a performance of a Monk tune helped the audience hear it this way, and Perez cements this sense of reference with paramusical aspects of the performance.

FRED HERSCH: "I MEAN YOU"

Having considered Danilo Perez, who uses clearly audible references to Monk in his performances of Monk's music and shows relatively little anxiety about being charged with unoriginality, I now want to move on to Fred Hersch, whose playing provides a contrast to Perez's. Hersch plays Monk's music regularly, using more abstract references to connect his performances with Monk. As will become clear, this is partly a result of his concern about being labeled an imitator.

Early in the summer of 1999 I went to the Village Vanguard, in Greenwich Village, to hear a performance by Hersch. I had heard his name before but was entirely unfamiliar with his music. It was a Tuesday night, the opening night of Hersch's trio's run at the Vanguard, and I was excited at the possibility of hearing something new. I sat down at the bar and began talking with the bartender, Tom Dylan. I asked him what he thought of Hersch, what he played, and what I could expect from the evening's performance. He told me that Hersch was an excellent pianist with an unusual business acumen, and as a result of these two qualities, he had managed to build a following. Dylan described Hersch as a "romantic" sort of player who played mostly standards, and who has a lush, accessible trio sound, strongly reminiscent of Bill Evans (Dylan, personal communication).

The first piece Hersch played, a medley of Cole Porter's songs "All of You" and "So in Love," bore out this description. I was surprised, then, when he started playing Monk's composition "Work" and the feel of the set changed. Hersch adapted his musical style to the material, presenting the piece with a less "impressionistic" harmonic language, a more unpredictable rhythmic approach, and an attempt to convey humor in both musical and physical language. My surprise was in part a result of my expectations, which were based upon a brief description of Hersch's playing. I might have been more prepared for this change of sound if I had known at the time the range of Hersch's performing history.[7] However, my surprise was also a result of the immediate juxtaposition of very different styles and sounds in that context. In my experience it is uncommon to hear such dramatic shifts in musical style in a single set. Because generic style expectations form an important frame for musical interpretation (though one that is not often analyzed), such a shift can be momentarily disorienting, but it can also be an effective performance strategy.[8] In this case Hersch's variation of musical style was effective: it successfully boosted the collective energy of the evening, made the audience more actively involved with the performance by challenging our expectations, and helped establish Hersch's versatility as the leader of the trio. It was also effective in invoking Monk's presence, more because the second piece contrasted with the earlier style of the evening than because of the piece's close relationship to Monk's voice itself.

As Danilo Perez did in his performance at Birdland, Hersch used nonmusical cues to underline this changed performance frame. His distinctly playful approach to "Work" was in part expressed through musical aspects of the trio's playing—the arrangement and solos—but Hersch also reflected it with a more informal personal presentation, bobbing his head along with the music and clapping along with Drew Gress's bass solo. This should not be seen as a suggestion that Hersch attaches less importance to, or ascribes less seriousness of musical purpose to, Monk's music than to the Tin Pan Alley tunes he plays. Rather, this sort of presentation is a way for Hersch to connect with and communicate a playfulness he says he has always heard at the heart of Monk's music (Hersch 1999).[9]

Although Hersch has been active in the New York jazz scene since the late 1970s, he began to receive significant recognition as a soloist and bandleader only recently, a fact he attributes to his professional integrity. Hersch, like many jazz musicians, dislikes playing with unfamiliar bandmates in an "all-star" package—"billboarding," as it is known in the music industry—insisting instead on working with his own trio. As he puts it, "I'm sure I could have been working at the Vanguard many years before I started working there regularly if I was willing to play that game; but I was not willing to play that game. So when I started working there I started with my own trio. And that's the only way I wanted to do it. It took me longer, but it was much more gratifying" (Hersch 1999).

Hersch shows such personal and professional integrity in a number of ways, all of which may well have made the road to professional success more difficult. His commitment to integrity was particularly evident when he chose to come out as a gay man as he was building his career. When he was diagnosed with the HIV virus in the mid-1980s, he took this potentially devastating illness as an opportunity to take a stand. In addition to coming out, Hersch began work to combat the disease and raise public awareness. In the years since then he has given numerous benefit concerts and organized benefit recordings within both the jazz and classical music communities.

Hersch, like many musicians, takes inspiration from Monk's example of personal and artistic integrity. The fact that Monk had to endure years of invisibility before landing a significant recording contract, and that he suffered from insensitive critics during the 1960s and early 1970s yet still maintained his belief in what he was doing, makes him a model for Hersch, particularly given that Monk's music and image ultimately survived these trials. In Hersch's words, "I think the fact, just the fact that he dared to be different . . . that he really, you know, stuck to it. I think that's inspiring" (Hersch 1999). In Hersch's description of why he is inspired by Monk, the personal and artistic aspects of Monk's integrity are interwoven. Hersch points to Monk's long association with Charlie Rouse, even in the face of critical opposition, as particularly admirable. He feels that an important part of Monk's legacy is "that he wasn't swayed by all the people who said, 'You should get another saxophone player. We're sick of hearing Charlie Rouse.' Whatever it was. Or that 'You need to do something different.' Or, 'Gee, people are tired of hearing . . .' He didn't give a shit. He said, 'Well, this is my vision. I'm sticking with it. Fuck you' " (Hersch 1999).

Hersch's approach to combining his voice and Monk's when playing Monk's music tends to grow out of the abstraction of particular formal processes he hears in Monk's compositions (and performances of them) rather than from borrowing surface details of Monk's voice. At least, he tends to see the abstractions as the most significant aspects of Monk's music and tends to downplay the surface resemblances between his voice and Monk's. When discussing how he interprets a Monk piece, Hersch noted that success depends on finding out what kind of story the tune tells and then expanding on that story. He made it clear that although for jazz standards this story may be narrative, with Monk's music the story is the expression of some specifically musical formal issue: "Every tune—or any work of art, whatever it is, that is a real work of art—but any great tune sort of has . . . its own world. It has certain features that are unique to that tune, whether it's a harmonic feature, a motivic feature, or something about, you know, just the way it unfolds, or that it's formed, that makes it distinctive" (Hersch 1999). Hersch's commitment to an aesthetic of unity is clear here, and this commitment is a significant factor in the way he ultimately negotiates the intra- and intermusical aspects of his solo improvisation.

Hersch's solo performance of "I Mean You," from the album *Thelonious,* is an example of the integration of intra- and intermusical concerns in improvisation as well as a superb performance (Hersch 1998). As mentioned above, for Hersch, making a Monk tune half Monk's and half his own is a matter of finding something in the piece itself and then finding a story of his own to tell with it. In the case of "I Mean You," this "something" is a very particular relationship between the melody and bass voices. Although there is significant variation in the many recordings Monk made of "I Mean You,"Monk typically plays, or at least suggests, a characteristic bass part. Rather than walking, or providing a standard harmonic foundation in half notes, as is common for the bass in a bebop or post-bop performance during the head chorus, the bass line in Monk's arrangements of "I Mean You," whether executed by the bass player or Monk's own left hand, usually consists of chord roots or, commonly, roots and fifths in combination on beats two and four, as a punctuation for the melody. The melody for this piece works by shifting accents within the bar against a basic backbeat $\frac{4}{4}$. The bass punctuation, then, functions as a foil for the melody's metric fluidity.

Hersch presents an abstraction of this polyrhythmic interaction of voices in his solo rendition of the head chorus of this performance (ex. 8). Rather than fill out the harmonies with the sort of lush pianistic sound he uses elsewhere on this CD, Hersch adopts a sparse approach, highlighting the stratification of melodic lines. At first he limits the arrangement to the two principal parts, an unadorned melody line and a bass part in open intervals, mainly fifths. Here Hersch references Monk through an abstraction: although this is not a specific use of a Monk arrangement of the head, the stripped-down, two-part texture references Monk's often-noted simplicity and clarity of texture. As the head chorus progresses Hersch begins to add some contrapuntal lines to the melody, but throughout the first two A sections he seldom plays more than two or three notes at a time. In the bridge Hersch changes the texture in accordance with the melodic and rhythmic change in the melody. He plays the long tones in tight harmony (as they might be played by a trumpet section in a big band arrangement), and he changes the rhythm of the open fifths in the bass. Nonetheless, he maintains the general relationship between the two parts, even throwing it into greater relief. In the final A section of the head chorus Hersch expands his use of moving inner lines somewhat, since the simpler framework of melody and bass voices is already well established.

Example 8. "I Mean You": Fred Hersch, head, A1, A2, and bridge
(Fred Hersch 1998, track 11, 0:0–0:33).

In this arrangement there is very little that sounds as though it were taken verbatim from one of Monk's recordings of the piece. Rather, Hersch invokes Monk through musical devices associated with the composer more generally. The arrangement's sparseness and its occasional stark, exposed use of dissonance both clearly call to mind Monk without necessarily referencing a particular Monk performance. Even Hersch's open fifths in the bass, which are prominent in a number of Monk's versions of "I Mean You," never relate directly to one model. Instead, he finds a new way of playing them—one that fits well within his own solo piano language even as it references Monk's.

Hersch takes up this polarity of bass and treble voices with Monk's characteristic open intervals in the bass, as a central feature of his improvised choruses following the head. He plays three choruses and then a final chorus that brings back the main melody at the third A section, and then extends the chorus with an additional A section. Of these choruses, the third makes the most of the bass in open fifths together with a more active melodic line. Now, however, the bass is released from its role of maintaining the backbeat and instead creates a rhythmic instability through a polyrhythmic counterpoint with the upper line. Throughout these choruses, in addition to using this characteristic texture, Hersch references Monk's approach to improvising on his own compositions by playing with small motives from the melody, establishing and playing with musical relationships within the thirty-two-bar chorus structure by moving motives from one place to another. This is notable in his extension of the closing motive from the last A section of the head into the beginning of the next chorus. Here a motive that fits harmonically is used to obscure the large-scale formal unit because of its syntactical meaning. It sounds like the continuation of the previous chorus, not the beginning of a new one, especially since one might be expecting the tag Monk often played here. This subtle playing with formal expectations allows Hersch to reference Monk without fear of sounding imitative in any way.

Following the final, elongated chorus, Hersch plays the tag that Monk often used as both an introduction and conclusion. This is an almost self-conscious way of reflecting on the place of Monk's voice in Hersch's arrangement of the piece. By ending with this tag, Hersch reinforces its absence elsewhere—at the beginning, and at the end of the head—where Monk commonly played it.

Hersch's description of his involvement with Monk's music contrasts with the relatively uncomplicated picture Perez paints of integrating his voice with Monk's when performing Monk's compositions. While Perez has a relatively unencumbered approach to playing Monk, freely invoking Monk through surface resemblance without fear of being accused of imitating him, Hersch, on the other hand, speaks in much less carefree terms about using Monk's music in his working repertoire. It is indicative of Hersch's attitude that he stressed to me the seriousness with which he views the sense of fun in Monk's music, and the hard work he feels is required to understand the playfulness and simplicity in Monk's performances (Hersch 1999).

In order to understand Hersch's discourse about playing the music it is necessary to consider it in relation to where he stands within the jazz community. Race is in the background of Hersch's discussion of his engagement with Monk's music. This is not surprising, since this complex, highly charged construction is at the heart of much of the discourse on jazz and on the social, cultural, and political life of America in general.[10] As a white musician, Hersch is uncomfortable with what he sees as a reverse racism in the jazz world. He is critical of what he perceives as an advantage that African American musicians have in jazz, singling out the Thelonious Monk International Jazz Competition as an institution that treats mainstream black performers preferentially and perpetuates the idea that they are more legitimate interpreters of Monk's music (Hersch 1999).[11] This is a problematic argument for a number of reasons, not the least of which is that the winners of the competition have by no means all been African American. Nevertheless, Hersch's feeling that race plays a role in creating a more favorable environment for African American musicians in the jazz industry cannot be ignored. It is particularly significant in this context because it informs the way Hersch describes his interaction with Monk through his music.

In an interview for this project Hersch described becoming interested in Monk's music early in his study of jazz. He had studied classical piano as a youth and at Grinnell College, but he left Grinnell to work on jazz in his native Cincinnati. In reply to a question about how he first learned the compositions and whether at first he tried to play them just like Monk did, Hersch said:

> Since there was nobody around to teach me, and I figured things out myself, what I would do is, I would sit at the piano and try to imagine that I was Monk, or Bill Evans, or Wynton Kelley, or Ahmad Jamal, or whoever my hero was at the moment, or whoever I was listening to. Where I would

listen to a side and then go to the piano and try to just . . . channel them in some way. But I've never transcribed any Monk, or any solos, for that matter. I just try to get inside how they think. (Hersch 1999)

Hersch continued this thought, saying that when he approaches a tune, he analyzes its structure, tries to figure out what it is "about," and then tries to "see how can I filter it through my experience, so that it's half them and half me" (Hersch 1999). Note here that there is a potential tension in having one's performance of a tune belong half to oneself and half to someone else, in the desire to avoid copying any one else's interpretation, and in the drive to "channel" Monk without appearing derivative.

When discussing his recordings of Monk's music on the album *Thelonious: Fred Hersch Plays Monk,* Hersch explicitly denied that he imitated, or even directly borrowed from, Monk's specific way of performing particular compositions. I asked Hersch whether he felt it was necessary to preserve the integrity of Monk's compositional voice by referencing his arrangements of the pieces, and his inner voices, in particular. He was adamant in his reply:

No. And, and frankly, you know, the inner voice movement and stuff, I mean . . . for me it, it didn't even come from Monk. I mean, Monk knew good voice leading and I know good voice leading. You know, Bach knew good voice leading. It's all the same; it's all pretty obvious. And there's times when . . . Monk had, you know, a very good solution, and I might have used essentially the same solution, but I didn't think of it as, "This is what he did." . . . But I hope there's nothing on *[Thelonious]* that's in any way imitative. (Hersch 1999)[12]

He was much more comfortable when I described his approach on that recording as more referential than imitative.

Hersch's description of his approach—that is, as referential rather than imitative—is best understood in the context of jazz aesthetics and racial discourse about jazz in the recent past. Jazz musicians, particularly as they have adopted various aspects of modernism in the past half century, have stressed the importance of individuality and originality. As noted previously, one of the strongest criticisms that can be leveled against a player is that he or she is an imitator of another's sound. This use of the term "imitation" or "imitator" itself is fraught with racial baggage, because the history of jazz generally portrays black musicians as the originators of jazz and whites as "merely imitators" (see Sudhalter 1999, xvi, xviii). This perception has been fostered at one time or another by musicians and critics alike, and by members of both races.

There is not room here to fully critique the various positions related to this argument, but, in a nutshell, it seems that any categorical position on the question will fail. What seems obvious is that the music derives from African American communities and sound worlds, and that, from the start, because of the long history of connections between black and white Americans, members of both races (to say nothing of various other Americans) have been involved in jazz as creators, innovators, imitators, and everything in between. That said, I would like to consider one of the effects of a racial discourse of creative authenticity. In practical terms Hersch and Perez have worked toward similar goals: getting far enough into Monk's music to make their performances of it "half him and half them," so to speak. Yet, in talking about their approaches to playing the music, Hersch downplays his indebtedness to Monk's performances of the pieces while Perez amplifies his. Undoubtedly, this is a matter of differing personalities and styles of self-presentation, as well as different understandings of the precise meaning of the term "voice" and differences in the two musicians' career trajectories. These two different styles of self-presentation, however, gain resonance from being situated in a world of cultural discourse in which race is a constant presence.

JESSICA WILLIAMS

If discourses of race are one of the most significant factors in many musicians' engagement with Monk's legacy, Jessica Williams's experience also points to gender as a significant factor in the attempt to integrate one's own voice with Monk's. Like many jazz musicians, Williams has spent decades working as an accompanist and soloist but has not received significant attention as a leader. She has recorded prodigiously with the small Canadian label Jazz Focus, and recently she began her own label, Red and Blue, in order to enhance her creative freedom and revenue stream. Williams's recordings first received little attention from the critical press, until she found a champion in Pat Hawes, a reviewer for *Jazz Journal International*. Hawes offered enthusiastic praise of Williams, describing her as "probably the finest improvising pianist in jazz today" (Hawes 1995, 6). As reviews of her work slowly appeared in more prestigious magazines, Williams felt reviewers often heard her playing as related to that of other female jazz musicians, but never to that of the men who largely form the canon of jazz masters. In her words:

> I always had good reviews, but the reviewers always said, she sounds like this one on this one, she sounds like this guy on this one, and, and then a whole bunch of reviewers always lump women together, would say, "oh, she sounds like Joanne Brackeen, oh, she sounds like Marilyn Crispell," even though I never did, of course, but they would do that, because, how could I possibly sound like Art Tatum, you know. And then, well, I *can't*, but they would go through this whole thing. (Williams 1999a)

Williams has recently made a solo piano recording that is a tribute to Monk, in part conceived to publicly recognize the importance of Monk's precedent in her own music making (Williams 1999b). The album consists of seven compositions by Monk, from the relatively obscure "San Francisco Holiday" to the well-known "Pannonica." She also included two standards closely associated with Monk, "Just a Gigolo" and "I Love You (Sweetheart of All My Dreams)," and three originals, two dedicated to Monk and one to Charlie Rouse, with whom she had a long musical association. As Fred Hersch pointed out, it is dangerous to make a solo piano recording of Monk's music because of the strong example set by Monk himself (Hersch 1999). I asked Williams if this was a concern for her, and she replied that in the end she did the album solo because of the exigencies of recording, saying "You really don't have a choice in situations like this, because: it was set up by the producer, it was in Calgary, I would have had to use two local musicians, I don't think the budget would have afforded it, it was all those kinds of things, you know. Little teeny budgets for little teeny record labels. Let's put it this way: [the producer] wouldn't have been able to afford it, because I charge what I'm worth" (Williams 1999a). Despite all of this, she was ultimately very satisfied with the project and felt that she managed to say something with the music, bringing her own voice to it while allowing what she hears of Monk in the pieces to come through at the same time.

Williams's own descriptions of this aspect of her performances of Monk's music are complicated. They show her in the somewhat problematic position of navigating a number of unsatisfactory discursive strategies for presenting her relationship to the music. On the one hand, she wants to avoid disappearing in an overly close relationship with Monk, becoming viewed as a clone. On the other hand, however, she wants to publicly recognize the debt she feels she owes his music, and thereby tap into the cultural capital associated with it. All of this is further complicated by her second-class status as a woman in an overwhelmingly male scene. In the liner notes she wrote for her album, she begins with what can best be described as an "open letter to misguided critics":

> While I'm not in agreement with critics who cite Monk as my main influence, I *am* willing to concede that his compositional style and "home-made" technique [have] had a lasting effect on the way I hear and play. . . . Monk had a distinctive "taste" as did Miles and 'Trane, and it is that existential "taste" that has influenced me. . . . I never copied his solos (or anyone else's) or intentionally studied his comping style or chordings. I just absorbed that "taste," and that's what the critics hear because it's like garlic or oregano; very identifiable. (Williams 1999b; emphasis in the original)

Note the similarity to Fred Hersch's description of "channeling" Monk, of trying to "get inside the way [he] thinks" without copying verbatim Monk's voice leadings or solos. Williams contests the critics' use of the term "Monkish" to describe her own performances of Monk tunes, saying that it fails to interrogate what she does with readily identifiable formal units that index Monk's style—whole-tone runs, tritone-based harmony, and sparse dominant chord voicings that incorporate the minor seventh and minor ninth. Williams again recalls Hersch's description of playing Monk's music when she says, "The truth is that . . . a musician playing a Monk tune sounds like Monk because Monk tunes sound like Monk tunes. They're authentic, genuine distillations of Monk's musical point of view, and they inevitably affect the course of improvisation that any musician might take playing them" (Williams 1999b). Williams's statement, like Hersch's, makes it clear that Monk's voice is so deeply embedded in the works themselves that it asserts itself, regardless of the interpretation. Therefore, she thinks the issue on which to focus is the work the interpreter does adding her or his voice to Monk's. This helps explain what Williams means when she says of the album, "It was not a Monk album, it is a Jessica Williams album with Monk as a special guest" (Williams 1999b).

Like other musicians such as Steve Lacy and Michael Weiss, Jessica Williams has at times found the presence of Monk in her performances of his tunes an impediment to developing her own voice. She describes growing up with Monk's music and playing it early in her career, but getting to a point where it was limiting. Like others, she then stopped playing it for an extended period of time. She explained:

> I had an affinity for that sort of playing, so it was like a sort of Monk tag that stuck to me. And so when I get reviews and stuff, you know, in magazines, they'd always say it sounded a little like Monk, even if it didn't, you know. Just 'cause, I think sometimes, that's what they expected to hear. So for a while I stopped playing Thelonious's tunes altogether, because I wanted to get rid of that tag that I had stuck to me. So there was a period of about eight—five to eight years, I can't remember exactly how long—where I didn't even play his music at all. Because it was beginning [trails off] his music is really powerful. (Williams 1999a)

Despite the vehemence of Williams's rejection of the common critical approach to finding "influences" in an artist's work, she was quick to affirm that she does in fact feel that Monk was a strong influence on her, as were the musicians he played with, most notably Sonny Rollins and Charlie Rouse, with whom she played regularly at one time. What she objects to are the limitations she believes the idea of "influence" often puts on a musician's reception. As she told me, "I just don't want to be [pause] see, when you do a tribute album it tends to typecast you in a certain role, and, you see, I'm not comfortable with the role, maybe, of being a Monk clone, or having *grown* out of his music, or something" (Williams 1999a).

BROADENING THE CONVERSATION: FROM TWO VOICES TO MANY

In addition to fearing sounding like Monk clones, jazz musicians also have a broad range of feelings about the weight of these compositions' histories. Some focus on playing Monk's less well-known compositions, in part from a revivalist or preservationist impulse—some want to bring neglected tunes back into the general repertoire—and in part because they offer more room to maneuver without laboring under the weight of a history of performances. In an important sense, Monk's is the only other voice that must be dealt with when interpreting a piece like "Gallop's Gallop." In comparison, musicians face a far heavier weight when performing, for instance, " 'Round Midnight." Although every musician I spoke with for this book knows the piece very well (as does virtually every jazz musician, from amateur to professional), many exclude it from their regular performing repertoire. Kenny Drew Jr. described his reservation about performing

" 'Round Midnight," saying, "I've always been kind of playing, well, some more obscure things, rather than the things you hear all the time. I figure they've already been done enough. Like, for instance, I don't play ''Round Midnight.' Of course I *know* it, and I'll play it with other people, and if somebody requests it I'll play it. But, you know, it'll never be a part of my regular performing repertoire" (Drew Jr. 1999). Some, such as Fred Hersch, play it with reservations, noting the danger of failing to say something truly new; of course, some play it with no qualms.

What is interesting to note about such a song is that the panoply of voices associated with it—Monk's, the current performer's, and those of its various interpreters through time—become a part of the piece itself, or at least we can experience them as such. Whether an interpreter chooses to reference one performance or another, any performance may be a part of a listener's field of experience. This is truer for some performances than others. In the case of " 'Round Midnight," for instance, the recording by the Miles Davis Quintet has become part of the piece's textual field—the field of interpretive possibility—for many jazz listeners and performers. For each listener and each performer this field is unique, being formed by his or her own musical history; but across individuals this field has a dense center composed of those versions of the piece known widely, and diffuse edges made up of those performances known by relatively few.

These many voices are often in the foreground, even if they sometimes fade from musicians' consciousness in performance. Jessica Williams pointed in particular to Monk's tenor players, Sonny Rollins, John Coltrane, and Charlie Rouse, as important voices in her approach to various Monk tunes. For example, she describes Rollins as suffusing her interpretation of "Reflections" because of his performance of it with Monk on *Sonny Rollins, Volume 2* (Rollins 1957). Bob Porcelli was particularly explicit about his engagement with a history of performances of the music. I asked him whether this was important to him as an interpreter of Monk's music, and he interrupted me, saying, "Yes, yes, yes! I don't know if I think consciously, but yes, yes. . . . When I play a song like 'Ask Me Now,' I think I'm aware of these other guys. Yeah, yeah, I am. The answer would be yes for that" (Porcelli 1999). This extends from small-scale referencing of earlier performances to larger-level decisions, like using Miles Davis's changes for " 'Round Midnight," because he "came up so influenced by what Miles did with it" (Porcelli 1999).

Porcelli, who has lived in New York his entire life and has been an active participant in the jazz scene there since the 1950s, saw Monk play more often than many of the musicians who participated in this study. This profoundly affected his engagement with the music. In his words:

> Like, Monk tunes, I remember so well some of the songs I play now by Monk, I remember sitting there, listening to Johnny Griffin playing them with him. And there's a certain bouncy, a certain way of playing that music that seems to fit so well. Like a certain—I'm generally, I tend to play a little not on the happy side, like Cannonball was a "happy" player, I'm basically not a "happy" player, but, you have to put some of that in it to play that music, and I remember seeing Johnny Griffin do it, and I guess 'Trane, I can't categorize him that way, but that seems to have been set into my brain from hearing Johnny Griffin, a lot of a certain way of playing those tunes. (Porcelli 1999)

Fred Hersch sees this sort of relationship happening for him in a more abstract way. He said, "I think it, inasmuch as it's all sort of an oral tradition, you know, I'm not aware of that, so much, you know. It's probably in there, somewhere. I'm sure all of the things that I've listened to are in there somewhere. But, you know, what's nearest to the surface is what I'm dealing with at the moment, which is the materials at hand, and trying to make use of them in the service of telling a story, or creating something" (Hersch 1999).

Still, a number of other musicians downplayed the importance of voices besides their own and Monk's in playing his music. Hersch's description of this issue as something that generally lies beneath the surface but unconsciously colors his engagement with the music, seems to capture a common feeling. Additionally, it seems that downplaying the importance of other interpreters' versions of the pieces is a result of the value attached to Monk's own performances by virtue of their authenticity, and, by extension, a lower value and a lack of authenticity placed on others'.

CONCLUSION

Despite notable differences in the way Danilo Perez's, Fred Hersch's, and Jessica Williams's interpretations of Thelonious Monk's music sound, they are connected through a shared commitment to integrating something from Monk into their own performances of his music. Their descriptions of what they are looking for in Monk's example and how they want to integrate it into their own playing also differ. Perez singles out Monk's use of materials from the head in solo choruses, and often, at times self-consciously, references Monk's voice leading and chord voicing as a way to keep Monk's voice in the performance. By contrast, Hersch tries to keep

Monk in the performance by finding some inner essence of Monk's think-ing in a composition and exploiting that. He even goes so far as to dismiss audible reference to stereotypically "Monkish" sounds in current jazz mu-sicians' interpretations of Monk. In his words, "I was never one of these, you know, . . . somebody plays a whole-tone run and they think, 'Oh, it's Monk,' 'cause it's just one of his devices. . . . It's a cliché. It's like, you know, Groucho Marx and the cigar or something. But there was more to Grou-cho Marx than the cigar and the leer. . . . So I try to get [Monk's] spirit in there, and his spirit is *in the tunes*" (Hersch 1999). Williams navigates a middle path, recognizing the ways Monk's peculiar musical language crops up in her playing, particularly in interpreting his compositions, but down-plays the importance of such referential moments. The shared concern with a responsibility to the past in their playing is common to many other jazz musicians, as attested in interviews I conducted for this project as well as less formal conversations with jazz musicians in a variety of settings.

What will become clear in the following chapters is that the consensus about a basic need to maintain the past in the present—a historicist lean-ing in recent jazz—becomes enmeshed with factionalism when the ques-tion is posed differently and the frame of reference is moved to a different level. The following chapters will tackle the ways musicians and others have used performances of Monk's music and discourse about those perfor-mances in the service of power negotiations among jazz's subgeneric styles. Together these two frames of reference—microlevel discussions of the in-dividual's engagement with Monk's music and macrolevel discussions of how Monk and his interpreters fit into style history—say something sig-nificant about jazz historicity that might not be perceptible from only one position.

PART THREE

Inside and Outside

Monk's Legacy, Neoconservatism, and the Avant-Garde

FIVE

Defining a Genre

Monk and the Struggle to Authenticate Jazz
at the End of the Twentieth Century

THE 1981 "INTERPRETATIONS OF MONK" CONCERT, produced by Verna Gillis, was by no means the last monumental tribute to Monk. In 1985 drummer and bandleader T.S. Monk and arranger Doug Richards, at the behest of critic Martin Williams, undertook the creation of a collection of authoritative scores for Monk's music. In a letter to T.S. Monk, Williams wrote, "Your father's best pieces are not 'lines' or 'heads' with chord changes attached, but they are *compositions* in the strictest sense— the way Ellington's were, or for that matter, the way Beethoven's were. So they should be preserved as close to his own conception, in *strict* detail, as they can be" (Williams 1985; emphasis in the original). The pieces were to be published, in score and parts, for a standard sixteen- to eighteen-piece big band and would include all of Monk's playing from a particular recording of a piece, scored for the horns. The envisioned arrangements were eventually completed and were first performed on May 11, 1986, at the Smithsonian Institution as part of their "Great Jazz Composers" series. In a letter to Dan Morgenstern promoting the concert, Williams wrote of his excitement about the big band arrangements. From his description it seems Richards fulfilled Williams's original vision quite well, incorporating all of Monk's playing on the Blue Note version of "Misterioso" into the horn parts, for example, and avoiding extended solo improvisation. In his letter to Morgenstern, Williams clarifies his motivation for preparing these arrangements and producing the concert:

> There are two reasons for doing this. One of course is to make good music. The other is our hope . . . that these arrangements and others like them, will be the means by which Monk is performed and preserved in performance. Otherwise his better pieces might only become a series of "tunes" or "heads" for any kind of small group playing . . . a limited thing compared to his full contribution. They will also be a vehicle . . . for ensembles (and audiences) to *learn* Monk more fully. (Williams 1986; emphasis in the original)

Monk concerts and other projects involving his collected works are generally attempts to construct and lay claim to Monk's legacy. In Pierre Nora's terms, they become *lieux de memoire,* sites through which memory is concentrated and put to particular social ends. This chapter is concerned with the connections between various approaches to Monk's legacy, which, though distinctive in their own right, nonetheless approach a common goal. They construct Monk as a key figure in the history of a jazz mainstream, and as a significant predecessor of "inside" players today. Through various narratives about Monk, through an attempt to create canonic texts for his compositions, and through consensus on how his works should be performed (if not how they actually are performed), this mainstreaming practice has been a part of a process of theoretically reifying both Monk and the music of his mainstream admirers, regardless of genuine divergences when theory gets translated into sound. As part of a more general reinterpretation and reconstruction of jazz as an analogue of European classical music (a project emblematized in Grover Sales's book *Jazz: America's Classical Music*), jazz critics, scholars, and musicians associated with jazz's institutional centers have emphasized a classicizing model of Monk and his music. This approach constructs Monk as a mainstream composer in a lineage that leads from Jelly Roll Morton, through Duke Ellington and Monk, to the contemporary mainstream—the "neo-boppers"—as the sole legitimate heirs to the tradition.

In the process of "classicizing" Monk, this discourse downplays Monk's contributions as a performer, or views them through a lens that insists on unity, coherence, universality, and, in some cases, formalist detachment from context—that is, from the social process of his performances and from their cultural contingency. One aspect of this reification is the treatment of

Monk's compositions as relatively fixed texts, only open to interpretation and innovation within relatively narrow boundaries. This is commonly expressed with some variant of the idea that to play Monk's music, you have to play it "his way." Significantly, musicians often describe the process of interpreting Monk's music as finding and developing its inherent characteristics rather than using it as a neutral vehicle for less contingent explorations. Thus, performances of the music convey the interpreters' visions of what kind of composer Monk was.[1] The great irony of this process is that it either ignores or inverts the stock historical construction of Monk as a musician who was marginalized precisely for not being part of his moment's mainstream, denaturing much of the radical quality many musicians and commentators have heard in his music.

That said, it is important to note that the meaning of the term *mainstream* is less obvious than it might appear at first blush. Commonly used to describe both musicians and a set of musical approaches, the word refers to a free-floating collection of ideas that is rife with internal contradictions. The term may be deployed by various people for different strategic purposes. As such, because of the implication that there is, in fact, a center to the jazz scene, the term may be used by almost anyone for centering self-presentations.[2] This is at the core of difficulties other writers have had with locating a center, or with adequately characterizing the contemporary jazz mainstream; ultimately, it is connected more with the performance of ideas than with any essence. There is generally some slippage, some play, in the relationship between the actual sonic, musical practices of particular musicians and the cultivation of an association with the mainstream (in all that the word means). In what is a perfect example of the sort of pastichelike process Jameson and others have shown to be indicative of the postmodern condition, free improvisation—the stock-in-trade and most distinctive feature of one era's avant-garde—can be claimed as one of the resources of the new mainstream, while a musician like Don Byron can perform Ellington's through-composed early work without in any sense becoming a mainstream repertory musician.[3]

The idea that all musical culture is engaged in the sociopolitical life of the community that nurtures it, if only implicitly, has been central to ethnomusicological work since at least the 1980s.[4] Although this case can be interpreted as demonstrating the general point, it is also distinctive in the way that it engages with the politics of establishment and counterculture in late-twentieth-century America, the "culture wars." During the late 1930s defenders of "revivalist" New Orleans–style jazz, and, later, defenders of bebop, used the language of leftist political engagement to connect their music to a valorized counterculture, as well as to connect swing to a maligned—even fascist—mainstream, as Bernard Gendron has noted (Gendron 1995, 45–46). These same connections—between less commercially viable music and the counterculture, and between more commercially viable music and an implicitly or explicitly right-wing mainstream—was repeated, in the 1960s, the 1970s, and more recently. There is, and has been, a tendency to associate aesthetic progressivism with the political left (seen clearly in figures such as Charles Mingus and Archie Shepp, but less so in Ornette Coleman, for instance), and aesthetic conservatism with conservative cultural politics. Steven Elworth says as much in an article on the canonization of bop: "If admissible standards have shifted to allow for different styles of dress and behavior, one can see the real reactionary nature of the Marsalis *Time* cover. The suit has become an image of seriousness that props up outworn images of masculinity" (Elworth 1995, 71–72).

A close consideration of the case of jazz in the 1980s and 1990s ultimately undercuts any attempt to draw distinctions between "progressive" and "reactionary" in a straightforward way. There is simply too much involved. Is a predominantly white avant-garde jazz scene on the Lower East Side of Manhattan representative of a "progressive" musico-political sensibility more or less than a predominantly black repertory orchestra on the Upper West Side? One problem is that the use of the term *progressive* in political and aesthetic movements suggests a connection that may simply not exist. A further problem is that different groups' political and musical interests may exist in nonintersecting planes rather than on a continuum. In any case, the politics of any given recording, musician, or style is overdetermined by his, her, or its contexts of race, class, and so forth, as well as personal history.

In order to understand how an "establishment" Monk legacy came to be and to investigate that legacy's life within the jazz community, I will first look at Monk as the object of institutional jazz culture. My analyses will consider the building of a jazz canon in general, and how scholars and jazz institutions such as the Thelonious Monk Institute (TMI), Jazz at Lincoln Center (JLC), and the Smithsonian Institution's jazz program have been involved with this process. The following chapter will then complicate this picture by looking at three rather different instances of "mainstream," "inside" performances of Monk's music: Marcus Roberts's *Alone with Three Giants*, Wynton Marsalis's *Standard Time, Volume 4,* and T.S. Monk's widely acclaimed, star-studded album *Monk on Monk*, three examples that show the remarkably variable musical consequences of a classicizing approach to remembering and memorializing Monk.

How did Monk's legacy come to have the particular shape it does? It appears from a limited survey of the broad array of musicians who have entered popular discourse as cultural icons that a certain malleability of image can be an important part of the general construction of legacy. This is undoubtedly the case for Monk. Those who emphasize his compositional output and discuss his compositions at length as fixed texts claim him for a jazz heritage according to the classical model favored by JLC and the Smithsonian. Moreover, those who emphasize fidelity to Monk by playing it "his way," in a hard-bop/mainstream style, whether they intend to or not, help construct an image of him as belonging to a historical jazz mainstream. Others, however, who emphasize his departures from earlier models, and even from the contemporaneous bebop style, claim him as a father figure for further experiments in avant-garde jazz. These are by no means the only possibilities, but they represent the most common discursive approaches to Monk and his music. Naturally, each musician or writer who constructs a narrative about jazz history places his or her own spin upon it, and some find other metanarratives altogether in which to place Monk.[5]

The first section of this book emphasized the ways Monk's compositions and his playing satisfy both modernist and vernacular aesthetics. I would like to suggest some further aspects of his music that make it particularly subject to these varied interpretations. More than anything, Monk's music is an unusual mix of the recognizably traditional and, at the same time, the undeniably groundbreaking and breathtakingly innovative. This could be said of the music of most jazz innovators, but for few is the contradiction so stark. As a composer Monk often stayed close to the large-scale formal models of his predecessors. He composed numerous short pieces based on twelve-bar blues or in thirty-two-bar AABA song form. Moreover, although he greatly expanded the possibilities for composing within a functional harmonic context, he very seldom left that context entirely behind. Nevertheless, his pieces are not easily mistaken for generic Tin Pan Alley tunes, nor even for standard jazz pieces composed in the prevailing style.

"Ruby, My Dear" is an interesting example, characteristic of the way Monk innovates while clearly referencing the tradition of song composition with which he was so familiar. A performance of the piece by Monk with John Coltrane (ts), Ahmed Abdul-Malik (b), and Roy Haynes (d) recorded in 1958 provides an example of how Monk interpreted it (Monk 1986, disc 5, track 6). "Ruby, My Dear" is a thirty-two-bar song in AABA form. It shows Monk demonstrating what Roswell Rudd refers to as his "total understanding of convention as well as un-convention" (Rudd 1999). The piece, as Monk performs it, suggests a layered orchestration: in the A sections a lyrical melody on the top (suggesting a syllabic text underlay, "Ruby, my dear," for the first four notes) is accompanied simply. This melody contrasts with dense interjections in a similar motion suggesting a horn section—saxes or trombones in a conventional big band arrangement—forming a call-and-response pattern with the main melody. The bridge reveals contrasts in melodic material, tonal reference, and harmonic movement, but it retains a similar textural layering. Monk emphasizes the contrast between the sections in his 1958 recording with John Coltrane by playing the bridge with a double-time feel, maintaining the basic meter but superimposing a second metrical sense that is twice as fast (an eighth note sounds like a quarter, and a sixteenth note sounds like an eighth). In this case, the bridge is also swung.

If the melody and implied arrangement of "Ruby, My Dear" are standard jazz song fare, its harmonic character is not. Monk clearly references the harmonic language of the Tin Pan Alley song, but he twists it in a surprising way. Most of the piece's changes can be heard as part of a ii–V–I sequence, the building blocks of any standard pop song. However, in their combination, and in the song's larger-scale harmonic construction, this standard tonal practice is at once referenced and undercut. The first eight measures comprise a move from tonic through dominant, or at least begins with a progression whose goal is E♭, the global tonic, and ends with a B♭7 chord that functions as a dominant—a momentary resting place, but one demanding some continuation. Measures 1 and 2 begin with a ii–V–I ending on the large-scale tonic, E♭ on the downbeat of measure 2. The next four measures repeat this opening motivic gesture, with ii–V–I's ending on F and A♭. From the end of measure 6 Monk takes a circuitous route to a structural dominant, a B♭7 chord in measure 8. The intervening changes, B♭m7–AM9/B–Em11–Em11/B defy a functional harmonic analysis. Rather, they arise out of a linear movement.

As with any song following the AABA form, the harmonic and linear moves of the A section are repeated immediately. The second time through, the effect of the first ii–V–I progression is heightened: the sound is already strongly end-directed the first time, pushing on toward E♭ because of the common practice of moving around the circle of fifths. It is even more strongly end-directed the second time, however, because of the expectation of a tonic resolution of the B♭7 at the end of the first A section.

The bridge begins with an unexpected move to A major. It is typical for Tin Pan Alley songs to move to a brighter key, often a structural predominant, at the beginning of the bridge and then move to a large-scale dominant by the end. A major is certainly much brighter than E♭, particularly on tenor sax, the horn Monk overwhelmingly favored for his quartets; but as sharp IV in relation to E♭, A major does not serve a standard tonal function, nor does Monk make it do so through a clever modulation back to the original key. Instead, after extending A as the tonic with a ii–V–I progression, Monk moves by diatonic and chromatic steps back to E♭ by the end of the bridge. Here again Monk creates a compelling phrase that cannot really be explained by recourse to standard tonal theory. It is much better understood as the result of contrapuntal lines. It may also serve as a kind of obscure musical in-joke. The focus on A major, as flat-5 to the tonic if understood enharmonically, may be heard as a winking reference to the significant melodic and harmonic use of flat-5 in bebop. This shows Monk drawing on his contemporaries' work, but altering it, extending it.

The final A section ends open, as had the first two, on the dominant, B♭7. Only at the end of the piece does Monk suggest some resolution to this dominant. He follows the final statement of the head—the "out chorus"— with a coda. In this coda, which one expects to finally bring the piece to a conclusion on the tonic, Monk undercuts the listener's expectations (and one of the basic premises of tonal music) by playing a long cadenza over a ii–V–I that ultimately lands on D♭, not E♭.

In contrast to "Ruby, My Dear," which subverts the tonal harmonic system in the context of an otherwise classic jazz standard/pop song, a composition like "Evidence" undermines every convention of rhythmic and melodic writing with its spare, jagged, pointillistic top line, but it does so in combination with the borrowed changes of a pop tune of Monk's youth, "Just You, Just Me," by Raymond Klages, Jesse Greer, and David Wolpe. This is indicative of Monk's style: his innovations are always counterbalanced by a sincere engagement with traditional or mainstream practice. He was not given to an outright rejection of convention, but to its reconstitution.

As discussed in chapter 1, various aspects of Monk's life as a public figure also fed into the radically varying constructions of who he was and how he fit into the broader sociocultural trends of his time. As house pianist for the jam sessions at Minton's in Harlem, Monk was central to the development of bebop, but he was not a bebopper per se. He did not achieve the recognition that his contemporaries, Charlie Parker and Dizzy Gillespie, did, at least not in the 1940s. Ultimately, although his harmonic and rhythmic ideas played an indisputable role in the creation of the bebop sound, his own style bore little resemblance to those of the mainstream bop artists (see Gillespie 1979).

This stylistic peculiarity was probably an initial factor keeping him from achieving wider recognition, but it was the loss of his cabaret card—a license required by the borough of Manhattan to perform in establishments that served alcohol—for nearly a decade that obscured him from the public eye for much of the 1950s (Gourse 1997, 85–89, 165–66). One of the most important, though seldom noted, consequences of the loss of his cabaret license was that, unlike the image of virtually all of his contemporaries, Monk's image was, for the most part, built on his recordings. Most jazz musicians at the time kept up rigorous performing schedules, playing in New York's well-known jazz clubs or on the road almost continuously. This meant that they became familiar to audiences around the country, and increasingly around the world, as actual people. Since Monk was unable to play in Manhattan and was averse to touring (and, moreover, it is not clear he could have successfully done so in the 1940s and 1950s), audiences could not become familiar with him in a humanizing way. Instead he existed on albums, in the pictures on their covers, in interviews, and occasionally in news stories. This is the stuff of mythmaking, and Monk quickly became a mythical figure, even, to some extent, to other musicians. Those who did not know him personally had essentially the same access to him as fans. As a mythical figure Monk was less complex in the public eye than some jazz musicians, and more obscure. As a result, it has been possible to spin his image in any of a number of ways.

Finally, one has to look at changing cultural contexts in which Monk was claimed by a number of opposed parties. In the 1950s and 1960s Monk was seen as representing the "furthest out," most obscure possibilities in jazz (Kelley 1999, 136; McKinney 1959, 21). As discussed later, Monk was, as a result, attractive to an iconoclastic audience that was interested in claiming him as an icon of their own countercultural, marginalist stance. As Robin Kelley has shown, there was a convergence of avant-garde interest in Monk across the arts in this historical moment; in the 1950s and 1960s painters, writers, musicians, and dancers, all looked to Monk as a guiding example for their own experiments (Kelley 1999, 139–40). Throughout the 1960s, however, the goalposts for experimentation were shifted back a number of yards by a flowering of avant-garde work, and by the middle of the decade Monk had begun to look mainstream to many critics and fans. By the 1970s he was routinely dismissed in the jazz press as hopelessly old-fashioned. In the 1980s, after his death, the mainstream status Monk had slowly acquired in the previous decades was consolidated and its tarnish polished off by his inclusion in a growing canon of past masters. Indeed, Monk's death contributed to the canonization process and the building of his legacy, as might be expected. After all, nothing builds a well-known artist's cultural capital like dying. Reissues, repertory bands, and historians of various stripes all had a part in creating a mainstream picture of Monk and his music.

The Origins of a "Classicizing" Vision of Monk

A classicizing model of Monk's music, emphasizing his work as a composer to the near exclusion of his work as a performer as well as the admonition that his music must be played "his way," did not arise ex nihilo upon his death. It has its roots in the writings of Nat Hentoff and Martin Williams from as early as the 1960s. Both writers were intent on reconstructing the image of jazz in the American public's mind and cementing the idea that jazz was a finely crafted art music. The two writers came from different aesthetic and political positions, but they shared a deeply felt love of jazz and the belief that it deserved the sort of serious intellectual consideration that was usually reserved for Western classical music. Williams in particular, having pursued graduate studies in literature at the University of Pennsylvania and Columbia University, was swayed by the text-centric ideology of the New Criticism as an approach to a serious understanding of jazz (see Gennari 1991, 476–77; Morgan 1988, 626). This accounts in some measure for his tendency to look at the music exclusively as a collection of unified, autonomous, and even hermetic musical objects and to largely ignore musical performance as a process, and also helps explain his strong interest in the creation of a collection of authoritative texts for Monk's music after the composer's death. Although Nat Hentoff's work as a jazz writer is consistently more socially motivated than many others', he, too, was involved in the formalist move in jazz criticism in the 1960s, particularly as cofounder with Williams of the periodical *Jazz Review* (Gennari 1991, 476).[6]

Both writers produced significant articles in the early 1960s, when Monk was just making the jump from recognition within the jazz world to broader recognition in American culture at large. The first sentence in

Hentoff's 1960 article for *Esquire* magazine, "The Private World of Thelonious Monk," set the tone for how Monk would be represented: "Outside his music there is little but trouble; inside, little but genius" (Hentoff 1960, 133). By this time Monk's personal trials were fairly well known and already part of his mythology, but calling his music a product of genius began a new program. The word "genius" is undoubtedly used incautiously by critics, but it is not exactly generic praise. It is a term carefully chosen in this instance because of its implications: that Monk's music is not "mere" entertainment, it is art; that it is not of the body (as black music is often stereotypically portrayed in American culture), but is of the mind—both a product of great intellect, and a music to be enjoyed through contemplation, not dancing.

Hentoff's feature article for *Esquire* was intended to familiarize a broad audience with Monk. It is the sort of piece a magazine runs when the subject has already begun to have a significant presence in the popular eye but is not yet an icon. It serves to consolidate and cement the subject's public image and guarantee him or her a more lasting popularity. The article serves this purpose very well, using materials largely recycled from articles published previously in the jazz press to provide a summary biographical sketch and a description of Monk's music that taps into recognizable aesthetic discourses to position Monk for the magazine's hip, middle-brow, mostly male American audience. Hentoff's discussion of Monk's music is most notable for its seriousness—particularly when it is compared with the sensationalist approach that was standard fare for the discussion of Monk's playing in the 1940s and 1950s—and for its use of a highbrow conception of the music as a modernist art.

The single most striking aspect of this article is the way the term *composition* surfaces in it. Hentoff quotes an anonymous musician saying, "when you learn one of his pieces, you can't learn just the melody and chord symbols. You have to remember the inner voicings and rhythms exactly. Everything is so carefully inter-related; his works are *compositions* in the sense that relatively few jazz 'originals' are" (Hentoff 1960, 137; emphasis in the original). This programmatic use of the term *composition* is interesting because of its relative novelty in 1960s jazz discourse and because of its staying power since then. Hentoff does not use *composition* in its most general sense, in which it simply refers to a distinct piece of music, but draws on its association with classical music, opposing it not just to improvisation, but also to the idea of a piece with relatively fluid characteristics. He uses the term to set Monk apart from the majority of his contemporaries in the jazz world in two ways: he argues that Monk is distinct from beboppers both because his compositions are often completely new—that is, Monk composed both a melody and new changes instead of fitting a new melody to preexisting changes—and because it is often possible to point to a motivic unity connecting Monk's accompaniment and solos with melodic material in the heads. Moreover, as "compositions" Monk's pieces can be described as distinct and concrete entities, not to be changed at a performer's discretion, but to be interpreted with fidelity to a conceptually fixed original or authentic form.[7]

Martin Williams reinforces this picture of Monk as a composer and his music as compositions in this programmatic sense in an article published in a 1963 issue of the *Saturday Review,* "Thelonious Monk: Arrival without Departure." Like Hentoff's article in *Esquire,* this piece was intended to foster an understanding of Monk among a general audience that was, by then, at least somewhat aware of him. Williams lauds Monk here on even more explicitly formalist grounds than Hentoff did, suggesting a clear relationship between his music and the aesthetics of classical music. When recommending Monk's recordings of standards to the readers of the *Saturday Review,* Williams says, "He can convert the most ordinary 'tune' into a two-handed *composition* for piano. . . . In more extended performance, Monk is apt to build blocks of subtly organized melodic variations, finding eight minutes of music in, for one very good example, rephrasings of the melodic line of 'Just You, Just Me' " (Williams 1963, 32; emphasis in the original). Williams reinforces this impression when discussing Monk's own pieces. "Even more important is Monk the jazz composer," Williams declares, "for he is, I think, a major jazz composer, the first since Duke Ellington" (33). The evidence he marshals for this assessment is noteworthy because it conforms to aesthetic values clearly drawn from the highbrow "art music" tradition. It is not the number of pieces Monk could claim credit to in 1963, nor their diffusion within the jazz world, nor even their quality that Williams points to, but that they are "compositions for instruments," "truly instrumental pieces," as opposed to songs, and that they are complete, fixed entities (32). Williams recognizes that these compositions are different from their classical counterparts in that they require performance and extension through improvisation, but, nonetheless, the factors he singles out for praise are precisely those that have analogues in classical music. Furthermore, by emphasizing their "instrumental" character, Williams highlights a modernist value system that elevates music that is abstract, that does not have semantic meaning.

There is ample evidence that Monk himself would have agreed, at least to some extent, with the idea that his pieces had fixed features to which performers should adhere when interpreting them. In the few opportunities he took to comment publicly on performances of his music by others, such as the incisive and subtle remarks he made to Leonard Feather in a "blindfold test" published in *Down Beat* in 1966, he was principally concerned with changes the musicians made, whether intentional or not, to his tunes. Odd tempos, changes in the melodies, and substitute harmonic progressions, for example, he saw not as interpretive decisions, but as mistakes arising from carelessness (Feather 1994, 78).

Another interesting aesthetic informs Williams's assessment of Monk's music. In discussing the direction he saw Monk's music going in the 1960s, when he had newly signed with Columbia records, Williams suggests that Monk's quartet did not live up to the requirements of his music, a criticism that would become nearly universal as the decade passed. He criticizes saxophonist Charlie Rouse for "settling," that is, for playing solos too obviously composed of repeated formulas and not searching for radical innovation with each performance. Most interestingly, he dismisses Frankie Dunlop's drumming, claiming, "Monk's music cries out for complex percussive interplay, beyond time-keeping accompaniment and even beyond intermittent snare and cymbal commentary that Dunlop provides" (34). Whatever the aesthetic validity of this position, it clearly contradicts what Monk thought about his own music. By and large, Monk sought out drummers who played solid, traditional time, and although his recordings with Roy Haynes—perhaps the most experimental drummer Monk recorded with—are excellent, it appears that Monk himself thought Haynes's playing was too busy for the music. An opposition to popular elements in Monk's music underlies Williams's dismissal of Dunlop's playing and celebration of the putatively instrumental (as opposed to vocal) quality of Monk's music. Dunlop's playing draws Williams's disapproval because it is too close to the drumming in rhythm and blues and even rock and roll. According to Williams's aesthetic context of rigidly drawn art/entertainment dialectic, the drumming is irreconcilable with Monk's indisputable artistry.

It should be borne in mind that this critical agenda was applied from outside the culture of the musicians. Monk was not committed to such a rigid, hierarchical categorization of genres. Indeed, some of his earliest performing experiences, like those of many African American musicians, were with gospel music, as an apprentice organist in New York and as a pianist in a touring medicine show (Gourse 1997, 10–11). Moreover, he was very fond of the Harlem stride pianists, a group of musicians whose work is almost impossible to locate on one side or the other of the putative division between art and entertainment. None of this is to deny the artistry or the value of gospel or stride music, nor is it intended to suggest that Monk and other jazz musicians do not view music with a hierarchy of value. Indeed, Monk, like most of his peers, was rigorously discriminating in his musical tastes.[8]

MONK AND THE CHANGING PLACE OF JAZZ IN THE 1980S AND 1990S

Becoming "America's Classical Music"

The image of Monk that Hentoff and Williams propagated came to be the basis for the institutionalization of a "mainstream" Monk. This process, however individual, is best understood in relation to the social and political context in which jazz found itself at the beginning of the 1980s and the changes it experienced in the following decades. This context forms a backdrop for the notion of "mainstream" as it is currently used, not just as a stylistic description, but in reference to a cultural and political position. The apparent downturn in fortunes seen by "inside," acoustic jazz in the late 1960s and early 1970s began to reverse in the late 1970s. This trend accelerated in the 1980s with the meteoric rise of a number of young musicians dubbed the "Young Lions" (Gioia 1997, 381–93). The most prominent among them, Wynton Marsalis, established himself as a member of Art Blakey's Jazz Messengers and released a number of solo recordings, starting in the early 1980s, with Columbia records (386). As the 1980s wore on, mainstream jazz drew attention on a scale unimaginable in the 1970s, though it remained a small part of the music market in comparison with any of the principal popular genres (rock, country, and hip-hop, for example). This trend continued into the 1990s, and jazz's cultural cachet skyrocketed. With the HCR 57 bill the U.S. Congress designated jazz a "national treasure," and the music—specifically a hard bop/cool jazz sound—began to be used in advertising to signify opulence, luxury, and highbrow culture generally (Gabbard 1995c, 1).[9]

In 1989 Manhattan's Lincoln Center, home to some of the most prestigious classical arts organizations in the world, including the Metropolitan Opera and the New York Philharmonic, instituted a summer jazz miniseries under the direction of Wynton Marsalis and Stanley Crouch, a jazz critic, historian, and erstwhile drummer. This series, Jazz at Lincoln Center (JLC), was successful and drew accolades in the jazz press.

Down Beat writer Kevin Whitehead reviewed both of JLC's first two seasons, in 1989 and 1990, and although his reactions were generally positive, they were interlaced with a criticism that was to grow as the series gained prominence and became a part of Lincoln Center's yearly programming in the early 1990s. Noting the overall quality of the performances but an exclusion of the avant-garde from a program intended to cover the history of jazz, Whitehead asked hopefully in his review of the first series, "next year, an evening of large-ensemble pieces by Braxton and Anthony Davis, perhaps?" He also couched a criticism of Marsalis's historical orientation as praise, writing, "If Marsalis must keep his back to the future, this is the way to do it" (Whitehead 1989, 52). In the following year's review Whitehead appears to have sensed the direction the program would take. "Classical jazz will surely return to Lincoln Center next summer," he wrote, adding, "It'd be a shame if Crouch and Marsalis got into a rut, producing a surefire boiler-plate festival every year. . . . Knowing their tastes, one hardly expects them to pay tribute to Albert Ayler, but it's tempting to think of what they could work up" (Whitehead 1990, 58). Marsalis has indeed continued to use JLC as an opportunity to extend the idea that the future of jazz lies in a return to its roots, constructing a narrative that leads from New Orleans to hard bop and from there to the "neo-boppers." He has been at the forefront of writing the various experiments of the 1970s out of the tradition with a historical narrative that sees fusion, electronica, and the avant-garde as dead-end tributaries at best, still-born because of their purported neglect of blues-derived aesthetics and shuffle groove–oriented rhythmic frameworks (see West 1983, 10).

The dismissal of the avant-gardism and fusion of the 1970s and the lionization of a return to older, acoustic approaches to jazz is one of the most widely shared criticisms of the monumental documentary *Jazz*, directed by Ken Burns. Though a number of scholars participated in the project, some on camera and others as off-camera consultants, the most prominent voices winding through all ten episodes are those of Marsalis and Crouch, both of whom consistently press for a historical interpretation that leads inexorably to Marsalis's own music. Predictably, the final episode climaxes with its penultimate scene, which casts Marsalis as the savior of jazz, the young lion eager to light the way for the future. The final montage of the series suggests a much broader view of what jazz sounds like today, showing snippets of Gonzalo Rubalcaba, Geri Allen, and Ron Carter with French MC Solar, among others, but it is strangely detached from the historical model that precedes it.

Ted Gioia has made a good case for revising the notion that the acoustic jazz revival of the past two decades began with Marsalis, pointing to the increase in reissues and the beginnings of a profusion of repertory bands in the Smithsonian Institution's activities in the 1970s, as well as the fact that gifted musicians had occasionally been taking up older, pre-bop styles with great seriousness (Gioia 1997, 381–85). As he points out, the ascendance of Marsalis and the other "Young Lions" in the 1980s and 1990s was a matter of a bright, talented individual hitting the timing just right and making the most of it, coupled with Columbia records intelligent promotion of Marsalis's work (385). Nevertheless there is little question that without this consolidating moment neither the Smithsonian's repertory concerts, nor Norman Granz's efforts in the 1980s to record older, forgotten masters on Pablo records, nor Warren Vaché's and Scott Hamilton's pre-bop approaches, would have been enough to propel the so-called "neoclassicism" into its current prominence.

Canonizing a (Neo)Classical Monk

After Monk left Columbia Records, in 1968, the jazz press devoted less space to him. This is not entirely surprising considering that he recorded very little in the following years, performed less often than he had in the early and mid-1960s, and eventually went into total seclusion in 1974. Thus there was little opportunity to write about him at this stage, save noting reissues of his earlier recordings. His death in 1982 created a flood of media attention in the form of obituaries and hagiographic memorials. Since then Monk has been transformed from a faded past master into one of the canonical artists of the jazz tradition. He has been presented as a timeless figure whose music, like that of Bach or Beethoven, is thought to transcend its historical position and speak in an unmediated way to the listener of the present.

In the process of this transformation parts of the image of Monk projected by Martin Williams and Nat Hentoff became an orthodoxy, and the corollary idea, that to play Monk's music you must play it "his way," gradually took on the quality of received wisdom. Canonization per se is really nothing new in jazz. There is a long history of vernacular canonization, characterized by the creation of a group of essential jazz musicians and of a body of essential recordings by them, either through musical reference or in the jazz press. This sort of canonization, however—one that relies on canonical texts and fidelity of interpretation—is new. It is important to recognize the reasons the different parties have had for being involved in the transition from a vernacular to an official, institutional canon formation in jazz. Most simply, all of these people have been involved with placing Monk into a jazz canon because of a deep respect for him and his music and a desire to see others share that respect.[10] Ultimately, the specific form of Monk's canonization owes more to the possible models for canonization than anything else. For the musicians involved with this official canonization, though, there are more concrete reasons. The development of an institutional valorization of their art is useful in the process of making it economically viable. Moreover, when jazz is seen in the context of the troubled history of race in America, it becomes clear that this institutional valorization helps balance the lingering reality of institutional racism. Sadly, it may be the same enduring logic of white supremacy that prompts those who would lionize Monk to do so on Beethoven's terms.

As discussed previously, one of the most explicit attempts to canonize Monk's music came in the arrangement for big band and the subsequent performance of authoritative versions of Monk's music, a Monk *denkmal,* or collected works, by Martin Williams, T.S. Monk, and others. The great irony about Williams's justification for this project is that for Monk the compositions were, above all else, heads, pieces for extensive playing in a small group format. Williams's model of Monk's "full contribution," and for how audiences and musicians might "learn Monk more fully," by contrast, is recognizable not in jazz (at least not in its first seventy years or so), but in classical repertory, in which the individual composition is a finished, hermetic object, to be re-created but not changed.

For the most part jazz critics ignored this concert. The only review of it appeared in the May 14 edition of the *Washington Post.* The reviewer, Royal Stokes, gave it a cursory, if generally positive, review (Stokes 1986, C13); otherwise the concert passed unnoticed. The attempt to canonize Richards's versions of Monk's compositions as authoritative texts was thus unsuccessful, but the idea that Monk's musical legacy should be understood as a collection of fixed musical objects that speak in a universal musical language has retained a salience over time.

In addition to the growth of "neo-bop", developments in jazz in the 1980s and '90s include an increasingly comfortable place for the music in colleges and universities. Student jazz combos and jazz concert programming have long been part of the college landscape, but the music was on the fringes of serious musicology until recent decades. Thomas Owens's dissertation on oral-traditional composition in Charlie Parker's music, finished in 1974, was an early attempt to address jazz within the academic sphere. Since then an increasing number of books, articles, and dissertations have investigated issues in jazz, often focusing on formalist concerns, particularly the problems of delineating texts for analysis and finding a suitable language with which to discuss them (Gridley 2000; Kernfeld 1981, 1995; Koch 1983; Larson 1987; Schuller 1989; Williams 1992). In the 1990s and the current decade a number of works have brought a new sophistication to jazz scholarship, suggesting the interconnection of formal musical detail and social organization and questioning the use of tools, techniques, and frameworks originally intended for European classical music in the analysis of an African American music (see, for example, Ake 2002; Berliner 1994; DeVeaux 1997; Jackson 1998; Monson 1995, 1996, 1999; Porter 2002; Ramsey 1994; and the essays in Gabbard 1995a and 1995b).

The first application of music-analytical techniques to Monk's music in a scholarly vein is Lawrence Koch's article "Thelonious Monk: Compositional Techniques," published a year after Monk's death in the 1983 issue of the *Annual Review of Jazz Studies (ARJS)*, a journal published by the Institute for Jazz Studies at Rutgers University in Newark. The journal is notable for its attention to the details of individual compositions and jazz improvisations, generally publishing articles that approach jazz history and theory through the analysis of musical detail in jazz recordings as an end in itself, at times to the exclusion of other, more contextual issues and other sources of knowledge. Koch's article is no exception: he notes a number of stylistic markers common in Monk's music—that is, in the heads, the parts of Monk's music most recognizable as his "compositions"—and presents them as a picture of Monk's compositional style. Koch's observations are interesting, but they leave many questions not only unanswered, but also unasked. Perhaps most problematic, Koch's analysis presents Monk's compositions in the abstract, as conceptual objects akin to classical compositions when they are considered outside the context of their performance. This reinforces the idea that Monk's compositions are fixed things, abstract and to be approached with a fundamental concern for fidelity to the abstract model.

This problem is equally, if not more, apparent in a later article from the *ARJS*, Mark Haywood's "Rhythmic Readings in Thelonious Monk" (1994–95). Haywood takes the analytical step of comparing abstracted versions of a number of Monk's compositions with even more abstract "paradigmatic" versions—simplified models conceived as conceptually prior

Example 9. "I Mean You": Rhythmic interpretation, mm. 2–4
(from Haywood 1994–95, 34).

a. "I Mean You"

b. Prototype

states for analytical purposes—in order to explain Monk's odd rhythmic moments and accentual patterns as displacements of simpler models. For example, Haywood proposes interpreting the opening melody of "I Mean You" so that the two rising figures that complete the first subphrase (C–D–E and D♭–E♭–D♭–F♯) have similar conceptually prior rhythmic profiles (ex. 9) (34). To do this, he suggests hearing an extension of measure 3 by either a half beat or a beat and a half. Haywood uses similar reasoning to propose regularized interpretations of numerous other Monk melodies, including "Monk's Mood," "Bolivar Ba-Lues-Are," and "Rhythm-a-ning."

Leaving aside the issue of whether or not this interpretation actually captures the experience of Monk's imaginative rhythmic play, one might ask what these analyses suggest about the ontological status of Monk's music. It is from what Haywood does not explicitly address, rather than from what he does, that one can best see his conceptualization of the music. It is clear that to Haywood these pieces are best addressed in their anterior, abstract status as conceptual objects rather than in the form in which we typically perceive them, as contingent upon performance. Haywood never refers to specific performances of the pieces in this article, not even to look for interpretive nuances to support his argument for a particular assessment of the melodies. This allows him to ignore the contingent, improvised aspects of any given instantiation of the pieces, just as an analyst writing about a Schubert song might ignore the effects of vocal type or pronunciation on the experience of the piece. This is a hallmark of "serious" approaches to music in the postwar musicological (and particularly music theory) genre.[11]

The implication is that music worthy of study has a platonic form that resists change, and that individual performances of that music are to be judged in relation to conceptual perfection.

A recent article by the classical composer Bruce Samet makes a strong case for considering Monk's music as part of a universal musical canon. He draws on literary theorist William H. Gass's description of various kinds of avant-gardism, locating Monk in Gass's "permanent avant-garde" (Samet 2000, 2). This category is, at its heart, a formalist canon of works (in any art) whose purpose "is to return the art to itself . . . in order to remind it of its nature (a creator of forms in the profoundest sense)" (quoted in Samet 2000, 2). The works Gass and Samet offer as examples—J.S. Bach's solo violin sonatas, Beethoven's Sonata No. 32, op. 111, Liszt's Transcendental Etudes, Varèse's *Poème électronique,* Ornette Coleman's *Free Jazz,* and Thelonious Monk's performances of "Evidence" and "Epistrophy"—qualify principally on their distinctiveness. They are avant-garde in a purely formal way, because they stand out in the context of their genres' style histories. Ironically, categorizing these works as examples of the "permanent avant-garde" involves an aspect of radical decontextualization. Samet's universalizing interpretation of these canonical works relies on a sense that they need no longer be interpreted within the context of their creation. He writes, "As the meat grinder of cultural attention has passed over these works, and such composers, and moved on . . . what is winnowed out and left prominent for us to consider . . . [is] the stuff of our permanent avant-garde; and for me . . . such works are independent of 'category' " (2).

Samet is clearly sympathetic to what he hears in Monk—a kindred musical thinker of the highest caliber—as his remarkable, thought-provoking analyses bear out. He is sensitive to the intricacies of internal construction, evolving in the moment of performance, that characterize the works he discusses, as well as to the importance of such insider aesthetic values as call and response and other interactive aspects of musical creation in jazz. What makes Samet's excellent analyses problematic is their justification. Samet, in an interesting reversal of historical value hierarchies, proposes that Monk might be introduced to music students as part of this universal canon because his music speaks in a way that is at once complex and unimpeachably artistic yet also approachable. But is the canon universal? In fact, Samet valorizes Monk over most other jazz musicians he might have chosen, and in his interpretation of Monk he privileges those qualities that are most recognizably similar to the established classical canon. Monk is, as it turns out, a hip Beethoven, or perhaps a hip C.P.E. Bach. Monk's music is to be studied as an " 'essay on the true art' . . . of thinking in music," notable principally for its large-scale formal sophistication (2). As Samet puts it, the 1971 recording of "Misterioso" (Monk 1971) is "a case of direct, improvisational thinking-in-music, which is quite straightforward . . . and which I think as a composition could be considered respectable by any 'classical' standard" (9). While Samet's analysis of how Monk and his trio create a compelling large-scale work in this performance is exceptional, it ultimately ignores those aspects of Monk's music, and, more broadly, jazz and African American music in general, that do not fulfill the aesthetics of Western classical music.[12]

The study of jazz performance has been even more significant than jazz theory in establishing what works are canonical and determining jazz's place in institutions of higher learning. David Ake's study of the ways John Coltrane is taught to aspiring jazz musicians in a university setting paints an unflattering picture of the ideology of classicism, which tends to displace any other sense of the music. He argues that Coltrane's unprecedented position within the canon of great jazz masters in collegiate jazz education programs is colored by the permeating ideologies of the conservatory setting. As he says, "certain musical and extramusical aspects of [Coltrane's] work challenge the guidelines of 'good music' set by most schools. Consequently, these aspects get brushed aside as aberrations or ignored altogether in college jazz ensembles and improvisation classes" (Ake 2002, 113). Moreover, since jazz education programs play a significant role in producing professional jazz musicians today, the vision of Coltrane, and jazz in general, that this supports has a lasting impact on the jazz played (and the ways jazz is heard) in the world outside those ivy-covered walls.

The central point of Ake's study of Coltrane in collegiate jazz education is that his hard work ethic and the extremely complex approach to harmony that characterize his work from around 1960 have become enshrined as the sum total of his musical legacy, and, in some ways, they are considered the crowning achievement of jazz, the thing toward which all development of harmonic sophistication in the music's history builds. In this musical world there is no place for Coltrane's more "outside" playing from 1965 and thereafter, nor for his later music's patently spiritual, mystical framework (129–40). This leads to a further-reaching problem, which is that avant-garde music becomes written out of the history, the present, and perhaps the future of jazz because it does not fit the jazz educator's model of "good music," and because it is exceedingly difficult to teach effectively (and to grade) in the conservatory setting (142–44).

John Murphy argues that Ake's analysis of the breadth of jazz instruction in the collegiate environment is missing a key component (Murphy forthcoming). Murphy suggests that by focusing exclusively on the pedagogical tools of jazz harmony, Ake has missed other aspects of the total ecology of a jazz education experience, which also include private lessons, student ensemble playing, gigging outside school, and, at least for the top musicians—those most likely to go on to professional careers as jazz musicians— experience as apprentice-level sidemen with professionals. Both studies are limited, of course, Ake's to published pedagogical materials and to the specific case of Coltrane, and Murphy's to an ethnography of jazz education at a specific moment, the early 2000s, at the University of North Texas. A much broader historical and ethnographic study of jazz education in the United States and abroad remains to be done. At present, my own rather unscientific impression is that, indeed, the ecology of the jazz program at a college conservatory is complex and multifaceted, and it differs in many ways from place to place, but, nevertheless, a profoundly conservative, harmony-centric, "rationalist" ideology pervades these programs, generally marginalizing "outside" playing and reinforcing the notion of a jazz canon.

WHY A JAZZ CANON?

The projects of jazz canonization in the academy and in artistic institutions such as JLC have been intertwined since 1980. Both have been intent on providing a consistent and compelling narrative about the past that legitimates jazz as a high art, worthy of respect and a place in education and performance alongside Western classical music. The cultural capital that can be developed as a result of this consolidation is particularly important if, as the common wisdom suggests, jazz is no longer able to support itself economically.[13] There is at least the appearance that few jazz recordings other than those by a handful of stars such as Wynton Marsalis are particularly profitable for either musicians or their record companies.[14] Accordingly, many jazz musicians rely on jobs in higher education to supplement their incomes. What is certain is that jazz is not economically remunerative in the way that any of today's popular musics—rock, country, rap, and soul— are, and that, as a result, competition for any cultural capital is significant. In this context the importance of control over the canonical history of jazz becomes apparent. A particular approach to the music may be marketed—or simply lionized—as "authentic" because of its ability to construct a picture that places it at the center of the tradition. The telling of history is an undeniably powerful tool in this process, and musical performance becomes a primary enunciative mode for telling that history.

Considering the value of canon formation to the jazz tradition, or at least to some of its members, the question as to why the canon has taken its particular form remains. Why would a canon developing in the final years of the twentieth century, for an African American music that is itself a product of that century, follow a number of modernist aesthetic ideologies more reflective of nineteenth-century European music? Here Foucault's theory of discourses is eminently valuable. He makes the case that all "enunciative acts" participate in larger "discursive formations," and that these discursive formations, or simply discourses, are themselves constitutive of and contingent upon their situation within social and cultural histories. He elaborates this point, saying, "Not all the positions of the subject, all the types of coexistence between statements, all the discursive strategies, are equally possible, but only those authorized by anterior levels" (Foucault 1972, 73). Foucault argues that discourses are "not deployed according to an unlimited autonomy," because of the discursive history in which the object of discourse exists and that in which the discoursing subject is situated, as well as the interrelations between these and other levels of discourse within any given formation (73). The point is that there are only so many options possible for a person to argue for the canonical status of jazz. This particular one has a lock on the activity of elevating the status of the music because it is deeply ingrained in the culture at many levels, and is durably instilled, generally beginning in childhood.

The other compelling question that all of this suggests is whether the discursive field represented by this canonization, the rhetoric about it, creates an equally uniform field of musical practice. Foucault presents a state of affairs in which webs of meaning are so densely overdetermined that many readings of his work have led to a denial of the possibility of any human agency in working with discourses. Foucault cautions that "systems of [discursive] formation must not be taken as blocks of immobility, static forms that are imposed on discourse from the outside, and that define once and for all its characteristics and possibilities" (73–74). Thus, while discursive formations may have a certain determining power, in practice interventions may be made, new conceptual relations construed, but within a context in which any given subject has limited agency. The following chapter provides an account of three musicians' approaches to this problem, showing how the construction of a "mainstream" Monk has played out in musical performance. Notably, it is in sound, in enunciation becoming text, that musicians have been able to negotiate creatively within and at times against preexistent discursive frameworks.

SIX

"Classicism" and Performance

IF THE STRATEGIES OF CANONIZATION discussed in chapter 5 were the provenance of critics and historians alone, they would be relatively circumscribed in their importance. Similar ideas, however, run through the intellectual community of jazz musicians (to some extent through dialogue with other commentators), impacting musicians' discursive stances and performance practices with regard to Monk's music. Through an analysis of musical performances, official public discourse (such as published interviews), and other, less official public and private speech (including stage talk, private interviews, and conversations), it is possible to find out to what extent jazz musicians have accepted or rejected a "classicized" view of Monk and his legacy. Not surprisingly, there is no consensus; the community of musicians has come to a range of positions on it, and in fact individual musicians hold what can appear to be contradictory opinions. Many do subscribe to the canonical ideal, that Monk's music has to be played with fidelity to some original version. However, few accept the idea that their own playing is orthodox, or is circumscribed by tradition. Moreover, they are loath to see their own performances as conventional. Given the jazz community's deeply felt valorization of innovation and novelty, this is hardly surprising. On the other hand, it is not hard to find musicians who criticize other jazz musicians' approaches to Monk's music as conventional recreations of someone else's interpretation—either Monk's or, in the case of a tune like " 'Round Midnight," Miles Davis's or some other well-known version. Often this opinion is expressed in general terms—"no one else (but me) has anything to say with this music"—but at times specific musicians were singled out. One piano player in the study criticized another who had recently released an album that consisted largely of songs either composed by or strongly interpreted by Monk, saying that he didn't intend to bother listening to the recording because he had heard her play Monk before and thought her playing was too "Monkish."[1] His often-echoed reasoning was, "Why should I listen to [that musician] play Monk just like Monk when I can just as easily go listen to the original?"

This resistance to conventional performances of Monk's music can be contextualized by a reading of Paul Berliner's description of the process of learning to play jazz in his book *Thinking in Jazz*. Guided by Walter Bishop Jr.'s description of learning to play, Berliner writes of a three-step process many musicians follow as they mature, working from "imitation," through "assimilation," and finally to "innovation" (Berliner 1994, 273). It is during the assimilation stage, as he describes it, that musicians are most likely to play Monk "like Monk." This is the stage at which musicians, "whose keen ears enable them to absorb an idol's precise style, but who improvise exclusively within its bounds" (273), are often described as "clones." While most, if not all, jazz musicians study the work of predecessors by extensively imitating and assimilating their style, such work is generally commendable only if the musician progresses beyond that stage and finds his or her own voice. Berliner quotes trombonist Curtis Fuller, saying, "It is 'great for a musician to walk in the shoes of the fisherman' because imitation is a great compliment, but, he cautions, 'I wouldn't want to lose my personality or shut down my development that way.' Otherwise, he says, 'I wouldn't have enhanced what's been done before. I would rather be an extension than a retention'" (121).

A great many musicians, particularly pianists, may well have gone through a period of playing in an excessively "Monkish" way as they developed as musicians, but few commercial recordings have documented performers at that stage, because it generally precedes acceptance as a full-fledged professional. Woody Shaw's recording *Bemsha Swing*, released posthumously in 1997, is interesting because it provides a glimpse of one such performance (Shaw 1997). Recorded live in Detroit in February 1986, the disc features a local rhythm section that includes Geri Allen, who was then near the beginning of her career. The recording pays Thelonious Monk significant attention, and includes three of his compositions and a tribute to him by drummer Roy Brooks. This recording is particularly interesting because it captures a performance by Allen that is clearly a step along the way to maturity as an artist. In an interview for *Down Beat* magazine, Allen described learning from Monk's recordings and the importance of honoring him and other predecessors in her music (Mandel 1994, 17–18). In her recordings from the late 1990s, to the extent that Monk's influence is discernable, it is thoroughly integrated into a personal voice that is immediately recognizable. On this recording, however, Allen's playing, particularly on the tune "Well You Needn't," sounds "Monkish" in a way that suggests an incomplete assimilation of his voice.

If playing Monk "like Monk" is easily heard as an immature stage in the development of a jazz musician, then one has to ask why musicians who have achieved acceptance as performers with their own voices would advocate the canonical ideal I have described. The following examples suggest a complicated answer, which might be summarized as follows. For some musicians this kind of reproduction-oriented approach may be one of many that they use, depending on the circumstances, and they might feel this approach is more appropriate for Monk's music than for others'. In other cases they may describe the goal of playing Monk "his way" but in fact find their own ways of playing his music, if within somewhat circumscribed contours. In very few cases do musicians working at the highest levels of jazz take a stylistically derivative approach as their only one.

Of the musicians involved in this study, pianist Michael Weiss stands out for his commitment to the idea that Monk's music has to be played Monk's way. He described his process of coming to this conclusion in an interview, saying, "I just learned through the process of doing it. I'd compare one recording to another of the same composition. I began to hear certain things that were always there—things that Monk played, the way he voiced a certain chord. That made me realize that you can't just play any type of E-dominant seventh chord, or some type of chord type at a certain place, 'cause just the generic sound doesn't give the flavor that he was looking for at that moment" (Weiss 1999). Weiss expanded on how to arrive at a reliable picture of what Monk intended for each composition, saying, "See, if you're going to learn a Thelonious Monk tune, you have to get all the recordings of a tune and make a comparison—compare one melody to the next" (Weiss 1999). Like many musicians, in addition to emphasizing the importance of fidelity to Monk's originals when playing the heads, Weiss noted how soloing on Monk's compositions is fundamentally different than doing so for pop standards, for example. He emphasized that an improviser approaching this music has to take a lesson from Monk, building a solo using the melodic material from the heads as germinal motives (Weiss 1999).

T.S. Monk is the musician most closely associated with orthodox interpretations of Monk's compositions, particularly for his work in the 1990s. This is a goal he set for himself, but his approach has also led to criticism, including charges that his recordings are unoriginal and that they bring nothing of himself to the compositions. T.S. has a complicated position within the jazz world: because he is Monk's son, he is scrutinized very closely and almost constantly held to the standard of his father's music. He is in a double bind of sorts: when he plays his father's compositions he may be dismissed either for adhering too closely to his father's playing or for not being true to his father's legacy. One musician with whom I spoke eloquently expressed the former criticism: "Yeah, I heard that group, and all that. Well, I thought it was a re-creation; and I'm not too partial to recreating things, or music as a recreative thing, a recreational thing, either. It sounded as though it was a copy . . . it sounded to me like he was trying to be what he was not. . . . We don't know what he is, really, 'cause he's got that *role,* you know. He's playing a role." The same musician softened this critique, expressing an understanding of the difficult position T.S., as Monk's son, inhabits in the jazz community. Although this sympathy, which is expressed by a number of people, seems reasonable, T.S. adamantly rejects it (Monk 1999).

T.S. Monk has an unusual past in the musical world. He occasionally traveled on tour with his father as a young boy, but he was not involved with the music. Indeed, he says his father never brought up the question of whether T.S. would play music of any kind. When he was in high school T.S. began playing drums on his own initiative (Monk 1999). More than a year later he spoke with his father about his musical aspirations. "At that point he said only two things to me," T.S. recalled. "He said I needed to learn how to read music and I needed to practice, because I was starting late. And so he then went and got Max Roach to give me my first drum lessons" (Richards 1994a, 10). Three years later, in 1969, when T.S. was twenty years old, his father invited him to join his touring band. The professional association between the two Monks lasted five years, until Monk senior retired from active music making. T.S. describes feeling frustrated when that job was over and he realized few young musicians were playing jazz. His contemporaries were drawn to R&B, a genre that had more listeners and was much more lucrative at the time. Monk followed suit and started a soul band under his own name with his sister Barbara Monk and his partner, Yvonne Fletcher. The band recorded regularly and was successful, scoring a dance hit with the tune "Bon, Bon Vie" (Monk 1999). After the deaths of both Barbara Monk and Yvonne Fletcher in a period of five months between 1983 and 1984, T.S. stopped performing and began actively pursuing the creation of a foundation in his father's honor (Monk 1999). Almost a decade later, in 1990, T.S. began to play drums again, this time in a jazz context. He has led a sextet comprised of journeymen musicians playing in a mainstream/hard bop style since 1991.

No single entity has done more to create and maintain a public image of Monk than T.S. Monk's organization, the Thelonious Monk Institute of Jazz. A brief glance at its past and its profile in the jazz world today shows its commitment to the creation of a Monk orthodoxy. The institute is distinct from most other organizations in the jazz world in that it is a more of a virtual entity than a brick-and-mortar organization. It sponsors educational programs, concerts, documentaries, and the renowned Thelonious Monk competitions, and although it runs a program through the University of Southern California, most of its life is not tied to a conservatory campus. Its principal permanent face to the world is its web site, www.monkinstitute.com. It is hard to determine what, exactly, was the guiding principle behind the Monk Institute at the start, as it appears to have shifted and grown in response to changing circumstances and the addition of new programs. A press release from early in the institute's life, most likely written in 1987 or 1988, describes it as "not only . . . a permanent memorial to a jazz figure, but . . . a standing monument to jazz—'America's' classical music" ("Thelonious Sphere Monk Cultural Center" n.d., 3).

The "classical music" model of jazz was particularly important in the institute's rhetoric from the 1980s and early 1990s. The first and largest sponsor to support the project was the Beethoven Society of America, in Washington, D.C. The Beethoven Society's founder and chair, Maria Fischer, appears to have been particularly interested in this project because Monk was often described as the preeminent composer of modern jazz, allowing him and his music to be discussed in a manner similar to analyses of Beethoven and his work (3). In 1988 the society and the institute produced a fund-raising concert that brought attention to the Monk Institute, which at the time was attempting to develop a Monk Center for the Arts, a permanent brick-and-mortar home in either Washington, D.C., Rocky Mount, North Carolina (Monk's birthplace), or Los Angeles. The event was arranged for the most part by David Amram, a French horn player who has worked in both the jazz and classical worlds and was closely involved with the Third Stream movement of the 1960s with Gunther Schuller and others.

In a review of the 1986 concert, singer Jon Hendricks told critic W. Royal Stokes, "To me the solos of Bird, the compositions and arrangements of Duke Ellington, the things done by Basie, Dizzy's solos, Art Tatum's solos are also *classical*, so to use that term to differentiate one type of music from another is discriminatory on a cultural level. To have the Beethoven Society recognize, through the music of Thelonious Monk, the classicality of jazz music is the biggest step that jazz has taken in the United States so far" (Stokes 1986, 8; emphasis in the original). It is particularly interesting to see how Hendricks intervenes in the use of the term *classical*, demanding that it be used adjectivally to describe music of value rather than nominally to define a specific musical tradition. He explicitly refers to the ways aesthetics encode racial meanings in his rejection of the nominal use of *classical* as "discriminatory on a cultural level."

The Monk Center as it was conceived at the time—a single venue incorporating a conservatory-like education center, a museum, a cultural center, and an archive—never came to fruition. Instead, the institute has taken a more decentered approach to achieving its goals. The most important incarnation of the Monk Institute is the annual Thelonious Monk International Jazz Competition. Through this competition, at first only for pianists, but over the years showcasing various instruments and jazz vocalists, the institute has become one of the most important sources of competitive funding in the jazz world.

Because of the resources the Monk Institute commands and the manner in which it redistributes a portion of them, it is subject to some criticism. Fred Hersch voiced a concern that appears to be widespread. He felt that the competition favored technically brilliant, but conceptually derivative, conventional performances of Monk's music, thereby consolidating an institutional view of what Monk's music should be and how it should be played (Hersch 1999). This is a debatable point: all of the musicians who have won the competition have been technically proficient, and all have played largely within a post-bop/hard bop style, but to dismiss them outright on this basis alone seems problematic. It certainly appears, however, that the competition tends not to show an interest in avant-garde performance and performers. What is most interesting about Hersch's criticism is that it is couched in terms of Monk's legacy: Hersch argued that because this competition takes place in Monk's name, it should be true to Monk's approach to jazz. The judges should therefore be looking for the most innovative, most novel approach to his compositions and should not be swayed by technical considerations. In essence, he saw the competition as playing a notable role in making the historical image of Monk, and saw it as reinforcing a view of Monk that he considers inaccurate: as a mainstream jazz musician whose compositions are vehicles to be interpreted within rigidly proscribed constraints. The perception of Hersch and many others is that, because of the resources it commands (and, thus, the media attention it receives), the Monk Institute is socially situated in such a way as to make its view of Monk and his legacy the dominant one—to make it an orthodoxy.

How does a discourse of authenticity about Monk based on the creation of and fidelity to authoritative texts play out in musical practice? There are probably a number of answers to this question, given the fact that practice is often far more varied and even self-contradictory than discourse. I would like to focus on three examples: T.S. Monk's large-ensemble recording project, *Monk on Monk;* Marcus Roberts's solo recording, *Alone with Three Giants;* and, finally Wynton Marsalis's Monk tribute album, *Standard Time, Volume 4.*

MONK ON MONK

Monk on Monk was not T.S. Monk's first attempt at recording his father's music, but it is distinct from his earlier recordings as a concept album dedicated entirely to his father's compositions. In other respects, however, the recording is continuous with his total output. When recording each of his albums he recognized both the potential benefit of using his surname as well as the potential dangers. Although the Monk name was a marketing asset, he was also keenly aware of the possibility that he would be seen as riding his father's coattails to success, and that he would be held to an unusually high standard: he would be expected to play on his father's level, and to actively cultivate his father's legacy without being seen as derivative (Monk 1999). T.S. Monk's first three albums, *Take One, Changing of the Guard,* and *The Charm,* all released on Blue Note Records, worked within a mainstream, groove-oriented, hard-bop aesthetic. T.S. explained the conception of his first three albums this way: having thought about what was essential to the music he liked, and having considered what audiences seemed to want—that is, what he thought he could sell—he concluded, "I have to make a record that has tunes with haunting melodies; every tune has to have a groove; it's got to be tight as shit; and the soloist's got to be a bitch" (Richards 1994b, 17). T.S. Monk's ideas for marketing his work were based on a sense of audience psychology. Having produced his first album himself, T.S. took it to Blue Note Records looking for a contract. He reasoned, "I'll take it to Blue Note Records 'cos that makes marketing sense. . . . They got all Monk and Monk is synonymous with Blue Note and Blue Note is synonymous with classic jazz" (17).[2] The extent to which this chain of signifiers works in precisely this way for the listening public probably varies widely, but the statement clearly shows T.S.'s marketing strategy.

The first three albums were all recorded by the same working band, with T.S. Monk on drums, Don Sickler on trumpet, Bobby Porcelli on alto sax, Willie Williams on tenor and soprano saxes, and Ronnie Matthews on piano. The band played regularly and their recordings were reviewed in jazz magazines—if not always glowingly—but these albums were apparently not particularly successful in economic terms. In 1997, before the recording of *Monk on Monk,* Blue Note dropped the band from their roster (Koransky 1998, 29). Nonetheless, T.S., the consummate promoter and businessman, had little difficulty finding a new label to release the tribute project. Although he continued to try to get the album out on Blue Note, it was eventually released by the multimedia production company N2K, now called Encoded Music (29).

The project of *Monk on Monk* consisted of more than just the music recorded on the album. From the beginning it was a package that included the music, a multimedia CD-ROM, a tour, lectures, and an exceptionally good public relations campaign. In T.S. Monk's descriptions of the project, and in the timing of its placement within his career's trajectory, music and marketing are constantly intertwined. His description of why he chose to record a tribute album of his father's music at that moment is a good example. T.S. Monk recognized that many people expected him to make that album first, at the beginning of his career as a jazz recording artist. It would have been a logical move, allowing him to capitalize on the instant recognition of his name and on the market for tribute albums in general. "But that was the album I absolutely would not make," he said. "I could have done it and fucked it up five, 10 years ago. But then no one was familiar with my playing. Now was the time to make that record" (Koransky 1998, 29). He may have been concerned with his own musical development and perhaps did not want to make such a demanding album before he knew his playing was up to it, but he was at least as concerned with the exigencies of living within the jazz community and the impact capitalizing on his father's legacy might have in that context. Jazz musicians are notoriously critical of one another's playing, and T.S. had no doubt that if they thought the project lacked credibility he would bear the heaviest criticism for it as the leader of the date. In addition, he recognized the potential for economic success in such a record and wanted to time its release in such a way as to maximize the rewards—neither releasing it too early, before he could make a case for the record's authenticity as the product of a recognized jazz artist, nor too late to make a splash. Finally, T.S. underscored the importance of his own name recognition in the timing of the release of *Monk on Monk*. A public relations campaign that focused on him rather than simply on the album or on his father could help him sell later projects that might not have the same built-in market value. A tribute album released before building his own status could have run the risk of overshadowing his own contribution, giving him little surplus public relations with which to build sales of later projects.

Despite the extent of T.S. Monk's calculation in the creation of *Monk on Monk*, it would be a mistake to dismiss the project as the result of crass commercialism, as though art and commerce are always and necessarily at odds with one another. Charles Hamm was one of the first to detail how an ideology of musical autonomy gradually became a hegemonic discourse over the course of the nineteenth century: that the value of a musical work was to be found in its decontextualization, its appearance of standing apart from various kinds of sociocultural uses. In addition, pieces in the Western classical tradition were understood to be the product of a lone genius, a matter of inspiration, not calculation (3). Scott DeVeaux thoughtfully critiques the "anticommercial stance" in modern jazz historiography, noting that it significantly misrepresents the realities of jazz musicians' own conception of themselves, their art, and its place in American culture (DeVeaux 1997, 12–16). Considering T.S. Monk and the process of actively building a career in jazz points to the difficulty one confronts trying to sustain a conceptual separation of art and commerce. The considerations he kept in mind are clearly economic, but they are also unquestionably necessary in creating an environment in which he could achieve his musical goals. They are the sorts of concerns that any musician has to address, though few are as forthcoming as he is in discussing them.

"Ruby, My Dear"

Before addressing the layers of discourse surrounding this project, it will be instructive to look more closely at a track from *Monk on Monk*. T.S. Monk chose compositions that his father wrote for friends and family members as an organizing theme for the recording. Thus, the CD includes "Little Rootie Tootie," composed for T.S. as a young boy, "Crepuscule with Nellie," written for Monk's wife, and "Boo Boo's Birthday," dedicated to Monk's daughter, Barbara, nicknamed "Boo Boo," among others tracks. All of the compositions were arranged for large ensemble—not the standard eighteen-piece big band that Martin Williams envisaged, but a more variable group, generally having three to four saxophones, two trumpets, and a trombone at its heart, and occasionally including a tuba or French horn. The scoring echoes the two ensembles Hall Overton worked with for Monk's big band concerts, the first of which was low and dark-timbred, including two tenor saxes, tuba and French horn, and the second of which was high and bright timbred, including soprano sax and cornet. In addition to these ensembles, *Monk on Monk* draws on the solo talents of some of the brightest young stars and established masters, including Geri Allen, Ron Carter, Herbie Hancock, Roy Hargrove, Jimmy Heath, Dave Holland, Danilo Perez, Wallace Roney, Arturo Sandoval, Wayne Shorter, Clark Terry, and Grover Washington Jr. and vocalists Kevin Mahogany, Nnenna Freelon, and Dianne Reeves.

The version of "Ruby, My Dear" on this recording, the fourth track on the disc, is representative of the ways T.S. Monk as leader, Don Sickler as arranger, and the rest of the musicians on the date worked to negotiate a double path, attempting at once to preserve a relationship to the piece as a "composition" while at the same time interpreting it in their own voices. The arrangement of the introduction, head, and coda is a nearly exact copy of the transcription and orchestration of Monk's performance of it with John Coltrane on the Riverside album *Monk's Music* (1957), discussed in chapter 5. The melody originally played on tenor sax is sung by Kevin Mahogany, with Sally Swisher's lyrics. Monk's piano chord voicings and "response" figures are scored, note for note, for soprano, alto, tenor, and baritone saxes, two trumpets, and trombone, with support from Ronnie Matthews on piano. In addition, the rhythmic nuance of Monk's version is reproduced remarkably well here, including, notably, a shifting between regular and double-time rhythmic feels in the bridge section of the head.

A comparison of this recording with the one discussed in chapter 5, played by Monk and Coltrane, clearly demonstrates the importance of parameters other than pitch and rhythm in creating the feel or experience and meaning of a performance. The rescoring of the accompaniment in this version, from Monk's piano to an ensemble of horns, creates a very different

Example 10. "Ruby My Dear": First chorus, A1, mm. 1–2
(T.S. Monk 1997, track 4, 0:09–0:14).

a. Thelonious Monk, standard

b. Kevin Mahogany

effect. The horns are capable of a legato that is impossible on piano, and that Monk did not attempt to suggest, in any case. Moreover, the sound of a horn section playing legato lines in close, parallel harmony implicitly references not the sound of a small bebop combo and the social and musical worlds that small jazz combos have inhabited since the 1940s, but the suave, "sweet," contemporary big band or the "cool" large ensemble recordings of the 1960s and 1970s. The vocalist here also draws this recording into the sound world of the "sweet" big band. Although Coltrane's tenor playing on the original recording is eminently vocal (though one never forgets that it is a tenor sax), such vocality is itself a kind of reference and is a basic part of instrumental virtuosity on the tenor sax going back to Coleman Hawkins, Lester Young, and Don Byas, among others. The actual singing voice on this recording, on the other hand, is part of a historical frame of reference that ties the recording in with pop singers and crooners of the 1930s through the 1960s and the resurgence of "sweet" pop music in the 1990s, all the more so because "Ruby, My Dear" is a love song.

Unlike the horns, which reproduce the melodic and rhythmic features of Monk's performance of this piece very closely, Mahogany's vocal interpretation makes some significant changes. He shifts the notes of the opening motive and its subsequent repetitions later in time, and alters the pitch of the third note (ex. 10). This small change has some interesting effects. By singing the notes later in time, Mahogany creates an impression of stretching time out, so that although the basic pulse of this recording is almost exactly the same tempo as on Monk's 1957 version, the overall rhythmic feel

Example 11. "Ruby, My Dear": Roy Hargrove's flugelhorn solo, A1, mm. 1–8 (T.S. Monk 1997, track 4, 2:07).

is as though it were slower, more languid. In addition, by moving the third note into the second measure and by lowering it a half step, Mahogany erases the strongest, and most characteristically "Monkish," dissonance, a minor ninth in combination with a minor seventh over the dominant seventh chord. It is a tiny detail of performance, a mere fraction of a second, a melodic shift of the smallest increment, and yet this little change has a significant effect, enhancing the "sweet" quality of the performance and giving it a less idiosyncratically marked harmonic profile.

Little space is given to instrumental improvisation in this recording, but Roy Hargrove's half-chorus flugelhorn solo is noteworthy. Hargrove plays through the first two A sections of the form, the first sixteen measures, with rhythm section accompaniment, including T.S. Monk on drums, Ronnie Matthews on piano, and Gary Wang on bass. In this section all of the musicians closely observe the form, but in a way somewhat different than the performers on Monk's 1957 version do. Hargrove plays a smooth, clear melodic solo that stays well inside the changes, drawing on the total sound world of the hard bop idiom. Unlike Coltrane's solo (or Coleman Hawkins's from another recording of "Ruby, My Dear," on *Monk's Music*), Hargrove's is not an ornamented version of the melody, but nevertheless it makes regular use of notes from the melody, ultimately projecting a clear sense of movement through the form (ex. 11). He plays through the two-measure ii–V–I progressions in the first six bars, emphasizing the shared diatonic collections for the harmonies in each two-measure span and downplaying the internal harmonic changes—a phrasing in keeping with both the melody's phrasing and with common practice.[3] Hargrove emphasizes the boundary notes of the repeated A-section motive in his improvisation. In measures 1–2 he focuses on B♭ and G, in measures 3–4 on A and C, and in measures 5–6, having created an expectation to hear these melody notes emphasized, he delays the C with an arpeggio of the B♭m^7 chord starting on B♭, landing at C on beat two, and then descends ultimately to E♭, the end point of the original melody in measures 5–6. An interesting effect of the way Hargrove moves through this solo is that, particularly in the first eight measures, he manages to clearly keep a sense of the form, and even the melody, in the listener's ear without sounding as though he is playing in Monk's idiom. He achieves this by playing through the changes without chromaticism that would emphasize the small-scale harmonic movement, instead playing diatonic melodies that emphasize the unity of larger-scale key areas over longer time spans. Like Mahogany, Hargrove emphasizes the boundary pitches of the motive but not the third pitch, the flat ninth over the V chord in the second half of measures 1, 3, and 5, thus avoiding the tritone/minor second relationships that permeate this part of the melody. In addition to maintaining a sound that indexes a prominent post-bop style, this helps avoid explicitly indexing a stereotypically "Monkish" sound.

Monk on Monk *and a Discourse of Authenticity*

The PR materials for *Monk on Monk* strive to produce an aura of authenticity to legitimate the project. In the interviews included as part of the "enhanced" CD-ROM version of the album, T.S. discusses his guiding philosophy as an interpreter of his father's music, claiming, "I felt it has been one of my responsibilities, because of the type of ensemble that I have—a sextet, basically—to approach my father's music in sort of an archival fashion. That is to say, to perform the music as close to his original conception as possible. Because, outside of Thelonious himself, it's very rare that you hear his music performed as it was written" (Monk 1997).[4] Part entertainment, part scholarly production, at least in its presentational style, this recording claims legitimacy at least to some extent through the power of a historical frame of reference.

In a similar move, Don Sickler, the arranger responsible for the big band versions of the compositions on *Monk on Monk,* emphasizes his careful study of Monk's recordings as the source of his claim to an authentic version of the music.[5] In an interview he made it clear that he considers it his mission to preserve the jazz of the 1950s and 1960s, through transcription, arranging, and promotion. I asked him whether he saw himself as a scholar, a historian, and his response was enlightening. He explained that although he enjoyed playing and composing, his true calling was his work as a publisher, and he said, "So yes, I am a *music* historian" (Sickler 1999).

It is worth noting the significance of the discourses of scholastic achievement and historicism in these two musicians' descriptions of their interaction with Monk's music. Despite recent attempts to destabilize or demystify an understanding of the kinds of truth to be found in the discipline of history, the explicit invocation of a historian's engagement with the past (as opposed to a more personal, informal understanding of it) is a powerful authenticating discourse. The use of a language of academicism doubly authorizes the work, both through the truth-value associated with official history and through the cultural authority represented by the academy.

Given this emphasis on the music of the past, it is not surprising that Sickler's musical goals as an arranger are thoroughly oriented toward capturing the intentions of the composer as he sees them. As he describes it, his process for writing arrangements of Monk's music for sextet and big band involves listening to Monk's recordings as carefully as possible and then attempting to orchestrate as precisely as possible Monk's own piano voicings for horns. This is an admirable project, and Sickler accomplishes it remarkably well, as the *Monk on Monk* recording amply demonstrates. It is, however, ironic that Sickler and T.S. Monk (and their public relations representatives) would present this as somehow capturing the composer's intentions. With a few exceptions Monk was not terribly interested in large ensemble arrangements of his music. The vast majority of his performances were with a quartet, and in these recordings the piano and ubiquitous tenor sax almost always play the melody in unison or octaves for both the head and out chorus. Moreover, even when Monk had multiple horn players, he generally asked them to play in unison or octaves. Steve Lacy recalls, "It had to have a sound. . . . He wouldn't let us play harmony parts. He wanted us to play unison or octaves. He said, if you can do that, 'That's the hardest shit in the world,' he said. 'If you can do that you can always add harmony. That's nothing.' But to get that *sound* first. Playing the same note, the tenor, soprano, and piano, that's it" (Lacy 1999a). Monk's large ensemble performances (of which he appears to have been justifiably proud) featured arrangements not entirely his own but developed in collaboration with composer Hall Overton. While Sickler's arrangements are clearly both virtuosic examples of the craft and unequalled in the debt they owe Monk's recordings of the compositions, it is hard to make a case that they better or more authentically capture Monk's intentions than would a quartet performance.

While there is no question that re-presenting Monk's compositions in this sort of monumental form was based on a sincere belief that it would be aesthetically satisfying and would be a fitting tribute, there is also a clear pragmatic goal involved as well. The 1990s saw an enormous swell of jazz tribute recordings—so many that the trend has drawn criticism from musicians as limiting their options in studio recording. Given this glut of tribute albums, it was fundamentally important that T.S. find a way of distinguishing a project dedicated to his father if it was to compete successfully in a limited market. The ostentatious abundance of star soloists on this recording, as well as the use of a smooth big band arrangement style that taps into a potentially larger market than that for small group bebop-style jazz, was undoubtedly a marketing strategy as well as a musical one.

MARCUS ROBERTS: BLACK TIE MONK

Marcus Roberts's solo piano album *Alone with Three Giants,* recorded in 1991, shows perhaps the purest canonical approach to constructing Monk's legacy. The album, Roberts' third as a leader, tackles repertoire that is extraordinarily challenging, from a musical standpoint if not a technical one. A portentous air of seriousness pervades this recording so thoroughly that it becomes difficult to hear it in any other light. In a feature piece published in *Down Beat* shortly before the release of the album, Roberts describes the guiding principle of the recording as paying "homage to the great tradition that's been established by Bird and Duke, Ellington and Monk and all the other people who could really play" (Booth 1990, 20). Later he reiterates the theme of homage, saying, "The only thing that I can do is play the music that I'm trying to get together and to pay homage to the musicians who I consider to be personally motivating forces behind the philosophy that I'm trying to develop. I can only hope that the people who come into contact with that find some inspiration" (21).

If it seems that a "black tie" mode underscores nearly everything about this album (the somber tone of Roberts's interviews is echoed in the severe, formal cover art, a geometric study in black and white that shows Roberts's hands on a keyboard and formal portraits of the three composers featured on the album, Monk, Jelly Roll Morton, and Duke Ellington), Roberts is at pains to reiterate the "classical" bona fides that might account for it. In interviews at the time, as well as in interviews since, he directed critics of his approach to consider the fact that hundreds of years after their composition, the great musical works of the European tradition are still regularly performed in accordance with the way they were written. Surely, he argues, if this is the case, then the work of Ellington, Monk, and so on can be treated this way and remain relevant. If not, then, the "music actually has no value and had no value when it was created" (Birnbaum 1996, 22). There is really no more straightforward justification of the 1980s and 1990s repertory movement in jazz than this.

The music on *Alone with Three Giants* is no less serious than the images and the rhetoric surrounding it. On the broadest level, the concept behind the recording is to connect the dots linking the three composers as a triumvirate of jazz classicists. There are, of course, a number of compelling connections between Morton, Ellington, and Monk, not least to be found in their "orchestral" style on the piano and their ties to stride and ragtime. The individual tracks, which, as one reviewer suggested, sound like a series of "jazz etudes," tend to work through the fundamental concept in a thorough way (Stein 1991, 32). The pieces are not played strictly in a "repertory" fashion, which is to say they are never note-for-note reproductions of original recordings, nor even obvious paraphrases. "In Walked Bud," for instance, which is one of the more distinctive tracks on the album, presents Monk's tune on the changes of "Blue Skies" as a kind of multistrain piece. Roberts opens with a straightforward statement of the head, followed by a quiet, meandering chorus aided by the una corda pedal. He then bursts into a loud, brash stride chorus that overlays the chord structure of "Blue Skies" with an allusion to the melody of "Is You Is or Is You Ain't My Baby." The rest of the performance alternates between una corda and full-voiced stride until the last chorus, in which Roberts brings back the head just as he played it at the beginning.

In addition to the academic treatment of themes on this album, the most notable quality of the recording is its general, pervasive sound. In Roberts's touch at the keyboard, the mix, and even the choice of pianos there is a studied, careful quality. Roberts's approach to the piano produces a full, rich tone but tends to even out and tone down extremes. Staccatos are not as sharp or biting as they could be, dissonances tend not to growl as much as they might, and loud passages are seldom edgy. The recording quality has a similar character: the production and postproduction work is crisp, clean, and balanced; every note is clear, and the pianos' distinctive timbres are readily audible. This can hardly be criticized in principle, but it does tend to produce a blander recording than anything Morton, Ellington, or Monk produced, for better or for worse.

No musician has been more closely associated with the repertory jazz movement, with neoclassicism in jazz, and with the jazz canon in the last twenty years than Wynton Marsalis. In fact, because of his combination of chops, intelligence, and moxy, no other jazz musician has been as visible in the last twenty years in any way. As the primary mouthpiece for jazz, he has had prominent billing on the pages of major jazz magazines, weekly and monthly news and general interest magazines, and many high-profile daily newspapers. At times his pronouncements have enough logical slippage to be frustrating to try to parse, but a number of themes nonetheless emerge. Foremost among them is that fusion and the avant-garde were musical, cultural, and intellectual dead ends. According to Marsalis in one interview, fusion is "like rock itself. If you were there it was a great way to meet women and have a good time . . . but it's the death toll for jazz musicians" (Milkowski 2000, 33). In another interview it amounts to transvestitism, having "a dress on, a skirt, panties" (for a man, one has to assume) (Zabor and Garbarini 1999, 347). The avant-garde is not jazz, but rather, "a reaction to the European avant-garde," "trying to destroy our music by coming up with something nobody likes under the auspices of innovation" (Milkowski 2000, 38, 35).

If, as Marsalis argues, neither of the main directions jazz went in the 1970s is legitimate, then the answer is to go back in time, to a point before these problems, and work forward from there. For Marsalis it is not one point but three: the 1960s, which saw the hard bop movement; the 1930s, especially the Ellington band of the 1930s; and the 1910s, in New Orleans. These moments share a number of things. They are all points at which the music was popular, in the best sense—that is, that there was a substantial and appreciative audience; they all featured a type of jazz that was connected to accessible, danceable sounds; and they are all points at which arrangements had a role that was as prominent, if not more so, than solo improvisation. Although Marsalis officially rejects commercialism as a goal in jazz (one of the great sins of fusion), it should also be noted that these three periods were also points at which jazz musicians could expect to produce hit records and make more than just a meager living.[6]

This historical orientation led to some unusual consequences when Marsalis recorded an album of Thelonious Monk's music. The album, *Standard Time, Volume 4: Marsalis Plays Monk,* is one in a series of recordings that includes paeans to Jelly Roll Morton, the blues, and the legacy of American popular song. There is, in this album, a sense of walking a line between the primacy of the compositions and the work of the past master, on the one hand, and of Marsalis's ideas about where jazz should be going, on the other. Monk, of course, was like Morton and Duke Ellington, as the liner notes are quick to point out, in that he was a composer who chose mostly to play his own music. However, the difference between him and the other two, the fact that he was not an arranger, and presented his compositions mostly as heads for extended solo improvisation by the members of his quartets, has significant consequences when Marsalis attempts to craft canonical performances of Monk's music. It means that when Marsalis plays Monk, unlike if he were playing Ellington or Morton's music, it requires that he do something other than play the pieces as they were originally conceived, particularly because at the time Marsalis recorded the album he was intent on seeing the end of the bop-style head-solo-solo-solo-head format for jazz performance (Milkowski 2000, 30).

Marsalis solves the problem of giving Monk's compositions primacy on *Marsalis Plays Monk* while playing in a decidedly un-Monkish style by dedicating much or all of each track to constantly varying arrangements of the heads. So, rather than playing the head once followed by solos, Marsalis crafts three or four arrangements for a head that, when played one after another, give the piece as a whole a kind of dramatic structure. There are relatively few long solos on the album, Marsalis instead favoring a variety of improvisatory arrangements—a short solo followed by a long one, duets, polyphonic improvisation, and so forth. In the best tracks, such as "Thelonious," the first one, there is a fire and energy in the arrangements and playing that is palpable; in less successful ones, such as "Monk's Mood," complicated arrangements have the effect of obscuring simple, powerful melodic lines. On the whole, the album, like much of Marsalis's work from the time, sounds mannered.

Not surprisingly, the rhetoric around the album, including Stanley Crouch's emblematic liner notes, aims most significantly at interpreting Monk in terms of Marsalis's programmatic history of the music. Monk is thus connected to Louis Armstrong, if obliquely, through the overlay of Armstrong-inspired arrangements on Monk's compositions. Monk is also associated with Ellington, Coltrane, and Marsalis himself. Crouch describes him in terms that specifically distance him from the 1960s avant-garde, writing that Monk "teaches us how to be modern without stooping to the kinds of cacophonous clichés that have been misinterpreted as bold or futuristic." Crouch also describes him in terms that highlight Marsalis's two sine qua nons of jazz, blues and swing, claiming, "Monk brings us right down home for a meal of some blues and swing, two ingredients that cannot be avoided if one wishes to continually summon others to one's table." Finally, he describes Monk as a musician not incidentally like Marsalis: "To [Monk], music was something you had to revere but that reverence didn't stop you [sic] from being funny, though" (Crouch 1999, 2).

Unlike T.S. Monk's recordings of his father's music, the performances on this album are seldom taken directly from particular Monk versions. There are often distinctive inner lines and countermelodies, for instance, but they are almost always new, and not based on Monk's. And, unlike Marcus Roberts's versions, these performances are not bland. The sound of Marsalis's ensemble is remarkable. In particular, the combination of soprano sax on top and trombone on the bottom of many of the arrangements has a growly, piquant edginess that stands out. One feels, without being quite able to say why, that Monk might well have liked the sound. It is indicative of Marsalis's maturity as a musician when he made this album that no matter how much attention is meant to be paid to Monk's voice as a composer, Marsalis's voice is constantly present in the strong readings of each tune.

It is important to note that Marsalis's approach to playing Monk's music here is decidedly different from his earlier forays into canonizing jazz standards, as on the first two *Standard Time* forays. David Ake's discussion of volume two in the series, *Intimacy Calling*, considers how important the sedimentation of a "jazz" sound (acoustic, standard instrumentation, elevation of the soloist's role, and so forth) was for a younger Marsalis (Ake 2002, 152–59). While the intent of the earlier recordings and volume four are clearly similar—to argue that there is a tradition and that the lines between jazz and nonjazz are there both to keep the good in and keep the bad out—the approach to music making really is quite different. For all that Marsalis's Monk album seems precious, it is a less generic, less hidebound sort of project than much of his earlier work. Nonetheless, both do accomplish, as Ake suggests quoting Hans-Georg Gadamer, the process of "traditioning," of participating "in the evolution of tradition, and hence further [determining] it" (174).

AUTHENTICATING PERFORMANCE:
MONK AND EARLY MUSIC

The clearest equivalent to the canonical approach to playing Monk's music can be found in the "historical performance practice" (HPP) movement.[7] In the 1970s and 1980s (and arguably to the present), this movement involved a conscious attempt to replace the standard nineteenth-century approach to playing "early music" (that is, Western classical music composed before the nineteenth century) with one based on a re-creation of the music's original sound, using historical instruments and putatively historical approaches to the many decisions required to interpret a written score. The extent to which HPP musicians fulfilled and continue to fulfill this approach is an argument for other venues, and in fact has taken up volumes of vitriolic prose in the pages of the *New York Times* and *Early Music,* among other places. It is notable, however, that for a while now HPP performers have recognized the limits of historicism in driving musical choices. Thus in HPP as in jazz, historicism is invoked but often not followed through in any rigorous way. Not only that, but when historicism is strictly applied, it generally results in dull, lifeless recordings.[8] In this context I would simply like to highlight two similarities between these two performance traditions that I believe are helpful in understanding claims on Monk's legacy. The first comes from the work of one of the strongest critics of claims of "historical authenticity," Richard Taruskin. The second has to do with the use of the label *authentic* as a selling point.

Taruskin's critique of claims of historical authenticity, collected in the book *Text and Act: Essays on Music and Performance,* comes largely from a reaction to a fundamentalist ideology of "historically authentic" performances in which musical interpretation is subjugated to the supposedly accurate. In such a situation, HPP performers have taken the interpretive stance that "that which is not permitted [in the surviving historical documents] is prohibited" (Taruskin 1995, 95). The musicians have thereby given up their responsibility as interpreters of the music, offering nothing but a void in its place. Taruskin, himself involved in the performance of Renaissance vocal music in an HPP style at the time, regularly argues that the fundamental notion of authenticity involved in the debate is misguided and occasionally argues against the use of the term *authentic* as a descriptor. His argument rests on the notion that two sorts of meanings can be ascribed to *authentic,* the first being that derived from art history, textual criticism, and paleography—correct, genuine, or accurate—and the second from moral philosophy. The first can really only apply to objects, which can be authenticated; the second can be applied appropriately only to subjects and their actions.

Though one might sympathize with Taruskin's apparent desire to be rid of the whole question of authenticity once and for all, it is, in fact, a very difficult notion to simply abolish. Indeed, Taruskin himself returns to it repeatedly, generally favoring a notion of authenticity derived from moral philosophy, according to which performers make, and take responsibility for, strong interpretive choices based on a thorough engagement with music in all its aspects—a sort of "to thine own self be true" kind of authenticity. This notion—that the point of performances in the HPP tradition should be "open-mindedness, receptivity to new ideas, and love of experiment" (62)—is surprisingly similar to an approach occasionally suggested by jazz avant-gardists. Both of these models of authenticity, that based on the composer's intentions and that based in moral philosophy, are used to justify performances of Monk's music as ways of staking a claim to his legacy.

The other way in which these uses of the term *authenticity* are congruent is related to the reason for broaching the discussion in the first place. In his critique of what he sees as HPP orthodoxy, Taruskin complains that the term *authentic*, "when used in connection with the performance of music . . . is neither description nor critique, but commercial propaganda, the stock-in-trade of press agents and promoters" (90). It is one of the central tenets of modernism that art and commercialism exist at opposite poles and are associated with the moral dichotomy of good and evil, and this appears to spur Taruskin's rejection of this particular use of the term *authenticity*. Nevertheless, it must be noted that the use of the term *authentic* that Taruskin prefers is equally intended as a way of touting favorite performances. His use may not be intended to sell albums, but it is at least intended to build cultural authority. The designation of a thing, whether a work of art, a musical performance, or some other cultural performance, as "authentic" is powerful in that it necessarily confers some kind of value, either economic, cultural, or, more likely, both. This accounts for the widespread use of the term in both the context of early music and by those laying claim to Monk's legacy.

A substantial and noteworthy difference emerges in the ways the HPP movement and jazz musicians dealing with Monk mobilize the idea of "authenticity." While the HPP movement embeds a clash of canonical and anticanonical impulses, its various proponents generally suggest a sort of countercultural position.[9] This may take the form of a lingering connection to the "do-it-yourself" amateurism of an earlier phase of the movement, a penchant for informal dress in public presentation, an interest in world music, or an association with Renaissance fairs and other "creative anachronist" circles (Shelemay 2001, 11, 18–21). The repertory jazz movement, by contrast, uses very similar discourses about authenticity and historicism in the service of a socially mainstreaming self-presentation.

CONCLUSION

The creation of a jazz institutional mainstream—or, really, the creation of jazz institutions at all—is quite possibly the single most significant thing to happen in jazz in the 1980s and 1990s. It clearly overshadows anything else—the efflorescence of the Lower East Side scene, for instance—in terms of visibility, energy, and the power to command resources. Chapter 5 considered the creation of jazz institutions and their approaches to the construction of an enduring historical Monk through the creation of authoritative musical scores, interpretations, and other fairly academic pursuits. While that has been an important, even indispensable, aspect of the project of pulling Monk's historical legacy into the camp of the contemporary "mainstream," its power has been magnified exponentially by the work of musicians occupied with parallel goals. The connections between these two sets of actors—musicians and "jazzerati"—are noteworthy.

The lesson learned from a close look at the musical and extramusical activities of musicians like Marsalis, Roberts, and T.S. Monk is that what appears at first glance to be fairly straightforward is in fact quite complex. Each of the musicians considered here has made manifestolike statements in interviews, op-ed pieces, and liner notes, advocating a "right" way of playing Monk's music along similar lines, and each has borrowed extensively from the cultural legitimacy of the Western classical tradition in the process. That this has not led to the creation of even remotely similar musical documents may come as no surprise, but should be considered a starting point for thinking about how the "mainstream" has constructed its own position in jazz today at the intersection of the new and the old through laying claim to the legacy of a musician like Monk.

Although much of the discussion in this chapter has dealt with the intertwining of mainstream approaches, repertory jazz, and the impact of ideas from the Western classical tradition, it is useful to disentangle these strands in order to see to what extent they represent distinct components of the institutionalization of a jazz mainstream in the 1990s. The first and most ambiguous of these terms is *mainstream* itself. It is a problem, at best, to swallow uncritically the notion that one musician or another represents the "mainstream." On what terms is that to be judged? The term has come to be associated with acoustic jazz that works within the stylistic language of bop and post-bop, eschewing more or less programmatically both fusion and the avant-garde approaches of the 1960s and 1970s. As such, it has a legitimate cause to associate itself with Monk's legacy, at least on the finer points of musical style. It is no small matter, though, to remember that in 1945 or 1955 these styles were at the cutting edge of jazz, and not easily absorbed by uninitiated ears.

Not all of the new mainstream, or "neo-bop," as it has been called, is repertory jazz. Rather, the repertory movement has made more popular the idea that in addition to making new music—composing in the moment, so to speak—jazz could also include as one of its practices re-creating earlier performances. This approach goes hand in hand with the time and energy spent by academic figures producing authoritative texts for Monk's music, as detailed in chapter 5. It is worth spending a moment to consider how singular the overt, explicit canonizing moves of repertory jazz are. While recordings themselves have always been a significant source of enduring culture (and a tool for enculturation) in jazz, only recently have significant figures at the forefront of the music suggested that the end result of a close study of recordings ought to be an approach to performance that treats them as the limits of style, much less suggest they be copied note for note. While this has been carried out as a part of the neo-bop program, it is significantly more extreme than run-of-the-mill neo-bop, and in fact represents a distinctive and hitherto marginal or even nonexistent kind of jazz historicity. It elevates its object, in this case Monk, from the role of potential equal—or, perhaps better, the role of mentor—in jazz history to something else, putting in place the paired roles of creator and re-creator.

It is partly in the adoption of these roles and the various ideas associated with them—notably, though not exclusively, that of the creator-genius—that basic ideas from the Western classical tradition have been incorporated into this particular vision of jazz. This is a tricky issue because the ideas brought in from the classical tradition are not, strictly speaking, foreign to jazz. Jazz has long had a canon of sorts, if a vernacular one made up of the recordings and musicians deemed great by their followers; but it has not previously included an idea of musical texts as fixed works to be re-created as written. It has, from the very start, involved great respect for older musicians on the part of younger ones; but it has not generally included a categorical distinction akin to the composer-performer dichotomy found in the Western classical tradition. It has long included musicians who were thoughtful and serious about their vocation; but it has not always made seriousness its primary aesthetic position. Taken together, these three positions, as they variously inform the theory and at times practices in *Monk on Monk, Alone with Three Giants,* and *Standard Time, Volume 4,* create an institutional orthodoxy that circumscribes how Monk should be interpreted today and thereby how his legacy should be seen. Ultimately, this orthodoxy connects the dots between Monk back to Ellington, Jelly Roll Morton, and others, as well as forward to the neo-boppers to construct a vision of what jazz history is and should be.

What is at stake for those institutions and musicians who subscribe to a classicizing, canonical view of Monk? It is clear from Martin Williams's comments on maintaining Monk's legacy, Sickler's enthusiasm about marketing that legacy, and T.S. Monk's active use of the legacy, both in his sextet recordings and, even more clearly, in the large ensemble recording *Monk on Monk,* that a great deal is at stake. In one sense, there is clearly a level on which legitimate ownership of Monk's legacy is profitable. The ability to sell records, license recordings, and publish arrangements is aided by the ability to construct an aura of authenticity around one's relationship to Monk's music. On a deeper, and ultimately more important, level, the maintenance of an orthodox view of the Monk legacy has to do with cultural legitimacy. T.S. Monk, along with many other jazz musicians, voices a deep and heartfelt sense of pride in the fact that the music his father and now he has created is seen as one of the great arts of the twentieth century. This is a powerful statement when viewed in terms of the contemporary history of race in the United States. The ability to turn the logic of white supremacy on its head with a demonstration of the success of an African American musician such as Monk on precisely the same terms as the canonic figures of the European concert music tradition is undeniably powerful.

SEVEN

Monk and Avant-Garde Positions

ALTHOUGH "MAINSTREAMING" OR "CLASSICIZING" TENDENCIES in jazz culture and the conservative memories embedded in them have been most visible in the recent past, even a cursory survey of the jazz world since the 1980s demonstrates the abundance and richness of other approaches to playing the music and playing with its past. It is clear—explicitly so, in fact—that the musicians and intellectuals associated with preservationist and revivalist paradigms of contemporary jazz neoclassicism considered in the previous chapter make recourse to the past as a key marker of musical identity. This chapter and the following one grow out of a recognition that the same is true, if less explicitly, of musicians working outside the obviously historically oriented mainstream. Monk has been a particularly important historical point of reference for this diverse collection of musicians for reasons relating to both his music and his public persona. In a sense, he has been seen as a great ancestor figure by musicians of many stripes who have sought a musical alternative.

The primary alternative lineage that draws on Monk as an ancestor is that of the jazz avant-garde, which itself represents a spectrum of practices and political meanings. The second is a specifically Africentric approach, which has been an important orientation for musicians from many points in the jazz world. Finally, a number of musicians outside jazz entirely have made some claim on Monk's legacy. Although the orientations of these varied musicians are distinct from one another, I present them together in this chapter because they are linked by the impression of difference that informs their cultural position in jazz generally, and their claims on Monk's legacy in particular. At times this sense of difference has been self-imposed ("We are doing what others will not"), and at others times it is the work of the self-anointed mainstream ("They are not part of the true lineage of jazz"). In either case, these approaches serve to distinguish musicians as "alternative"—in jazz, and often in American culture more broadly speaking.

As in many such conflicts, it is in the relationships forged between the mainstream and countermainstream positions, rather than in one discourse or another on its own, that one can begin to glimpse the importance of these historical interventions to jazz's continued place in American culture. Many of the same issues come up in considering countermainstream claims on Monk's legacy as are revealed when looking at mainstream ones. These include negotiations over authenticity and work concepts in the interpretation of repertoire, the place of history in the construction of identities, and a palpable sense of the importance of race in the working out of cultural memory in jazz. The conflict between mainstream and alternative orientations in jazz and Monk's place in the conflict can shed light on a number of questions. It provides an interesting example of the uses of music in the making of sociocultural positions (an important part of what is often glossed in the ethomusicological literature as "identity") and the specific place of history in that process, and it allows for a consideration of alternatives to the classicizing model of historical jazz repertoire.

This chapter deals specifically with the ways Monk has been significant to contemporary avant-garde jazz. Musicians following in the footsteps of the 1960s avant-garde—including older musicians still active, who comprise an "old guard"—make up the most visible subgroup or alternative to the mainstream in the jazz world, and the one with the most interest in demonstrating their legitimacy as carriers of the tradition. Though they comprise a relatively small part of the jazz scene, they hold an important place in a music that has, for much of its history, been concerned with being at the cutting edge.

A PARTICULAR AVANT-GARDE
AND OPPOSITIONAL CANON BUILDING

Before considering the avant-garde's claim on Monk's legacy in discourse and in musical practice, it might be helpful to delimit exactly what I mean by *the avant-garde*. Defining the term, however, is at least as problematic as defining jazz itself (or, for that matter, any musical genre or movement with many participants). There is at least some agreement within the jazz world on the existence of this category. The concept surfaces in the jazz literature, in publicity, and in conversation under various names, including *the avant-garde, free jazz,* and *the New Thing,* among others. The category, like many, is denser in the center than at the edges; nonetheless, there is general agreement that the term *avant-garde* implies a particular relationship to harmony, rhythm, timbre, and other musical parameters. Musicians whose playing consistently pushes the boundaries of jazz's tonal, melodic, and rhythmic resources, or who often play in markedly nonmainstream circles, such as New York's contemporary "Downtown" scene or the loft jazz scene of the 1970s, are typically included. Musicians whose playing is less unified in style, or who play among different circles at different times, may be more or less clearly associated with the avant-garde, depending on the circumstances and the person who is doing the categorizing. Indeed, the case of a musician like Billy Higgins, who played extensively in and out of the avant-garde in the 1960s and beyond, should give us pause when attempting to rigidly link players with styles.

In this context, I, like most, use the term *avant-garde* to refer to those musicians involved in nonmainstream playing networks and who typically play in an "outside" style, such as the Art Ensemble of Chicago or Cecil Taylor. My use of the category, however, is somewhat narrower than most. I use it to denote a particular relationship between improvisatory performance and precomposed materials, and a distinctive, overtly self-conscious approach to generic expectations in the music. Particularly important here is the use of non-groove-oriented rhythmic and metric organization and timbral variation and pitch inflection as structural ways of organizing musical space, both in the context of a given piece and in drawing connections between pieces. For the purposes of examining musicians' interactions with Monk's music, I make a distinction between avant-garde and high-modernist approaches to the music, in order to highlight certain kinds of jazz work that fall outside both historical avant-garde sounds and the contemporary mainstream. Because musicians commonly play in multiple styles it is more useful to consider avant-garde approaches and specific avant-garde performances than to label musicians in a rigid way.[1]

While this particular jazz avant-garde has been typified by certain musical practices, it has also been part of a broader avant-garde in the arts in America and Europe, sharing a common set of ideas about art, creativity, and its role in society. Pushing the boundaries of what is beautiful and even, ultimately, comprehensible is an aesthetic orientation, and as an intervention in opposition to accepted ways of hearing, it has often been coupled with opposition to the status quo more generally. It has also been coupled with a willingness to push the boundaries dividing various arts, so that music is often part of a larger performance incorporating visual art, theater, dance, poetry, and so forth. Sun Ra and his Arkestra are a quintessential example of this orientation. They played music that was often very challenging, at the outer limits of what even the most adventuresome listeners were used to, marketed it through alternative distribution channels, lived for a time in a communal house, developed a spiritual as well as a musical profile, and experimented in concert with poetry, light shows, costumes, and dancers (see Szwed 1998). Charles Mingus's Jazz Workshop offers another, more overtly political example. Mingus's and the Jazz Workshop's music was at the cutting edge of jazz practice, developing out of collective improvisational approaches that were socially distinctive and undermining, at least to some extent, the idea of a hierarchy that divided leader and followers.[2] In addition, Mingus's work with the Jazz Workshop and beyond coupled musical explorations with liberation politics, as in the song "Fables of Faubus," and linked musical independence with independence in the music business.

It is important that while the avant-garde has pushed many boundaries since the 1960s, it has, for the most part, not detached itself conceptually from the rest of jazz. Instead, its practitioners have generally worked to maintain significant musical connections to the tradition, and have argued, often through the establishment of lineages, for its centrality to the jazz community. Amiri Baraka's work provides a precedent for avant-gardists today to hear Monk's music as avant-garde, and to claim him as a musical predecessor. The most widely published spokesperson for the jazz avant-garde of the 1960s, Baraka throughout that decade published essays in leading jazz and popular culture journals as well as album liner notes (collected in the volume *Black Music*) that argue strongly for avant-garde jazz as the only legitimate successor to bebop (or "the bebop revolution," as he and others at the time characterized it). In a 1963 article first published in *Down Beat*, "Jazz and the White Critic," Baraka explicitly compared the two musics, writing, "Bop was . . . a reaction by young musicians against the sterility and formality of Swing as it moved to become a formal part of the mainstream American culture. The New Thing . . . is, to a large degree, a reaction to the hard bop–funk–groove–soul camp, which itself seemed to come into being in protest against the squelching of most of the blues elements in cool and progressive jazz" (Baraka 1967, 16). Most importantly, in the same article, having just presented "Ornette Coleman, Sonny Rollins, John Coltrane, Cecil Taylor, and some others" as exemplary of a movement in jazz that took on "some of the anarchy and excitement of the bebop years," Baraka singles out Monk as the only bebop pioneer to have maintained "without question the vicious creativity with which he first entered the jazz scene back in the 40s" (16). Throughout the essays in this volume Monk reappears in connection with the "New Thing." In the article "New York Loft and Coffee Shop Jazz," for example, he appears along with Coltrane and Rollins as one of the only progressive jazz musicians with ample opportunities to perform (94).

What is at stake in Baraka's work is the need to claim a legitimacy for the "New Thing" *as* jazz in the face of hostility from critics, fans, and people in the music industry in the position to make or break the careers of avant-garde musicians. Baraka clarifies this by drawing a parallel between the terms of aesthetic engagement of the 1960s and those of the 1940s:

> Recently, [reactionary] attitudes have become more apparent in the face of a fresh redefinition of the form and content of Negro music. Such phrases as "anti-jazz" have been used to describe musicians who are making the most exciting music produced in this country. But as critic A. B. Spellman asked, "What does anti-jazz mean and who are these ofays who've appointed themselves the guardians of last year's blues?" It is that simple, really. What does anti-jazz mean? And who coined the phrase? What is the definition of jazz? And who was authorized to make one? (18)

Throughout this collection of essays Baraka's recurrent strategy for countering the characterization of the New Thing as anti-jazz is to claim that the New Thing is organically linked to earlier forms of jazz, particularly bebop. For example, in a 1961 article, "The Jazz Avant-Garde," Baraka defines the jazz avant-garde as "young musicians who have started to utilize the most important ideas contained in that startling music called bebop" (69).

The recourse to constructions of historical continuity as a tool to legitimate nonmainstream performing styles is characteristic of the work of more recent apologists for avant-garde jazz as well. David Such prefaces his ethnographic investigation of "out jazz" performers (his favored label for jazz avant-gardism) with a synoptic, teleological history of jazz from the beginnings of slavery in the sixteenth century, through various "precursory" musicians in the 1930s, 1940s, and 1950s, and finally to three generations of "out jazz" performers in the years between 1960 and the present. Such's table giving a "partial listing of the precursors, founders, and succeeding generations of out performers" is clearly a legitimating strategy (Such 1993, 42). Not only is it arbitrary in its selection of musicians (why Charlie Parker and not Dizzy Gillespie, why Monk and not Herbie Nichols?), but it is gratuitous as well. After a brief discussion of the various precursors, in which he occasionally, but not always, suggests how they were precursory, Such effectively drops the discussion of historical linkages between the avant-garde and other jazz styles.

The most substantive work thus far to deal with the relationship between the 1960s avant-garde and Monk is Robin Kelley's "New Monastery: Thelonious Monk and the Jazz Avant-Garde." Kelley shows the linkages between Monk and his avant-garde admirers and the deeply one-sided appreciation between the two, and he asks what explains this imbalance of affection. He notes the various sociological reasons Monk might have wanted to distance himself from the avant-garde, not the least of which was that he had only recently achieved a measure of economic success and might not have wanted to jeopardize it (Kelley 1999, 143–47).

Kelley describes the 1960s avant-garde's approach to Monk's music as one characterized by relatively free appropriation, showing how musicians like Cecil Taylor took from Monk's music only those stylistic aspects that appealed to them, leaving the rest out of their picture of him altogether. He describes Cecil Taylor's playing as extending Monk's conception of various parameters (rhythm, harmony, accompaniment) to the extreme limit. Thus, for example, Taylor's tone clusters can be heard as a development of Monk's use of dissonance, freed from the need to fulfill functional harmonic tasks. Most significantly, Kelley highlights Taylor's description of playing with Monk's tunes as a way to get outside traditional jazz frameworks. Nowhere to be seen is the deferential attitude common to many mainstream players today that Monk must be played "his way." Kelley quotes Taylor from an interview with A.B. Spellman: "We used a lot of Monk's tunes. We used to take the Monk tunes out of themselves into the area in which I was going" (Spellman 1985, 71; quoted in Kelley 1999, 155). This appropriation, which obscures many of the details of Monk's composed material—details Monk appears to have considered important—may have contributed significantly to his antipathy to the avant-garde, despite the fact that the practice of appropriation led them in some extremely fruitful directions.

Monk seems to have been particularly sensitive to the less than faithful attention other performers paid to his harmonic and melodic structures. This is clear in a blindfold test published in a 1966 issue of *Down Beat*. For this feature, Leonard Feather played for Monk performances of his well-known compositions by other musicians. Monk was particularly unhappy with performances by Art Pepper and Phineas Newborn because of their cavalier treatments of his compositions. This is not Monk's only concern in his reactions to the pieces, but it is paramount. He criticizes Newborn for sounding too much like Bud Powell, but when Feather tries to get him to say more about the piano playing on the recording, Monk says, "I enjoy *all* piano players. All pianists have got 5 stars for me . . . but I was thinking about the wrong changes, so I didn't pay too much attention to the rest of it" (Feather 1994, 78). Newborn's approach to the changes was probably thornier for Monk than it might have been for others because of the fact that so few people at the time appeared to share his conviction that his harmonic approach was perfectly intelligible within the established language of jazz.

It follows that Monk would have been even more uncomfortable with avant-garde performances that claimed to take him as an inspiration, but dispensed with his compositional structures altogether. Roswell Rudd, who played in a number of styles in the 1960s but is best known for his avant-garde work, remembers having the opportunity to play Monk's piece "Misterioso" for Monk backstage during one of Monk's concerts. He thinks of it as one of the finest moments of his life—the chance to pay homage directly to an idol—but also remarks that Monk was decidedly nonplussed. "He was polite about it," Rudd said, "but you could tell that he wasn't really digging it."

Despite the fact that Monk may not have appreciated Rudd's music, an important belief that unites avant-garde discourse and, to some extent, practice is that Monk's legacy is a matter of more than his compositions alone. Avant-gardists in jazz and rock—and, for that matter painting, sculpture, poetry, and so on—share the opinion that legitimate historical connection to Monk is to be cultivated not through playing his music, and particularly not by playing it in a way that is similar to his own performances, but by absorbing the totality of his professional persona as a model of tenacious nonconformity and using it as a basis for innovative playing. Such an approach can be an important tool in an attempt to recast the definition of jazz in toto and to place avant-gardists in a central position as the legitimate descendants of bebop.

As in the rest of jazz, there are many, many avant-garde musicians who never achieve the level of success that would make them well known as leaders, even to fans of the music, but who nonetheless maintain a commitment to their art and express themselves eloquently about it given the opportunity. My interest in avant-gardist claims on Monk's historical legacy was piqued by a conversation I had at the beginning of my research for this project with one such musician, Jim Leff, a trombone player and food critic. Leff is a well-respected sideman on the New York scene, playing regularly in swing and bebop contexts with Illinois Jacquet, Lionel Hampton, Cecil Payne, Sahib Shihab, Tete Montoliu, Ted Curson, and others, as well as in klezmer bands and many bands associated with the Knitting Factory, an eclectic club on Manhattan's Lower East Side. Leff is a self-proclaimed admirer of "radical" musicians and is outspokenly anti-corporate in all aspects of his life. He describes Monk as the most important role model for musicians today who want to push the limits of their creativity. He is particularly critical of the way that the institutional jazz culture has claimed Monk. In his words,

> That [Monk] is lionized today is just the most twisted irony. . . . As we've deified composers like Beethoven and Mozart, radicals of their day, we've also deified the great jazz musicians. And just as Beethoven, if alive today, would be thrown out of Juilliard (given a chance to internalize the intervening centuries of composition, he'd be writing some *really* crazy shit), Monk wouldn't be able to get a gig or pass the Berklee College entrance exam these days, when jazz is a dead music re-created faithfully and skillfully by devoted and highly trained automatons. . . .[3]
>
> Monk is lionized but not understood, and his spiritual descendants, the brave radical players (I'm not just talking about the "avant-garde" here . . .), are put down by the same established jazz scene figures who pay Monk lip service. (Leff, personal communication)

This is not *merely* an aesthetic disagreement, but rather the staking out of a subaltern position vis-à-vis the perceived power and capital of jazz's institutions. Leff's use of the phrase "spiritual descendants" is also interesting in that it emphasizes a relationship between today's radical musicians and Monk's legacy that skirts the issue of formal musical influence and moves the relationship between Monk and present musicians into a more rarefied, abstract area. Following this logic it is those musicians who most avoid playing like Monk who most deserve the title of heirs to his legacy.

Similar themes emerged in pianist Andrew Bemkey's view of Monk's legacy. In the late 1990s Bemkey, a self-proclaimed revolutionary musician, played regularly at Tonic and occasionally at the Knitting Factory, generally in bands fronted by other leaders. I met Bemkey at the Jazz Standard in Manhattan's Murray Hill district on July 22, 1999. We were both there to hear a performance by Andrew Hill's trio with Richard Davis. The Jazz Standard's programs are less conservative than those of more established clubs like the Blue Note or the Village Vanguard, but Hill's performance was the most outside—that is, the most experimental—I had heard there. Unlike other clubs that typically program outside styles, the Jazz Standard caters to a posh, wealthy audience: the shows and the menu are expensive, the lavish restaurant and bar upstairs are stylishly appointed, and the music the house manager plays over the PA system before the shows and during breaks is a mix of neo-bop and so-called "smooth jazz." These musics contribute to the atmosphere through their perceived inoffensiveness and their status as highbrow but not stodgy. Bemkey and I struck up a conversation at the bar after Hill's first set, agreeing that we both found the music on the PA system jarring when juxtaposed with Hill's energetic, reaching first set.

As we talked I found out that he was an aspiring young avant-garde pianist (he used the term "revolutionary" at the time). He had studied jazz at the New School and was currently working as often as he could, providing he could play only what he wanted. He described his attendance at Hill's performance as "studying," trying to "learn from a master." Since he seemed to have an interest in the stylistic continuity between older and more recent avant-garde jazz, I asked him whether he thought Monk was a significant stylistic predecessor of outside playing—of what he called "revolutionary" jazz. Bemkey's response was that Monk was a revolutionary, and that therefore *only* revolutionaries really hear his music and understand its lessons. " 'Stylists' don't get it. They aren't doing what Bird did," he said, "because they are just repeating what they've already heard. *Bird* created a new music" (personal communication). Bemkey's remarks were not terribly surprising, except for his reference to Charlie Parker. Until that time we had been talking only about Monk. In the end, his remarks reflect a view of jazz history: Bird and Monk are interchangeable as shorthand for the stylistic innovation in jazz in the 1940s. Despite their significant differences, a generalized likeness causes them to be understood as predecessors of contemporary avant-garde music without reference to specific formal similarities.

Bemkey's derisory description of the contemporary jazz mainstream as "stylists" suggests that the authentic or legitimate owners of Monk's legacy—the keepers of the jazz tradition—are not the musicians who play Monk's music, or that play in a style that reflects an internalization of Monk's formal approach to the music. Rather, they are those who resemble Monk least.

Bemkey stressed the fact that he knew Monk's tunes (as they are a part of the jazz canon), but that he would never consider performing them; that was the work of "stylists," re-creators, not creative musicians. He went so far as to dismiss outright the playing of music with a groove-oriented, steady rhythmic feel at all. Gesturing to draw my attention to the music playing over the PA system, he counted along with the meter, "one, two, three, four . . . ," and told me that, while there was something to be said for that kind of regularity, it wasn't a viable option any more, at least as far as he was concerned (personal communication).

Bemkey's use of terms like "revolutionary" and "radical" is only partially contained within the discourse of the jazz tradition, however. It is best explained as belonging to the ethics of the punk counterculture movement that spanned the 1970s and 1980s and lingered into the 1990s. An important aspect of Bemkey's oppositional position, like Leff's, is a distrust of corporate American culture. Bemkey fondly extolled the virtues of "alternative" jazz happenings in the summer as an antidote to the JVC Jazz Festival (sponsored by JVC, the Japanese electronics company), New York City's premiere (and most thoroughly corporate) jazz event. Like proponents of the punk movement in pop music, Bemkey highlighted an anti-corporate "do-it-yourself" ethic that characterizes the alternatives he posits to JVC. His dismissal of "stylists" was only partially on formal grounds. It was at least as important that he saw figures like Wynton Marsalis and T.S. Monk as complicit with corporate strategies of appropriation and control over vernacular expressivity and its profits.

PLAYING AVANT-GARDE MONK

It will be useful to consider some general aspects of what has constituted an avant-garde style in jazz since the 1960s before moving on to consider a specific example: the performance of Monk's " 'Round Midnight" by the Art Ensemble of Chicago. If the discourse surrounding avant-garde practices in jazz is relatively transparent to a scholarly reading, the music itself has been notoriously difficult for musicologists to write about. The most successful approaches, such as Lewis Porter's analysis of John Coltrane's *A Love Supreme* and Lynette Westendorf's dissertation "Analyzing Free Jazz," have used sociolinguistic and semiotic approaches in addition to more traditional music theories. These analyses highlight the ways avant-garde musicians rely on rhetorical structures, imitations of vocal sounds, and intermusical reference to make their improvisations intelligible, generally in the absence of more traditional precomposed frameworks. A number of recent ethno-musicological works that do not focus primarily on avant-garde jazz have enriched the theoretical framework for generally understanding music as a mode of communication. Although this chapter focuses on the differences between avant-garde and mainstream jazz performances of Monk's music, these writers' general theoretical models will be useful.

The central issue in "free jazz" is that of the relationship between pre-composed structures and improvisation. While some musicians, notably Ornette Coleman, saw pure improvisation, with no reference to (or con-striction by) precomposed materials, as an ideal, in practice few avant-garde performers strictly follow this approach. More commonly, one aspect of a composition or another—a particular lick or a collection of harmonies, for example—may serve as a point of departure and reference in improvisation, without determining the flow of events to the extent that chorus structures and chord changes do in mainstream practice.

The relationship between improvisation and preexisting materials in a jazz performance is more complicated than this implies, however. In a sense, much of *Thinking in Jazz* concerns this relationship, which Berliner conceives as an "eternal cycle" (Berliner 1994, 221). Precomposed pieces provide models for improvisation, and licks, patterns, and ways of com-bining them into larger units improvised in one performance can, over the course of multiple performances, become models for further improvisation and can even become compositions in their own right (222–30). Berliner's work deals primarily with players' approaches to improvising within chord changes or modal constraints, but his use of quotes from Kenny Barron and Gary Bartz make it clear that they use similar approaches to create coher-ent solos when using precomposed changes or more free styles. Bartz is par-ticularly emphatic: "I don't think [free improvising] is that different from what I ordinarily play because it's the same music, just another type of song, really, where you don't have the structure set up before you play. So, you work out your own structure as you play" (Berliner 1994, 225). What Bartz refers to as the similarity between the kinds of improvisation he plays is the use of preexisting materials, not necessarily taken from the piece he is play-ing, in a compelling combination to create a sense of structure. As Ingrid Monson has noted, this internally referential aspect of musical structuring is at times accomplished by intermusical referentiality. This can range from quotes to stylistic reference, including, but not limited to, harmonic, melodic, rhythmic, timbral, intonational, and textural features (Monson 1995, 188).

It is clear that while there is a general similarity in the improvisatory practices of various jazz styles, musicians and audiences recognize significant
differences between avant-garde and mainstream styles. It is my contention
that the avant-garde's manner of relating individual performances to precomposed pieces and the breadth of materials used in making coherent improvisations account for this impression. Avant-garde musicians and critics
deploy a discourse about this improvisation that downplays the centrality of
the composition's preexisting structures in favor of those precomposed and
newly composed materials each musician brings to the performance. This is
a fundamental difference, if perhaps one of degree rather than kind, between
their interaction with Monk's legacy and that of other musicians.

Avant-Garde Dreams: The Art Ensemble of Chicago's " 'Round Midnight"

In order to examine the connection between repertoire and improvisation
in avant-garde approaches to Monk's music more concretely and to investigate the relationship between the ways it is represented in discourse and
musical practice, it will be useful to consider the Art Ensemble of Chicago's
performance of " 'Round Midnight" from their album *Thelonious Sphere
Monk: Dreaming of the Masters, Volume 2* (Art Ensemble of Chicago 1991).
This recording bears extended consideration because it offers an opportunity to hear a particularly nuanced, unusually innovative engagement with
Monk's compositions within an avant-garde sound world.

A tension between object and process inherent in jazz recordings adds a
level of complexity to the analysis of the epistemological status of this performance. Jazz performances are fluid processes in which a number of musicians interactively create an "emergent text" (Sawyer 1996, 279). That is,
as a performance unfolds diachronically, the past becomes fixed and suggests, without fully determining, the possible future paths the musicians
may travel. Once such a performance is recorded, however, it becomes fully
textual, no longer truly emergent. In the case of the Art Ensemble's recording of " 'Round Midnight," the most fruitful analytical tactic is to approach
the album as a whole as an artistic object while at the same time retaining
a sense of the emergent performance that created the individual recordings
that comprise the album. While the avant-garde constructions of Monk's
legacy discussed above are particularly extreme in their dismissal of the importance of his music as a collection of compositions themselves, the Art
Ensemble's recording of " 'Round Midnight" suggests a much more grace-
ful interaction with Monk's musical texts (as, in fact, did a live performance

by Andrew Bemkey with Ori Kaplan and Susie Ibarra that I heard at Tonic a few days after meeting Bemkey). This is not terribly surprising; experience suggests that discourse is often more extreme than practice.

Dreaming of the Masters is designed in a way that enhances the tension between musical object and the representation of a process. The programmatic title strongly suggests that the album should be heard as a unit—in sum, as the Art Ensemble's and Cecil Taylor's collective dream of Monk. This unity is intensified by the placement of two short performances of the title piece, Joseph Jarman's "Dreaming of the Masters," as a frame around the main tracks. This framing is reminiscent of the form typical to most jazz performances, where extended improvisation happens between statements of the head. It is also reminiscent of pop concept albums since the 1960s, which have used similar methods to achieve a kind of unity and coherence. Through this aesthetic of unity, albums like the Beatles' signal *Sgt. Pepper's Lonely Hearts Club Band* pioneered the exploitation of the possibilities of the LP as a musical work per se.

"Dreaming," the title track, itself is complicated by the fact that it is presented as an excerpt, as are the second and third tracks, "Intro to Fifteen" and "Excerpt from Fifteen Part 3A." Together they argue against the autonomy of the recording as an artifact, or, at least, they complicate the recording's existence as a complete text: the recording becomes a text that specifically testifies to its own inadequacy as a representation of performance. As parts of larger musical entities these tracks point outward from the recording to a larger conception of the music. Howard Mandel's liner notes reinforce this sense: " 'One thing to remember about Mr. Taylor's performance concept and his musical legacy is he's not handicapped by specific concepts of time,' Joseph Jarman reports. 'To us a ballad may last five minutes; once Mr. Taylor starts, he could go on forever, until the music resolves' " (Mandel 1991). "Intro," as it appears on the CD, was distilled from three full days in the studio, and in live performance it can last hours.

Beyond the title and the inclusion of two of Monk pieces, " 'Round Midnight" and "Nutty," it is hard to find any concrete sense in which this recording is understandable in terms of Monk, and, indeed, this is intended. Lester Bowie, the Art Ensemble's late trumpet player, says in the liner notes:

"Of course, Cecil doesn't play tunes established by someone else; he didn't think he could play ' 'Round Midnight' and 'Nutty' better than Monk himself did. And we didn't press him. . . . This album wasn't intended as a Monk tribute so much as a 'thank you' for what we learned from Monk about being innovative." Joseph Jarman adds to this, "It is meaningless to repeat what one of the masters has done, note for note. . . . We need to play our own music and incorporate the master's ideas, but show they're an influence, not an affliction." (quoted in Mandel 1991)

There is a notable parallel between these statements and what other musicians associated with the jazz avant-garde said about playing Monk's music. There is the suggestion of a relationship with Monk's musical work, not so much as a storehouse of formal materials to be borrowed from and worked with, but as a surface representation or a single instance of deeper musical truths that are themselves the object of a serious artist's engagement.

Unlike most of the album, the Art Ensemble's performance of " 'Round Midnight" shows a clear relationship to a specific preexisting work that is readily associated with Monk. Indeed, over the course of the performance's seventeen minutes, very little happens that cannot be thought of as engaged with the composition. Nonetheless, there is a world of difference between this and mainstream performances, such as the ones discussed in chapter 6. It is my impression that the dialogue between the Art Ensemble and the past of " 'Round Midnight" is different from similar conversations because an entirely different set of topics are on the table. It shares with these other conversations the attempt to manage a relationship between the past and the present, but it does so by signifying with generic stylistic markers—such as timbre and rhythmic organization—that often seem taken for granted in more mainstream practice.

" 'Round Midnight" opens with a lengthy introduction that consists of nearly four minutes of nonmetric group improvisation (ex. 12). After the striking of a very low gong, the piece's opening moments offer a winking, indexical reference to the piece's title. Two chimes ring in a steady, even rhythm, a sound easily interpreted as representing the ringing of the midnight hour on a clock. Over the course of the introduction this clock motif is extended through the entrance of a deep, bell-like gong that resembles those used to ring the hours from a clock tower and a faster percussive motif reminiscent of a clock's ticktock. One minute and forty-eight seconds into the piece the ticktock is replaced by a steady thumping on the bass drum at one quarter the speed. This draws the clock sounds into a more traditionally musical sphere by engaging them in a simple, proportional rhythmic relationship; at the same time, it expands the extramusical referential framework of the piece. The bass drum pulse is felt as well as heard, particularly at a relatively high volume, and can be understood as a reference to the heartbeat, extending the sense of time from machines to the body.

Example 12. " 'Round Midnight": Schematic diagram of introduction (Art Ensemble of Chicago 1991, vol. 2, track 4).

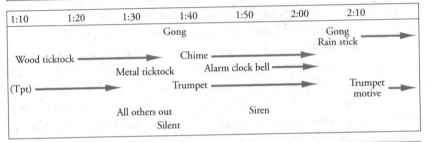

0:00	0:10	0:20	0:30	0:40	0:50	1:00

Gong   Cymbal crash

Chime 1 (even pulse) ——————→   Bell chimes ——————→

Chime 2 (even pulse) ——————→

Various metal percussion

     Trumpet motive ——→   Trumpet vocalistics   Trumpet motive expanded ——→

Drum ca. 1/4 ticktock

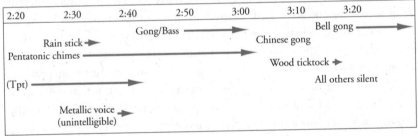

1:10	1:20	1:30	1:40	1:50	2:00	2:10

Gong   Gong ——————→

Rain stick

Wood ticktock ——————→   Chime ——————→

   Metal ticktock   Alarm clock bell ——————→

(Tpt) ——————→   Trumpet ——————→   Trumpet motive ——→

All others out   Siren

Silent

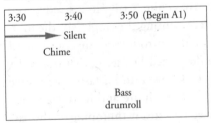

2:20	2:30	2:40	2:50	3:00	3:10	3:20

Gong/Bass ——————→   Bell gong ——————→

Rain stick ➔   Chinese gong

Pentatonic chimes ——————————→

Wood ticktock ➔

(Tpt) ——————→   All others silent

Metallic voice ➔
(unintelligible)

3:30	3:40	3:50 (Begin A1)

——————→ Silent

Chime

Bass drumroll

Example 13. "'Round Midnight": Introduction, Lester Bowie's versions of the opening melody (Art Ensemble of Chicago 1991, vol. 2, track 4).

a. 0:20

b. 1:03

c. 2:11

In addition to referencing time as a general framework, the introduction also develops a relationship to the melodic and rhythmic materials of "'Round Midnight." About twenty seconds into the performance Lester Bowie initiates a rifflike figure on the trumpet (ex. 13a). This figure is repeated again two more times (ex. 13b and 13c). As Bowie repeats the figure he transforms it, so that what initially bore only a suggestion of resemblance to "'Round Midnight" becomes its opening five-note figure, as played by Miles Davis. The timing of this motivic development is exquisite. All of the performers work as an ensemble to create a compelling structure for the introduction: it builds from the opening gong and gradually develops intensity through the addition of sounds, the creation of dense rhythmic relationships between the parts, and the unfolding of a melodic idea that climaxes at about two to three minutes into the music. If it were not for what follows, it would be easy to hear this as a self-contained performance, a highly abstracted rendition of "'Round Midnight" in and of itself.

The following thirteen minutes bear a much closer relationship to the precomposed structures of "'Round Midnight." The Art Ensemble plays three choruses of the tune in a more or less recognizable form and then an extended coda. Throughout the performance the musicians consistently work with the melody, not so much developing it motivically as reinterpreting and recontextualizing it. The first chorus is striking in its contrast with the preceding introduction. A bass drumroll bridges the transition from introduction to chorus, propelling the ensemble forward and strongly emphasizing the downbeat of the first measure. All of the instruments enter at once and begin an arrangement of the head (ex. 14). The bass and drums suggest a slow groove, but often break it up with odd accents off the beat. Malachi Favors Maghostut plays a fairly consistent two-beat bass pattern, clearly outlining the changes with notes on beats one and three. Famoudou Don Moye's drumming is less groove-oriented. He emphasizes beats two and four with the hi-hat cymbals and occasionally uses brush strokes on the snare drum for a traditional ballad sound, but he surrounds and intercuts these groove-defining patterns with less predictable melodic work on the cymbals. The changes implied by Maghostut's playing are clearly Monk's, but the languorous feel is much closer to that on the Miles Davis Quintet's famous recording (Davis 1987b). Indeed, references to that version in other places reinforce the ability of the slow groove to function referentially. Bowie's opening statement of the first five notes of the piece clearly reference the Davis Quintet's recording, both by using G♭ in the ascending and descending arpeggios and by filling in the space between the melody notes with a passing motion in a way unmistakably similar to John Coltrane's solo chorus on the quintet recording. Bowie, Joseph Jarman, and Roscoe Mitchell's contrapuntal version of the melody follows a standard conception of the tune closely, but it allows for more latitude in timbral and intonational variation as tools for expression than do the versions of most mainstream jazz artists.

Timbre and texture are at least as referentially significant as pitch and rhythm in this performance. Individually and in combination, they serve to reinforce the piece's structural framework through internal reference, and through intermusical reference they enrich the piece's relational meaning. In mainstream jazz practice, timbre, though more variable than in the classical idiom, is most often used to inflect basically melodic ideas. Moreover, although the classical idiom's striving for "pure" tone does not operate in jazz, only some variations are typical. Musicians may use a "dirty" or "growling" tone, but harsh, strident tones, wide, rapid vibrato, and an extensive use of honks, screams, and whistles tend not to be used. By contrast, these sounds are central to the timbral palette of many avant-garde musicians—most notably Albert Ayler, but also Lester Bowie and others, and timbre becomes an important musical parameter in its own right.

Lester Bowie's performance here relies particularly heavily on timbre for its effectiveness. In the introduction Bowie often plays on a single note,

Example 14. " 'Round Midnight": First chorus, A1, mm. 1–8 (Art Ensemble of Chicago 1991, vol. 2, track 4, 3:50–4:42).

(continued)

Example 14 *(continued)*

using variations in timbre that have strong associations with vocality, along with microtonal pitch inflections. These should be heard as a way of referencing both vernacular and learned aesthetic ideologies at once. Within the African diaspora there is a valorization of instrumental performance that captures the essence of vocality in one way or another: West African drummers mimetically reproduce the pitch inflections of their tonal languages; blues musicians use slides, wah-wah pedals, and a keen feel for the rhythms and inflections of African American English to make their guitars talk, sing, and cry; and jazz musicians explore nonstandard techniques to draw similar sounds from brass, strings, woodwinds, and percussion. Even in the absence of these mimetic devices, musicians keep a vocal model of form and expression in mind when improvising, holding in the highest esteem those musicians who are able to "say something." Like musicians working in the jazz avant-garde, composers in the Western classical idiom's avant-garde in the second half of the twentieth century have used instrumental techniques extensively to produce nonstandard sounds, and have used technology to bring new sounds into their music. In some cases these sounds and their combination have become central to the compositional process in the way that melody and harmony were in the preceding centuries. Jazz musicians, particularly those associated with the avant-garde, have generally been aware of these two strands of aesthetic practice in American culture.

In the transition from the introduction to the first chorus, the whole ensemble uses timbre and texture structurally. The introduction is characterized by timbral variety, both in Bowie's playing and in the various percussion instruments that he plays with. It is also notable for the aesthetic pleasure to be found in its textural density—that is, for the ways the shifting textures created by the many different combinations of instruments stand out as aesthetically compelling—a result of the kinds of percussion employed and their interaction in a nonstratified, nonmetric sound space. When the first chorus begins, the ensemble adopts a unified sound that is easily interpreted in terms of standard jazz practice. Maghostut's long, full tone on the downbeat, Moye's cymbal stroke, and Bowie's subtone sound on the opening note of the melody combine to produce an idiomatically recognizable timbral/textural complex. It is not so much that this section is less timbrally or texturally variegated or dense than the previous one, but rather that it can be heard and interpreted more readily in terms of a listener's past experience and thus fade to an interpretive background. This sound, not reducible to any one of its constituent parts, creates certain expectations, however, that are only partially fulfilled. It implies a move into a groove-oriented rhythmic space and a more mainstream frame for interpreting timbre. So strong is the effect of this moment that I listened to the recording many times before I recognized that Moye does not actually play a steady groove in the following measures but only suggests it. He accomplishes this by occasional, strategically placed references to groove-defining time-pattern bits. In measure 2 he hits the ride cymbal on beat three and the hi-hat on four, in measure 3 the ride on beat one and hi-hat on two and four. The distinctive sound of a brush stirring on the snare drum and the hi-hat on the backbeat solidifies this sensation in measures 5 and 6, as does the cymbal on beat one and the hi-hat on two and four in measure 7 (see ex. 14). Interestingly, Moye integrates his moves between more and less time-defining playing with Maghostut's bass work. Maghostut clearly outlines a two-beat pattern in measures 1 and 2. In measure 3, the first measure in which Moye strongly suggests a groove with the hi-hat, Maghostut takes the opportunity to relinquish some of his time-playing role by using more complicated, out-of-time melodic work. The same holds true in measures 5, 6, and 7.

In the bridge, trumpet and alto sax form a dialogue in call and response. The alto player (it sounds like Mitchell's timbre, but it is hard to know from the recording alone) responds to Bowie's initial melodic figure with a lick that begins as a reminiscence of the opening five-note theme of " 'Round Midnight" but melds into the melody of "and the livin' is easy" from "Summertime" (ex. 15a). This fragment, which may have arisen out of a free-associational play of sound, is continued in the second chorus by combining the opening motif from " 'Round Midnight" with the melody of "So hush,

Example 15. " 'Round Midnight": Alto sax combination of opening melody with melodic fragment from "Summertime" (Art Ensemble of Chicago 1991, vol. 2, track 4).

a. Chorus 1, bridge, 5:56

b. Chorus 2, A2, 8:35

little baby, don't you cry" from "Summertime" (ex. 15b). Here the alto player places the lick so that it is the primary melody rather than a response. As in the analogous place in the preceding A sections, the alto player uses G♭ ascending and descending, as in Davis's version of " 'Round Midnight." The relationship between Monk, Coltrane, and Davis is strongly evocative. Perhaps in response to this reference Bowie treats the thematic material in measures 5–8 of the bridge in a way strongly reminiscent of Davis's interpretation of the piece, playing the rising sixteenth notes and then holding the top note instead of playing the descending continuation of the melody. Interestingly, Bowie avoids one feature that would most clearly reference Davis's version of the piece, that is, playing with a Harmon mute. Perhaps this is because it would not have provided the kind of subtlety, fluidity, nor apparent spontaneity of allusion that the ensemble achieves here.

Following this chorus, the traditional convention of a head followed by solos is referenced but altered. The second and third choruses open up the improvisational possibilities, but, as with the other pieces on this recording, the entire ensemble continues to play, building off of one another. In addition, the horn players continue to present the motivic materials of the theme in roughly the places they originally appeared. The improvisational work is primarily a matter of surrounding and recontextualizing the original melody.

The most striking change marking the beginning of the second chorus is the alteration of the rhythmic feel. Throughout the first chorus the bass and drums maintain a groove-oriented metrical framework. At the beginning of the second chorus, however, both players begin to play more "melodi-cally." At times this allows for a suspension of the sense of meter altogether. Although there is a dissolution of the preexisting material's primacy at cer-tain moments, particularly in the accompanimental parts, the basic struc-ture of the piece is never significantly altered. (Note the fact that each sec-tion of the later choruses remains relatively consistent in total length, even when lower-level structuring may be largely unmarked.) This is achieved in part by the fact that at almost any given moment some member of the en-semble plays in a way that maintains the basic pulse. This near-ubiquity of the basic pulse suggests that even when the meter is entirely unstated, the musicians maintain a measured sense of the passage of time.

What is clear in the resulting piece is that the genre-defining musical in-teraction described by jazz musicians is central to avant-garde jazz as well as to the mainstream. How might one, as a listener, approach this interac-tion? In mainstream performances a shared referential framework—groove and chorus structure, including harmony and melody—makes it easier to understand what is going on and know what to expect. In the absence of this framework, the parameters musicians listen and react to in the perfor-mance are much broader and more idiosyncratic. A characteristic moment from the second chorus provides an example. The first A section begins with a statement of the melody by Bowie that maintains the basic pulse with a free-rhythmic accompaniment. At the end of the first A section no one states the basic pulse, and there is a feeling that time is suspended, or at least stretched. The alto takes a leading role, playing a quarter-tone tremolo around B♭, scale degree 5 in E♭ minor, the first pitch of the fol-lowing A section. He holds this tremolo while the bass and drums gradu-ally join with their own versions of the tremolo figure. Finally, the alto re-leases the tension built up in this moment by initiating the second A section. In the absence of any shared metric framework, this moment re-lies on close listening and common purpose to be effective. Had Magho-stut and Moye not responded to the saxophonist's figure, the performance would have been different. Had they responded in a similar way but with different timing, the result could have been less effective.

A similar moment happens in the bridge of the third chorus. After ex-tended non-groove-oriented playing, one of the musicians begins a re-peated rhythmic figure (ex. 16). Initially, this figure adds to the ongoing sonic texture, but as others join with a similar rhythm, the figure comes to define a groove. Finally, Bowie completes the process by playing a melody that conforms to the new rhythmic feel. Here again close listening and

Example 16. " 'Round Midnight": Percussion and trumpet creation of metric groove after nonmetric section (Art Ensemble of Chicago 1991, vol. 2, track 4, 11:40–12:19).

Example 16 *(continued)*

responsive playing by the ensemble members allows for the emergence of a coherent piece. This is similar to the kinds of interaction that take place in traditional jazz improvisation, but the direction taken by the emergent performance is less constrained by preexisting aspects of the composition. Additionally, the trend away from a hierarchy of soloist and accompaniment in this music makes the social organization of call and response even more democratic than in more traditional jazz.

The piece ends with a return to the arrangement from the head for the final A section of the third chorus and an extended coda. The coda in particular reinforces the sense of reference back to previous versions of " 'Round Midnight." Although it is drawn out over a period of minutes, the musicians work with melodic material originally used by Monk and Davis in their versions of the piece, ending with the standard melodic fourths descending by step. The material is extended and played in an affective rubato that, along with the horn players' use of very bright, open tone, gives the feel of an Albert Ayler–style "gospel-apocalyptic" treatment, a sound uniquely associated with the avant-garde in jazz.

Given the nearly constant references to the melody and, often implicitly, the harmonies of Monk's composition in most of this performance of " 'Round Midnight," how can this be said to represent an alternative position vis-à-vis the history of Monk performance, and, moreover, how can it be related to the discourses of the jazz avant-garde that surround it? Musicians and critics of the avant-garde describe the music in a way that highlights the idiosyncratic, internally referential aspects of the performance in order to distinguish themselves from less idiosyncratic mainstream performers. This should not blind the analyst to the profoundly intermusical referentiality of this and many other avant-garde performances.

The Canon in Action

The Art Ensemble's tribute album may be intimately connected to the moment at which it was recorded—the 1980s and 1990s were, after all, the era of the tribute album—but it is by no means an isolated example of an avant-garde jazz response to and adaptation of mainstream jazz repertoire as a starting point for outside explorations. Indeed, while avant-garde musicians may be more likely to perform their own compositions than any other jazz performers, there have been any number of remarkable avant-garde recordings of older repertoire since the style's heyday in the mid-1960s. This stands in stark contrast to the image of many avant-garde players as fiercely antiestablishment and committed to freedom from constraint, from the past, and from musical norms. A relationship with precomposed materials, however, is an important part of avant-garde jazz, both in intent and in action. Recordings like Cecil Taylor's *Jazz Advance* and Archie Shepp's *Fire Music,* for instance, from 1955 and 1965, respectively, show jazz repertoire playing two key roles in avant-garde approaches: as a point of origin and as a point of return.

Jazz Advance, Taylor's first studio effort, contains Monk's blues composition "Bemsha Swing" as the opening track, followed by an alternation of Taylor's original compositions and standards that include Ellington's "Azure" and Cole Porter's "You'd Be So Nice To Come Home To." The final tune, "Sweet and Lovely," was one of Monk's favorites and a regular in his recording repertoire. Steven Block provides a detailed account of the relationships between Monk's approach to "Bemsha Swing" and Taylor's on this album, taking particular note of the ways that the motivic quality of the composition and Monk's common approach to improvising on it provide a grounding in the tradition for Taylor's motivic explorations (Block 1997). What Block finds is that while Taylor's improvisation is largely unrelated to the changes, it tends to retain, through careful variation of pitch collections, both a relationship to the motive that characterizes the head and to the tonal center, C. It should, I think, be stressed that Taylor chose his repertoire carefully. "Bemsha Swing" is notable for having remarkably little harmonic content and a thoroughly motive-saturated head. Like a number of Monk's blues pieces, it is a repetition (in this case four times rather than the usual three, because of the sixteen-bar form) of a single motive, and one, for that matter, that is itself internally repetitive, both in its opening melodic leap (G–C in the first instance and C–F in the second) and in the opening and closing rhythmic figure (a quarter note on a stressed beat followed by a half note on an unstressed beat), which is emphasized by a similar rising contour (rising fourth G–C/C–F, rising half step B–C/E–F). The other pieces not by Taylor do not show any particular uniformity, but all do offer qualities that make them amenable to the kind of improvisation Taylor explored at the time.

In any case, the album as a whole neatly shows Taylor moving back and forth between a desire to push boundaries and a cognizance of the tradition that established those boundaries in the first place. This kind of dialectic is hardly limited to avant-garde jazz, but in fact seems central to the practices of almost any kind of artistic innovation. It is important that Taylor chooses Monk and Ellington out of the much larger pool of possible resources from the tradition to draw upon. They are, of course, paired by others (Marcus Roberts, for instance, as noted in the previous chapter), and in 1955 they represented the venerable and the hip.

By 1965, when Archie Shepp released *Fire Music,* the avant-garde was at its height, following seminal recordings by Ornette Coleman, John Coltrane, Cecil Taylor, and Charles Mingus. The avant-garde was also, by this time, a distinct subcategory and the source of controversy, particularly as a music that some saw as alienating listeners and even destroying jazz altogether. By then a significant number of people had come to see it as musically univocal, a voice of anger. No doubt there was musical anger and chaos in some significant pieces, notably Mingus's "Fables of Faubus" and "Pithecanthropus Erectus," but there was a great deal more, as well. In this context Shepp's *Fire Music* represents an interesting intervention. The central track, "Malcolm, Malcolm, Semper Malcolm" is clearly part of the emerging tradition of musical and social protest in jazz, but the following tracks, "Prelude to a Kiss" and "The Girl from Ipanema," as well as the opening track, "Hambone," are all intended to reconnect the avant-garde sound with jazz—again through Ellington, among others—and vernacular expressivity in popular and "folk" guises.

Shepp's decision to give so prominent a place to "inside" repertoire on *Fire Music* reflects a stated desire on his part not to "let the audience escape" (Hopkins and Houston 1965, 6). This concern was particularly on the minds of "New Thing" musicians in the 1960s, as musicians tried to make avant-garde art and remain committed to black nationalist political ideals, black populism foremost among them (Anderson 2002, 136–39). Shepp courted an African American popular audience, albeit unsuccessfully, for a number of years before accepting that avant-garde music was liable to have limited appeal. In any case, the use of repertoire on *Fire Music* to cement ties between Shepp's approach and the jazz tradition more broadly (and historically) and to African American vernacular music generally is remarkably similar to avant-gardists' use of performance today to lay claim to Monk's legacy.

The highest-profile examples of avant-garde tribute or repertory albums from around the time that the Art Ensemble of Chicago recorded *Dreaming of the Masters* are the World Saxophone Quartet's Ellington and R&B albums. Both of these recordings, but especially the first, are more straightforwardly repertoire driven than the albums discussed so far, inasmuch as original compositions play only a very limited role. Still, they share the same basic orientation, drawing together the music represented by the repertoire and that represented by the performers' avant-garde approaches and playing histories.

Avant-garde musicians' interest in Monk is relatively easy to understand in this context. For one thing, Monk's music serves as a set of vehicles for improvisation that extends the expressive registers available to performers. It is a gross oversimplification to suggest that avant-garde jazz was ever exclusively, or even principally, concerned with the expression of anger or chaos, but as musicians abandoned the clichés of genre they also moved away from the generally accepted cues for the musical expression of emotion. In this context, audiences can perhaps be forgiven for hearing principally negative emotion in the music. Monk's music provides a context in which it is easier to hear a range of musical meaning. There is reverence, humor, irony, and pure, unadulterated joy.

It is centrally important, when looking at avant-garde performances of Monk's music, as much as at neo-bop performances, to note that in addition to representing particular musical challenges, the pieces represent cultural or social meanings. What one finds is that far from distancing themselves from the jazz tradition, avant-gardists have sought, often through historical interventions, to draw themselves into it. In fact, they have often used Monk as lesson from the past, positing a reconceptualization of the last thirty years or so of jazz history to suggest that they, rather than the institutional mainstream, should be seen as the real keepers of jazz's core traditions.

EIGHT

Loving Care

Steve Lacy, Roswell Rudd, and Randy Weston

WHILE THE SO-CALLED "MAINSTREAM" has marked itself off as the jazz style associated with tradition and as the bearers of Monk's legacy into the present, any number of musicians who do not fit into the mainstream mold have found Monk's musical legacy an important point of reference and source of creativity. Chapter 7 looked at one such countermainstream claim on Monk's legacy, that of the contemporary avant-garde. This chapter looks at a number of others. Whereas the previous chapter considered something like a subgenre, this chapter looks at a diverse body of music from players who are not part of the neo-bop movement, but who also do not fit neatly into another particular subgroup. Each of the musicians discussed here, Steve Lacy, Roswell Rudd, Randy Weston, and a number of pop musicians who worked on a Monk tribute project directed by Hal Wilner, represents a piece of the whole picture of just how broad and varied Monk's resonance has been for later musicians.

Lacy, Rudd, and Weston are particularly interesting to consider when thinking about the historical implications of Monk's music and its ability to impact jazz over time because much of their work has dealt with Monk's music. Lacy is the best-known interpreter of Monk's music aside from Monk himself and a small circle of regular sidemen, and in some ways Lacy, of all the musicians considered in this book, developed a sound that is least like that of other jazz musicians. The others, and the pop musicians discussed at the end of this chapter, all play in a manner closer to standard models. Still, the surprising breadth of sound to be found in their music tells us something about the profundity of Monk's legacy. It also bodes well. Jazz is a music that thrives on diversity, and it is heartening to see that the historical orientation that has characterized the past twenty years has not necessarily led to a lessening of that diversity.

A DIFFERENT MODERNISM: STEVE LACY AND ROSWELL RUDD

Steve Lacy was one of the first musicians apart from Monk himself to play a significant quantity of Monk's music publicly, and he appears to have been the first to dedicate an entire album to Monk's compositions. Moreover, Lacy's repertory band in the early 1960s with Roswell Rudd and a revolving complement of bassists and drummers was not only the first group to dedicate itself exclusively to playing Monk's music, but also one of the very first jazz repertory bands of any kind. Although that band never formally recorded (there is one bootleg recording, released on LP by Emanem in 1975 and on CD by Hat Hut in 1994, as *School Days*), Rudd and Lacy recorded later, once in 1983, the fruits of which were released as an album of Monk and Herbie Nichols compositions, titled *Regenerations,* and again in the summer of 1999 (Lacy 1990, 1994b, 1999a; Rudd 1983).

These musicians are best considered together because of their long-term collaborative relationship, and because they have remarkably similar playing histories and approaches to the music. Both began playing during the traditional jazz revival of the 1950s, Rudd at Yale University and Lacy in New York; and both were involved in "New Thing" experimentation in the late 1950s and the 1960s, Lacy as a leader and Rudd as a sideman with Archie Shepp. Both eventually left New York City: Lacy went to Europe and settled in Paris, and Rudd went to Maine and later upstate New York. Both developed a playing style that expands the tonal, melodic, and referential framework of the music without extensive "free" playing. Lacy referred to the style as "poly-free," a term that he coined to suggest the possibility of freeing the improviser in various ways while maintaining the presence of the preexisting structure of the composition. The term makes obvious reference to the free jazz of the 1960s and recognizes one of the ultimate problems with that label. By using the prefix "poly-," Lacy captured the sense that "freedom" should apply to more than just playing without preexisting changes and without a regular meter. It pushes listeners to understand that musicians can cultivate freedom in many ways.

In interviews Lacy and Rudd both stressed the importance of their work with each other in the process of learning Monk's music. It is almost a commonplace now to say that in order to really get Monk's music you have to pay attention to all the parts—not just the melody and bass, but the harmonic lines as well—but Lacy was quick to point out that in the 1950s, when he started recording Monk's compositions, he was really only listening to the melodies, and the changes were more abstract to him. "Roswell really opened my ears to . . . to the inner voicings, the other lines in Monk," he told me (Lacy 1999a). When I followed that with a question about the importance of working with someone else over a long period of time, he didn't wait for me to finish my question to answer, interjecting, "Collaboration. Collaboration is the whole thing. All by yourself, you can't . . . you can't get too far. You can't get too far. And the risk of . . . it's risky to go it alone, for many reasons, really. You could fool yourself, and you could fool others, too. . . . But I mean, that, that collaboration is the secret of the whole thing" (Lacy 1999a). Lacy elaborated this point after describing some of the other collaborations that had been important to him throughout his life, saying, "So, that's very important, those collaborations. . . . Because, I mean, you can't take risks with strangers. . . . So you can't really have too much fun until you get to know somebody really well, and over a long period of time. And then you can start to take risks together, and . . . and to do more advanced play. That was what I learned with Roswell, you know" (Lacy 1999a).

As with the avant-garde players I discussed in the previous chapter, investigating the ongoing dialogue between improvisation and precomposition is one of the best ways to get at the way Lacy and Rudd's engagement with Monk's music was distinctive. Their concept of their repertory band was indicative of the two musicians' general approach to the music. At the time their idea was that by playing the music every day they could develop beyond what they had been able to do with those pieces in performance. They accomplished this through extended exploration of the many facets of Monk's compositions, both as interesting structures in their own right and as the seeds of further improvisation. This approach appears to have yielded mixed results for Lacy, as it turns out. In his book, *Findings*, Lacy notes that,

"There is a music that is only available through improvisation. There is another that must be composed. In jazz, the former is played, the latter, played with, extended, elaborated, embellished" (Lacy 1994a, 72). It seems that at one point Monk's compositions took on a kind of rigidity in Lacy's imagination that made them hard to "play with" for a time. I discovered this by asking Lacy if the amount of time he had spent with Monk and his music left him with a feeling of responsibility to the music, as an interpreter.

> Oh, *yeah*. . . . You know, I felt I was never, could never do real justice to his music 'cause it wasn't mine, no matter how much I played it. . . . I don't feel that way any more. Now I feel it's as much mine as it is anybody's. . . . But the thing is, most people don't play it very well, still. Very few. I hear an awful lot of corny versions of it, really. (Lacy 1999a)

The ways musical creation and the development of subjectivity are intertwined in Lacy's description of this experience are very important in trying to understand the relationship between music and identity construction. What might in the abstract be interpreted as a set of formal problems—how to play this piece, what makes a good interpretation of it—is also described in terms of selfhood. A good interpretation is one that is one's own. This can be described in terms of the interpretation's formal characteristics, but the meaning that those structural features create radiates out into a musician's sense of self.

Importantly, according to Lacy's description, an extreme dedication to the exploration of Monk's compositions as concrete musical models is a prerequisite for good interpretation. Having criticized the way other musicians interpret Monk's music, suggesting that they do not know it well enough to make it their own, Lacy explained that this is a matter of technical, formal detail. "Gee, I just heard one recently, some very corny arrangements, wow," he told me. "And you'll also see some publications *full* of errors, and fake books with versions of them just completely wrong; just amazing." "You know," he continued, "when we worked with Monk, he would never show us the music. The paper. He didn't trust the paper. He had it all written down on the paper, but he would not show it. And he would play it over and over again. . . . And he's right, you know. We misinterpret, you know; the paper is not . . . it's not sound" (Lacy 1999a).[1]

Lacy's insistence on the primacy of sound over representation in jazz is interesting because it can be interpreted on at least two levels. In a straightforward sense he was addressing a formal concern: that musical notation often fails to convey the rhythmic, melodic, and expressive subtleties of the music (for example, how to interpret eighth notes along the continuum from even to swung, how to release a note, or how flat to play a blue note). But Lacy's skepticism about the authority of notated music also suggests another level of criticism, one with social and historical underpinnings. Through his reference to the unreliability of fake books and the centrality of oral/aural learning, Lacy presented himself within the traditional sphere of jazz, and implicitly references the often repeated criticism that jazz is in danger because of the prevalence among younger players of relying on written materials and institutional education to learn the tradition.[2]

The centrality of Monk's music as a body of texts to learn and to learn from in Lacy's and Rudd's approach to music seems difficult to reconcile with the fact that freedom is the highest goal according to their description of learning Monk's compositions. Indeed, Lacy specifically criticized one well-received mainstream performer's approach to Monk's tunes as "a re-creation. . . . It sounded as though it was a copy, you know, it sounded to me like he . . . was trying to be what he was not" (Lacy 1999a). I asked Rudd how freedom and minute attention to the details of the preexisting composition, which I saw as two different, and potentially opposed, principles, were possible to satisfy at the same time. After all, much of the discourse about freedom in jazz, particularly in the 1960s avant-garde that Lacy and Rudd were once part of, has been about freedom from the constraints of precomposed musical texts—freedom from the chord changes, and perhaps even freedom from playing preexistent pieces at all. Although in practice he seems to have a clear conception of the role of freedom in his own musical goals, Rudd had to work to express it so that I could understand. The exchange went as follows:

GABRIEL SOLIS: What did that [freedom] amount to? Was it a matter of getting to a place where because you know the pieces so well you can take more liberties with them?

ROSWELL RUDD: The . . . the freedom is in . . . searching, probably never knowing, but in searching and feeling that you're really on the trail, that you're really on the tail of, of something. You know, [something] that makes sense, sounds right, sounds good, lifts you up. Yeah, for me the freedom was in the flight and the search. . . .

SOLIS: . . . So it's like a personal freedom? A freedom within the music rather than a freedom from . . . some kind of restraint?

RUDD: I, I couldn't say, I couldn't put the freedom separate from the, from, from Thelonious Monk, you know. It's . . . for me freedom is something that's defined and has, you know, for the moment anyway, a certain limitation, delimitation. . . . [Monk] gives you parameters, you know what I'm saying? And . . . like I say, the parameters are so finely wrought that they will forever change. People will forever search. . . . You'd think anything that was, you know, monumentally in place like this would be easy to see, find, touch, delineate, and . . . mark on your map, you know. But, man . . .

SOLIS: [laughing] . . . It's elusive stuff!

RUDD: [laughing] Yeah. The shit . . . it's . . . yeah. It keeps changing, nevertheless, it keeps changing, nevertheless. As colossal as it is, it's . . . for me the sands keep shifting, even now, even after it's been so long. Every time I go back to one of these pieces there's another layer. (Rudd 1999)

Rudd's definition of freedom is particularly interesting when understood in terms of his personal history. Rudd was one of only a very few white musicians to be accepted within Black Nationalist circles of avant-garde jazz in the 1960s, when he was hired by Archie Shepp as a trombonist and arranger. It seems plausible that one of the reasons he was well received by such musicians was his sophisticated understanding of what freedom might mean in a musical context. Far from solely indexing improvisation outside the constraints of a rhythmic groove, and without tonal reference, for Rudd freedom is largely a spiritual, personal goal. Unlike many of the Black Nationalist thinkers of the 1960s, however, Rudd conceives of freedom as largely apolitical. It is the feeling he gets from what he describes as "illuminata," or "moments of illumination," instances of deep, spiritual understanding from long-term, engaged interaction with music, among other things (Rudd 1999).

Lacy had a more straightforward response to the question of how to integrate freedom and a dedication to Monk's composed structures. He made it clear that the reason for learning the music very carefully was that the better he and the band got to know the music, the more they could find interesting ways to work within it and extend the given parameters. As he put it, "We could start to fuck around with it . . . and . . . have fun, and make mistakes, and try out different shit. And otherwise it was just, like, a stiff performance, you know" (Lacy 1999a). Lacy clearly differentiates between the kinds of mistakes he and his band made from what he hears in other, more conservative performances. "You know, a lot of people played those tunes completely wrong, because they copied the way Miles did it, or something. And Miles just did it in a sort of sketchy fashion. . . . And so other people . . . took the same liberty. You can't copy somebody else's liberties, you know, you have to earn them by yourself. You really have to work hard for your little liberties" (Lacy 1999a).

Lacy's comment about the work required to legitimately deviate from the precedent Monk set in interpreting his own tunes was perhaps the most interesting one he made regarding freedom and the interpretation of Monk's music. It struck me immediately, and I later brought it up a number of times to find out what other musicians thought of it. There was a general agreement with the spirit of Lacy's remark. Most interestingly, T.S. Monk and Don Sickler, stylistically conservative musicians, both remarked on how fitting it was that it was Lacy who made this point. Both think of Lacy as an exemplary musician who knew the history of the music and had irreproachable credibility within the community. Because of these qualities, they told me, he could explore the furthest-out possibilities suggested by the compositions without fear of negative judgments from the mainstream. Lacy's freedom came from an interaction of sociocultural and musical factors. Because Sickler knew that Lacy's background in jazz was solid, he trusted that Lacy's experiments would be rooted in the tradition and therefore legitimate.

MODERNISM, THE HISTORICAL AVANT-GARDE, AND JAZZ

To understand fully the aesthetic and cultural context that distinguishes Lacy and Rudd's approach to countermainstream performance of Monk's music from the avant-garde approach discussed in the previous chapter, it is necessary to consider their position vis-à-vis modernism and avant-gardism as larger artistic and cultural movements. It should be noted that there is a terminological issue to deal with as well. Some writers consider modernism and avant-gardism as separate movements, while others consider them two related sides of the same coin, seeing them both as reactions to middlebrow bourgeois culture of the nineteenth and twentieth centuries. I am sympathetic to the latter position, particularly because it allows an analysis of postmodernism as a movement that is itself part of a larger, overarching modernism.

In *After the Great Divide*, Andreas Huyssen describes modernism and the avant-garde through dualistic oppositions, characterizing their relationships with one another and with other social formations over the course of their history from the late nineteenth century to the 1980s. The two aesthetic movements share an opposition to previous bourgeois norms, but they construct the opposition in notably different ways. Modernism involves the construction of art as an autonomous domain, removed from the sullying effects of contact with bourgeois commercialism and explicit political engagement (Huyssen 1986, vii, viii–ix, 54). By contrast, the avant-garde positions itself in active opposition to the bourgeois institutionalization of the arts in order to oppose the political and cultural power structure that art historically has been used to legitimate (3–11). The difference between these two positions is particularly acute in terms of their relationship with popular, or mass, culture. Huyssen describes modernism and mass culture as locked in a Hegelian dialectic, like master and slave, in which the entire system is predicated on the existence of the two sides. Mass culture, then, is modernism's "repressed other," while modernism is "the straw man desperately needed by the system to provide an aura of popular legitimation for the blessings of the culture industry," which in turn creates mass culture (16–17). This dialectic is Huyssen's "great divide." He sees avant-gardism (in both its "historical" and its "postmodernist" expressions) as a radical challenge to "the theories and practices of the Great Divide" (x). By destabilizing the high/low dichotomy in the arts, avant-gardists seek to create a potentially energizing relation between the arts and the masses, subverting the culture industry from within to explicitly oppose the rule of the bourgeoisie.

Martha Bayles addresses the mystification of an elitist tendency in avant-garde arts in her book about pop music and aesthetics, *Hole in Our Soul.* Her destabilization of the notion that avant-garde and postmodernist artists have championed popular culture and aesthetics in a simple way is particularly valuable. In her view there is at least the appearance of a positive engagement with popular culture and the media in this branch of modernism (unlike in high modernism, which constructs popular, mass-mediated culture in pure opposition), but this engagement is of a second order. Bayles quotes from Rimbaud's *A Season in Hell* on his love of "maudlin pictures . . . old inn signs, popular prints . . . old operas, inane refrains and artless rhythms," and draws the clear connection with more recent "camp" and "postmodernist" aesthetics (Bayles 1996, 44). The wording is highly suggestive: note particularly the adjectives "maudlin" and "inane." For Rimbaud (and modern-day aficionados of camp), popular culture is enjoyed for its ability to titillate and arouse the aficionado through apparent degradation and transgression of bourgeois behavioral and aesthetic norms. When applied to the white American engagement with jazz, this has often been expressed through a valorization of the alleged depravity and transgression of bourgeois norms to be found in putatively "authentic" African American culture.[3] The classic expression of this position is found in Norman Mailer's "The White Negro." In this often-quoted article Mailer situates the origin of black creativity in deviant sexuality and violent rage. The African American, Mailer said, "subsisted for his Saturday night kicks, relinquishing the pleasures of the mind for the more obligatory pleasures of the body, and in his music he gave voice to the character and quality of his existence, to his rage and the infinite variations of joy, lust, languor, growl, cramp, pinch, scream and despair of his orgasm. For jazz is orgasm" (Mailer 1957, 279).

When jazz is considered within the context of these dominant paradigms of modernist aesthetics, high modernism and avant-gardism, the field of interpretation becomes even more complicated. As an African American music with its origins (and much of its history) uncontestedly within the realm of entertainment, jazz has a significantly different relationship with both dominant "high" culture and mass, or popular, culture than have any of the modernist or avant-garde artistic movements considered by Huyssen. For some jazz musicians in the 1940s, the adoption of some aspects of modernist discourse was an effective strategy in their struggle for legitimacy (I. Monson 1995, 410–11). Indeed, it quickly became apparent that in terms of technical sophistication, innovation, and subtle use of irony, jazz musicians often better fulfilled modernist aesthetics than did many of their "high art" counterparts (Monson 1996, 115–20). It is important to bear in mind that this appeal to "high art" legitimacy by jazz musicians in the 1940s was essentially a strategic use of discourse, not a radical break with their own past musical traditions. They were interested in changing the social status of jazz and the economic relations in the field of production, but not by abandoning the music in favor of a different aesthetic. It is a mistake to interpret the evolving language of modern jazz in the 1940s as motivated by an interest in entering the canons of "high art" as constructed by the dominant institutions of the time. Rather, it was the appropriation of terminology and the cultural legitimacy associated with it. While there were many significant changes to the language of the music introduced by the beboppers, some of which may have developed in part from their interest in modernist classical music of the early twentieth century, the movement as a whole must also be seen as an innovation within the traditions of black vernacular music, and in a profound, if often contradictory, relationship with modern technology and the mass media, as Scott DeVeaux has compellingly argued in *The Birth of Bebop* (DeVeaux 1997, 3–4, 438–47).

Over the course of the following decades there have been practical changes in the relationship between jazz and the listening public that flowed in part from the adoption of certain modernist aesthetic values, but modernism has never been the only set of aesthetic values at work in the music. The relationship between the jazz avant-garde—the kind of modernist jazz exemplified by Steve Lacy and Roswell Rudd, among others—and the jazz mainstream is explained, at least in part, as the intensification of certain aspects of modernism and avant-gardism in the different performers' practices and discourse. In some sense the position of the jazz avant-garde as expressed in formal and informal discourse, described in chapter 7, deploys some of the avant-gardist tendencies Huyssen describes. Most importantly, Amiri Baraka's writings and the conversations I had with younger avant-garde musicians stressed a connection between musical radicalism and leftist oppositional politics.[4] The musicians I spoke with saw themselves as explicitly engaged in counterhegemonic practice, rescuing Monk's legacy from the hegemonic grip of "stylists." Monk is particularly important in this argument at the present moment because of the enormous cultural capital with which he is imbued, because of how recently his work has reached canonical status, and because his music has significantly affected musicians from across the spectrum of jazz.

In contrast, Lacy and Rudd's position involved the intensification of high modernist aesthetic tendencies.[5] The most important constellation of modernist aesthetics in the two musicians' discourse involved the importance of scientism and formalism. Rudd described the process through which he and Lacy had been involved with Monk's music since the 1960s as "research." He qualified this statement to clarify that this research should not be understood as a detached process, saying, "[this is] more than some kind of . . . *academic* research project, you know. We really wanted to play the stuff" (Rudd 1999). For him, this meant learning, for instance, what improvisational possibilities Monk's polyphonic structures suggested. This is only part of the story for Rudd, however, because this sort of formalist language quickly led him to talk about the ways musical learning has led to personal and spiritual growth. This connects Rudd with a number of other jazz musicians interested in modernism and the connections between the scientific, mystical, and spiritual realms of obscure philosophy and religion, notably Sun Ra and Anthony Braxton. Monk, too, made reference to science, particularly mathematics, in various interviews, though it was never integral to his self-presentation, nor did he make connections between science and spiritual or mystical thinking.

Lacy even more explicitly brought into play the notion of science in talking about Monk's music. He had mentioned that he first became interested in learning Monk's music because each composition contained a lot of material that could be used in improvisation, and that he learned the "basic nature of music" from that (Lacy 1999a). In response to a question about Monk's penchant for motivic elaboration in his solos, Lacy said with enthusiasm:

> Yeah, yeah, yeah, yeah, yeah, no. . . . He . . . showed how it was done, really. And he invented those sounds, himself, really, through research. He did a lot of research at the piano. . . . And he had this mirror on the ceiling, and the top of the piano was . . . nonexistent—the piano was open—and he could see his hands in the mirror up there . . . and he would be doing research like that . . . with different sounds. He invented all these . . . jewels. . . . Those sounds he made were like diamonds, rubies, pearls, sapphire, marble, all kinds of elemental, elemental sounds. (Lacy 1999a)

MONK AND PAN-AFRICAN DIASPORIC THINKING

Lacy and Rudd's explorations in music led them down a number of paths, most notably toward a connection with improvisers from what is known as the "New Music" movement in Europe; but another important direction that musicians outside the jazz mainstream have traveled is through non-European improvised musical traditions. There is a significant history of explicit borrowings from African diasporic musics in jazz. This borrowing stretches back at least as far as the 1910s and Jelly Roll Morton's "Latin tinge" (Roberts 1979, 38–39). In the 1940s and 1950s, Dizzy Gillespie collaborated with Cuban master drummer Chano Pozo, and Art Blakey and Max Roach used Afro-Cuban rhythms in their playing and composing. In the 1960s John Coltrane used rhythmic and melodic ideas developed from his interest in African and Indian musics.[6] Of course, these examples could be multiplied manyfold. Often, though not always, this borrowing has resulted from collaborations between African American musicians and musicians from elsewhere within the African diaspora, such as Nigerian drummer Babatunde Olatunji, Pozo (only one of many Afro-Caribbean drummers to play with jazz musicians since the 1940s), Cuban bandleader Machito, and many others. Jazz's intermusical borrowing has continued and taken on greater resonance in the context of the "world music" phenomenon of the 1980s and '90s.

Not all of these connections and collaborations with other cultures have been explicitly politicized (and, like jazz generally, none of them have been exclusively political in nature), but many of them have been colored by Africentrism. As a philosophy and practice, Africentrism involves a rejection of status quo readings of history that would seek to divide African and African American people. The term *Africentrism,* coined by Molefi Kete Asante, denotes the most recent and self-conscious form of this philosophy, but it shares something with earlier pan-African, postcolonial ideas. Not necessarily avant-garde in its aesthetics, Africentrism is nonetheless inherently countermainstream, both in terms of American culture today and with respect to jazz's institutional mainstream.

Thelonious Monk has been significant for Africentrists in the contemporary jazz scene because of the extent to which some musicians hear his music as African or African diasporic in a way that transcends jazz's specifically American character in the popular imagination. Foremost among musicians who interpret Monk in this way is Randy Weston. Like Steve Lacy, Weston was close to Monk beginning in the 1940s (although, because they were both pianists, they never performed together). Weston first became interested in Monk when he heard him playing with Coleman Hawkins, then Weston's favorite performer, on New York's 52nd Street (Weston 1999). Although Weston was much younger than Monk, their careers began to blossom at roughly the same time, in the early to mid-1950s.

Weston's playing on his first recordings, with the Riverside label, is remarkably similar to Monk's at the time, using a similar harmonic language and approach to space. These recordings are particularly striking because of the fact that at the time few pianists publicly recognized Monk's greatness, much less attempted to play in a style similar to his. Whether Weston was self-consciously incorporating Monk's sound into his own or absorbing and using it subconsciously is hard to know now. In any case, unlike many musicians, Weston is quite simply untroubled by thinking of his playing as an amalgam of materials taken from his favorite models; it is understood that the act of amalgamation is itself creative. As he put it, "See, my first influence on piano was Count Basie, my second was Nat 'King' Cole, my third was Art Tatum, my fourth was Monk, and my fifth was Duke. I mean, put those together in a pot and stir it up, plus Africa, you have Randy Weston" (Weston 1999).

Weston's interest in Africa dates to his youth. In an interview Weston said that his father laid the groundwork for his later interest in African music: "He gave me Africa, told me I was an African born in America. . . . He said, 'look at us as African people. And look at the fact that we have thousands of years of history. That's the reason why we're able to adapt and create different kinds of music.' It goes back to a thousand years of tradition" (Weston 1999). Weston's early interest in African music also stems from his involvement with Ahmed Abdul Malik, a bass player of North African heritage. Weston explained, "I used to hang out with Malik, and Malik would take me to downtown Brooklyn, the Arab section, the North African section of Brooklyn. . . . So we'd hear the qanun and oud and all these instruments where you could play those eighth and sixteenth tones and whatnot" (Weston 1999). In retrospect, Weston says that having heard this sound, he began experimenting with the piano, trying to get something new to come out of it, and that as soon as he heard Monk he realized that Monk had found that something (Weston 1999).

Weston toured Africa a number of times in the 1960s, playing in the continent's newly independent nations. In 1967 he, like many of his contemporaries, played for an international tour under the auspices of the U.S. State Department. Although the intention of these tours was to present America as a paragon among nations to whom the emerging West African nations should look for a model of modernity, Weston clearly derived a different lesson from the tours. Like a number of jazz musicians who performed on these tours, Weston took an active interest in indigenous African music and culture and considered it a viable alternative to that of the West (Griggs 1966, 17, 38).[7] In 1965 he moved to Morocco, and he eventually settled in Tangier. Over a period of years Weston became involved with the economic and cultural life of Tangier, opening a short-lived jazz club and collaborating extensively with the local Gnawa musicians (Johnson 1990, 55).

In live performance Weston foregrounds his Africentric theory of the music through his stage talk, his addresses to the audience between songs. In a performance at the Iridium nightclub in August of 1999, Weston spent longer than is common for most jazz musicians—perhaps two minutes—explaining his inspiration for the composition "Brooklyn: African Village" to the racially mixed audience before playing it. He noted the way he has come to see Brooklyn as an African village in terms of its citizens, its social organization, and its "feel."

Despite Weston's long friendship with Monk (or perhaps because of it), he seldom performs Monk's compositions, and he has recorded them even less often. The notable exception to this is his 1990 recording on the Verve record label, *Portraits of Thelonious Monk*. This recording is part of a three-CD series of "portraits," one dedicated to the music of Duke Ellington, another to Weston's own compositions, and the third to Monk. Weston appears to be somewhat ambivalent about playing other people's compositions, largely because of the difficulty he has had over the years convincing the people who control the economic side of the jazz industry to let him play and record his own compositions (personal communication). When I asked him how he felt about the *Portraits* project, he told me he was pleased with it, despite the exigencies of recording on an extremely tight schedule (they recorded three CDs in only three days). He explained that to prepare for the recording, "what we did, we got all the guys together, put Monk's picture on the wall, and stood there, burnt incense, and everybody told Monk stories before we [recorded]. . . . And everybody was on the floor [laughing]. Some Monk stories are incredible. . . . It was a spiritual thing." I suggested that they were "calling on the ancestors," and he replied, "Yeah . . . calling them to help us. [Laughing] Come help me do this!" (Weston 1999).

Earlier in our conversation I had asked Weston if it was important to him to maintain a part of African American history through playing. "That's right," he said, "Because one thing I learned in Africa is that the musicians are historians. They keep the traditions alive. And I thought about Duke, thought about all those cats, thought, 'man, they kept those traditions alive.' All of them. Recording from 1926, or '23 . . . all the way up to Monk. So that's incredible, you know" (Weston 1999). This resonated with the fact that in one of our earlier conversations he had compared his work with that of the griots, African musicians who sing praise to their ancestors. Weston is by no means the only African American musician to compare his art with that of the griots. Gil Scott-Heron referenced the griot figure in explaining the relationship between his art and African American culture as early as the 1970s, as did the Last Poets. Rappers as well, perhaps taking a cue from Scott-Heron, have been described (and have described themselves) as griots. This is a significant act of cultural positioning because Mande *jeli*—the griots best known in the West—have great prestige within their own cultures. Most importantly, within African American culture griots represent a peculiarly African cultural complex, combining historical learning with oral/aural tradition and music. Reference to griots in this context bestows Weston's references to Monk and other figures from the past with characteristics of history telling as a practice that stands above individual memory while marking the whole complex as resolutely African.

This practice is countermainstream, but when Weston speaks, he does not have the stridently oppositional tone vis-à-vis the jazz mainstream as do the avant-garde musicians discussed earlier. This difference must be understood as a convergence of musical and racial conceptual frameworks. Weston has not been plagued by the accusation that his music is not jazz, as far removed as it is in its own way from the paradigmatic sound world of mainstream bebop/modern jazz of the 1940s and 1950s. As noted earlier, jazz is generally conceptualized as black, and Weston's music is clearly and consciously marked as Africentric. Note, by comparison, that even when the "New Thing" and its supporters have seen their music as Africentric, it has often been hard for audiences to hear the connection between it and African or African American aesthetics. Even the Art Ensemble of Chicago, whose music is more obviously engaged with core African American aesthetic practices than some, found it difficult to cultivate a jazz audience in the United States (and spent a number of years in Europe as a result) because of the distance between their music and the vernacular culture of the late twentieth century. It is principally Weston's use of a fundamentally groove-oriented aesthetic that has allowed him to explore musically as much as he has without alienating jazz audiences. Weston's way of talking about his music is situated within a context of implicit opposition to a history of white appropriation of black creativity in American culture. The frame within which his music is critically engaged is larger, in this sense, and it and his discourse about it must be heard in terms of their relation to that larger frame.

Current critical writing on African American culture has often taken one of two positions, the first based on an essentialist understanding of ethnicity in which black expressive culture is theorized as somehow pure, hermetically sealed off from the influence of outside culture, and the second based on a far too easy anti-essentialism, in which the contingency of race is used as a tool to theorize away its powerful effects. Paul Gilroy incisively criticizes these two tendencies in *The Black Atlantic* and, more recently, in *Beyond Race*. The first is problematic because it is used as a moralistic high ground with which to justify arbitrary political choices, and because "it overlooks the development and change of black political ideologies and ignores the restless, recombinant qualities of the black Atlantic's affirmative political cultures" (Gilroy 1993, 31). The second is equally unhelpful because, "in leaving racial essentialism behind by viewing 'race' itself as a social and cultural construction, it has been insufficiently alive to the lingering power of specifically racialised forms of power and subordination" (32). Gilroy proposes a third possibility, that of viewing African diasporic experiences of race and ethnicity as hybrid—neither natural nor essential, but nonetheless salient and powerful in the real world, and ultimately bounded.

Gilroy's groundbreaking work on this topic is essential to a developing understanding of the ways fundamental received notions of race entered the cultural studies literature largely unchallenged in the 1970s and 1980s. Moreover, his charge that scholars interested in the culture question have to consider music seriously because of its remarkable affinity for hybrid cross-fertilization has set the stage in an important way for much current writing on jazz. Building on his work, one must ask what is Gilroy's third possibility, his "anti-anti-essentialism" in actual practice, and how might it be expressed. Gilroy leaves the question relatively open. Drawing on Foucault, he proposes "an anti-anti-essentialism that sees racialized subjectivity as the product of the social practices that supposedly derive from it" (102). This is fertile ground. The first step in understanding how an anti-anti-essentialism might be constructed is to define the practices involved. Following Richard Fox's idea of "culture in the making," it is clear that rather than reified "traditional" practices, one should consider creative interaction with material conditions and the ways those actions are interpreted by a society (see Fox 1985, 1997). In the case of jazz and American society, musical performance is certainly an important practice to investigate, as is the telling of history. These practices become coherent as tools in the production of racial or ethnic subjectivity to the degree that they produce a feeling of "we" in the audience to whom they are directed. At precisely this point interpreting a given complex of practices as anti-anti-essentialist becomes intractably complicated. Because it relies on interpretation by an audience, there is always the possibility of varying reception.

Randy Weston's self-presentation could easily be seen as essentialist, according to Gilroy's description of the concept, but I would like to present an interpretation of it as anti-anti-essentialist. In our conversations Weston was at pains to clarify that what he plays, and what Monk played—jazz, blues, gospel— are all *African* music (Weston 1999; personal communication). When he told me this, however, Weston was not engaged in the construction of a hermetically sealed, pure culture, nor in the conflation of Africa and America as geocultural entities. He would no more have attempted to convince me that, for example, the piano is an indigenous African instrument than that Brooklyn is in a literal sense on the African continent. That level of meaning was, I believe, understood. What Weston wanted to convey was the notion that what Gilroy, following Raymond Williams, refers to as a "shared structure of feeling" unites his music with that of other members of the diaspora, and that its Africanness is neither incidental, nor lost in the experience of interaction with European-derived culture. His use of essentialist language links his music with Africa as a way of specifically combating an anti-essentialist metanarrative of African American music of the sort that uses the term "America's classical music" to erase the achievements of black culture through a universalizing interpretive move. Moreover, Weston is well aware of the essentialism issue. When confronted with it by interviewers, he has often retorted with a universalist vision of Africa—one variation or another on the idea that "we all came from Africa." This clever inversion of the commonly assumed universality of Western, modern culture is more than empty rhetoric. It offers a pointed challenge by suggesting that jazz music and African American culture is conceptually available to anyone, but only if one recognizes his or her common humanity with Weston on his terms. This, then, is a sort of strategic essentialism; to be understood the assertions must be heard in context.

What I find most useful in Weston's discourse is his recognition of the power differentials involved in the cultural process and his respect for the agency involved. Weston rejects the idea that there is a power-neutral hybridity in African American expressive culture. Just as I am reacting to a mechanistic understanding of influence, substituting in its place an active, humanized one, Weston describes African American music in emergent rather than deterministic terms: it is what happens when people with African musical sensibilities appropriate materials from outside their culture to make a new music. This is important because it allows for a reinterpretation of a common, overly simplistic conception of jazz's hybridity: that jazz's rhythms and blue notes are of African origin, and its harmony is European. While there is clearly something to this characterization that has made it salient for many years, it takes the mixing for granted. Weston's interpretation foregrounds the act of drawing on these various sonic possibilities as the fundamentally important step.

MONK AND POST-1970S POP MUSIC

Lacy, Rudd, and Weston's interest in claiming Monk as an influence, and in publicly declaring their connection to him—both verbally and in their performances—is fairly easy to understand as one of the ways they situated themselves within the jazz genre. In fact, it is one of the fundamental ways that a musical style becomes a genre, a "tradition." There are, however, musicians from other, less obviously connected styles who have found something useful and interesting in Monk's legacy to draw upon. The Kronos Quartet, for instance, one of the premier American chamber music ensembles, recorded an album of Monk's compositions that leaned heavily on the idea of Monk as a sort of jazz Webern, whose music could comfortably be recast outside the jazz genre.

Perhaps most surprising of the approaches to Monk's music that make a claim for his legacy outside the mainstream jazz orthodoxy are those by musicians within the pop and rock world. This approach exists outside the framework for mainstream and countermainstream approaches to Monk outlined in the introduction, but adds another layer to it. Marketing systems, radio formats, and music television broadcasting as well as audience consumption patterns have all conspired to keep the various forms of vernacular music in postwar America separate, and despite a number of crossover hits in the 1960s and 1970s such as Lee Morgan's "The Sidewinder," Miles Davis's *Bitches Brew*, and Herbie Hancock's *Chameleon*, jazz and pop and rock music have been distant for most of the last half century. It suggests the enormity of Monk's cultural diffusion that when his Blue Note recordings from the 1940s were reissued in the 1970s, a reviewer from *Creem* recommended them to his predominantly young audience, saying, "Thelonious Monk is surely one of the most admirable of American artists, and this is one of the most important collections of jazz recordings ever assembled" (Goldberg 1976, 59). In contrast to other jazz works that have gotten the attention of pop critics and audiences, Monk's recordings are not "crossovers" in the typical sense. They do not appeal to rock and roll fans because of an R&B shuffle groove, nor because of electronica or soul- or funk-oriented rhythmic and melodic structures. Instead they are recommended to pop audiences as "pure" and "authentic." They appeal because they are seen to carry with them some of the cultural capital jazz amassed in the post-bop context as highbrow, while also conveying a kind of opposition to mainstream aesthetics: Goldberg's strongest endorsement of Monk is that he "rocks," and he compares Monk with John Lennon and Charles Ives, a veritable pantheon of "far out" musicians from across generic borders (59, 60).

It is hard to say for certain whether this reviewer was addressing an audience unfamiliar with Monk's music, though it seems likely. When the review was written it had been nearly a decade since Monk had appeared in general interest magazines like *Time* or *The Saturday Review.* By that time jazz was already seen as an "adult" music, for aficionados, having been replaced among the young audience by rock and roll. There is reason to think that Monk had somehow maintained a presence, however, at least with rock musicians. Certainly Monk had significant cachet with a hipster audience in the 1960s, and it seems that he continued to maintain that cachet through the following decades and that it even continues to the present.

Vernon Reid, guitarist and former leader of the rock band Living Color, exemplifies Monk's presence in the rock world. Reid and I met before a show he was headlining with a band mixing rap, jazz, hard rock, and techno influences. We were in Thoughtforms, an arts space in New York's Tribeca neighborhood, standing in the gallery in front of the stage, surrounded by paintings and prints with Africentric themes. I had been introduced to Reid by Malik Yusef, the proprietor of the space, who had told Reid I was working on a project dealing with Thelonious Monk. Reid seemed interested, so I asked him whether he listened to Monk. He told me emphatically that he had listened to Monk for many years, and that he considered Monk a sort of role model. In particular Reid said he was impressed by Monk's artistic integrity, his playing according to his convictions despite opposition. This made sense in light of Reid's own performance history as he played in Living Color, a band that stretched listeners' expectations as an all-black band playing hard rock, a music commonly encoded as white.

Perhaps the most striking evidence of Monk's continued presence in the rock music world is the album *That's the Way I Feel Now,* produced by Hal Willner. This album, released in 1984 and billed as "A Tribute to Thelonious Monk," presents twenty-three Monk compositions performed by a mix of rock and jazz artists, including Todd Rundgren, NRBQ, Peter Frampton, Was (Not Was), Bobby McFerrin, Carla Bley, Randy Weston, Steve Lacy, Elvin Jones, and many others. The liner notes stress the fact that the rock musicians had been interested in Monk for some time: "When NRBQ performs, rarely does a set go by without the band playing at least one Monk composition. Donald Fagen salutes Monk in almost every interview he gives." Moreover, Willner's notes stress the fact that the jazz musicians were receptive to their interest: "When I played the Chris Spedding/Peter Frampton version of 'Work' for Steve Lacy, he asked to hear it again," Willner says (Willner 1984).

What stands out in the liner notes to this album, in Reid's descriptions of Monk, and in the review of Monk's Blue Note recordings in *Creem* is the importance of a discourse of universality regarding Monk's legacy. For all of these musicians Monk transcends genre to speak to musicians outside jazz, contesting the mainstream jazz world's claim to be the only legitimate heirs to Monk's legacy.

CONCLUSION

Not every claim on Monk's legacy, whether in the form of a verbal or musical tribute, has been an exclusive one. The neo-boppers and many in the avant-garde have often spoken about their art and their interest in jazz's history in ways that suggest that they and only they are the true keepers of the tradition. Outside these two poles, however, one finds many musicians working to make good and interesting music that is conscious of the past while simultaneously seeking to develop its impact on the present. All of this music plays an indispensable role in shaping our impressions of Monk as a historical figure and as a composer-performer with something to say to us now. Ultimately, all these musicians play a role in keeping his music in our ears, on stage, and on recordings. Though few of these musicians define their times or will become household names, they are a fundamental part of making a tradition.

Afterword

AN INTERVIEWER ONCE ASKED MONK where jazz was going. Monk replied, somewhat testily, "Where's jazz going? I don't know. Maybe it's going to hell. You can't make anything go anywhere. It just happens." In the recent past jazz has been looking carefully at its past and putting that past to use in many different ways. People who worry about "where jazz is going" often complain that, considering that jazz is a music that has been progressive in outlook throughout most of its history, this focus on the past is a sign of a moribund art. This book has been an attempt to come to terms with jazz's historicism, and to see why the past has become so important in this age of the putative death of history. The most striking conclusion that emerges through listening to people play and talk is that while the past may at times be a burden, perhaps even an overwhelming weight, it is much more often productive. Looking backward and looking forward are not necessarily mutually contradictory. To return to the quote from Ralph Ellison with which this book started, jazz's ability to place people in the present moment, the vantage point from which we look both backward and forward, is part of its "power to give us an orientation in time."

NOTES

INTRODUCTION

1. Scholarly works on jazz commonly open with the ontological question "What is jazz?" While such a question is useful in framing certain questions about the music (largely, it would seem, in pragmatically defining the entity about which the questions will be asked), the answer, if it is not to be qualified into uselessness, amounts to a tautology: jazz is the music jazz musicians play. Rather than attempting a better definition, I would like to leave the tautology, along with the ambiguity it represents, in place. I do this in part because I trust that readers of this book will be familiar enough with music to have a working ("I know it when I see it") definition of jazz in mind already, and that such definitions will be sufficiently similar to each other and to my own. Furthermore, I bracket the ontological question because a working definition is sufficient to engage the questions that make up the rest of this book.

2. Mark Tucker was writing a book on Monk's music when I first proposed this book. I happily looked forward to being able to use Tucker's thoughtful understanding of Monk as an aid in the analyses presented here. Sadly, the Monk book was unfinished at Tucker's untimely passing in 2000.

3. The anthropologist Marilyn Ivy, writing about memory in contemporary Japan, describes the events of the past as "phantasmatic," because their existence *as historical events* is always, necessarily constituted after the fact and out of traces rather than out of the thing itself (Ivy 1995). Dale Chapman argues in his dissertation that musical recordings can usefully be understood as "phantasms" in

the same sense, inasmuch as they are traces of originary performances from which we constitute historicity, rather than performances themselves (Chapman 2003, 148). Writing about rock recordings as audio art, Albin Zak has argued that recordings are, for musicians and audiences alike, the musical object themselves and not simply traces of a live performance (Zak 2001). Zak's work suggests that we should be hesitant to make too many generalizations about recordings per se and should instead be responsive to the ways they are used and understood in specific communities, a point I follow up in the article " 'A Unique Chunk of Jazz Reality' " (Solis 2004).

4. Here a note on the use of terms to describe musical scholarship and the scholars who practice it is in order. Often historical musicologists—music scholars trained in historical method or who study the Western classical tradition in a historical framework—refer to their study simply as "musicology," without any modifier. This usage is confusing at best, and problematic insofar as it implies, through the linguistic trick of using the unmarked category to refer to a particular group, that historical musicology is the universal study of music and the other subdisciplines are "other." In this book I use the unmarked term only when I am referring to all approaches to the academic study of music. Otherwise I use a set of marked terms, "historical musicology," "ethnomusicology," and "music theory."

5. For representative examples of this two-part process, which might be glossed as documenting and critiquing, or learning and understanding, see, for instance, Jane Sugarman's *Engendering Song* (1997) and Thomas Turino's *Nationalists, Cosmopolitans, and Popular Music in Zimbabwe* (2000).

CHAPTER 2

1. Richard Fox uses the terms "hyper-difference" and "over-likeness" in "Passage from India," an article dealing with the transnational flow of cultural styles, particularly those surrounding civil disobedience practiced by Mohandas Gandhi, Martin Luther King Jr., and a host of contemporary people worldwide. Fox derives this binarism from a set of misinterpretations that may arise in the movement of countermainstream practices and principles "from local to global and then to another locale" (Fox 1997, 67). In his terms, "hyper-difference" "depends on a magnification of difference, a supposition that a cultural practice located elsewhere cannot travel anywhere else." By contrast "over-likeness" occurs when the information saturation of contemporary life minimizes "real contrasts and . . . so [washes] out difference that we see similarity when it is not there." The one produces "an extremely exaggerated Otherness," while the other creates "a complete assimilation to Self" (67).

2. It is difficult to avoid confusion when referring to these two Thelonious Monks, as I do throughout this book. The younger Monk is often referred to in print as Monk Jr., although, as he points out, this is not technically correct. His

grandfather was also Thelonious Monk, making his father the second and him the third (and his son the fourth). I will use T.S. Monk to refer to the younger Monk and Thelonious Monk to refer to the older throughout, since these are the names most widely used on recordings and in print.

3. Here and throughout this book I have transcribed quotes from my interviews as accurately as possible. I have made no attempt to formalize spoken grammar and syntax, except to clarify meaning. In all such cases I have marked my changes in brackets.

4. For more on this and its relationship to music, see Radano 2000 (459 ff.) and Agawu 2003 (55), among others.

5. See the variation in tempo on this piece as recorded for Blue Note, Riverside, and Columbia. Perhaps most striking are the versions recorded with Gerry Mulligan, released on the CD reissue of *Mulligan Meets Monk*, released as part of *The Complete Riverside Recordings* (Monk 1986), on disc 6, tracks 2 and 3. Take 4 (track 3) is markedly slower than take 2 (track 2).

6. This is not to say that De Wilde has no experience with jazz outside of recordings, but that his work as a historian—his book on Monk—focuses solely on Monk's recordings and looks at them as uncomplicated documents.

7. It is difficult to say what importance Monk ascribed to his own recordings. He was reticent in interviews and left very little record of his personal tastes and ideals aside from his recordings. Other musicians, however, seem to have an ambivalent relationship to their recordings. While they are often justifiably proud of the achievement recordings represent and the permanence they provide, musicians often express concern that recordings fail to capture the best qualities of communication and spontaneity found in live performances.

8. For an enlightening discussion of jazz performance as ritual, see Jackson 2000.

9. For more on the interactive creation of a groove in jazz performance, see Ingrid Monson 1996.

10. Thelonious Monk, *Criss Cross* (1993), track 4. "Eronel," credited on this album to Monk alone, was the fruit of a collaborative process. Although it was originally composed by Idrees Sulieman and Sahib Shihab, Monk suggested a crucial change. Suleiman told T.S. Monk that the change consisted of only a single note and the title, yet Sulieman and Shihab felt that Monk's suggestions made the piece what it is, and therefore gave over the composer's rights altogether (Wittner and Braus 1994, 12).

11. Scott DeVeaux points out that this became increasingly common in Monk's recordings of standards in his later years. He also used this method in recordings of his own music, though perhaps not as frequently (DeVeaux 1999a, 174).

12. Phil Ford discusses a similarly harmonically ambiguous introduction in Monk's recording of "I Should Care" (Ford 2002, 63–64).

13. Thelonious Monk, *The Complete Blue Note Recordings* (1994), disc 2, track 6; disc 4, track 4.

14. This was particularly true in the past, but it remains a distressingly significant issue even today.

15. Some musicians who knew Monk well describe him affectionately as possessing a childlike quality, making the point that he was unencumbered by the trivialities of adult life. However, there can be no mistaking the vitriol in Bacon's statement for such a positive view of Monk.

16. Thelonious Monk, *Thelonious Monk* (1982), track 1.

17. Thelonious Monk, *The Complete Riverside Recordings* (1986), disc 2, track 3; disc 7, track 10. It is problematic to attach dates of composition to Monk's pieces, as with most jazz compositions. The best one can do, in the absence of a scholarly biography of Monk, which might be able to provide accurate dates, is to consider the date of first recording. The problem with this tactic is that Monk was actively composing throughout the 1940s, before he began recording, making any chronology on the basis of recordings of limited value.

18. Monk, *The Complete Blue Note Recordings* (1994), disc 2, track 5.

19. Monk, *The Complete Blue Note Recordings* (1994), disc 4, track 3.

CHAPTER 3

1. Interestingly, this double sense of the performance of identity meshes well with the theory of identity presented by the psychologist Erik Erikson in the essays that make up *Identity and the Life Cycle*. Erikson builds on Freud's informal use of the term *identity*, suggesting that a more formal theory might help explain some of the basic questions of psychotherapy. While Freud sees the relationship between the ego and social groups as antagonistic—based on the need to defend identity against the ever-present leader/mob mentality—Erikson suggests that there could be a dynamic, potentially valuable relationship between the individual and his or her social situation (Erikson 1980, 18–19). It is in order to satisfy the need to theorize this relationship between the self and others that Erikson introduces his idea of the "ego identity," or "personal identity," defined as "the immediate perception of one's selfsameness and continuity in time; and the simultaneous perception of the fact that others recognize one's sameness and continuity" (22).

2. "Rhythm changes" is the name for the chord progression from George Gershwin's Broadway tune "I Got Rhythm." This progression is the basis for innumerable jazz compositions, especially bebop tunes, such as Dizzy Gillespie's "Salt Peanuts," Sonny Rollins's "Oleo," and Charlie Parker's "Anthropology." Thelonious Monk's "Rhythm-a-ning" is also based on rhythm changes, as its title suggests. In a jazz context the blues provides far more than simply a chord progression. Only those pieces that use one or another blues-based harmonic progression, however, are referred to as "blues" tunes per se.

3. There is some conceptual slippage in the use of the term "jazz standard," but musicians seem to differentiate between those pieces, such as Sonny Rollins's "Airegin," Horace Silver's "Song for My Father," and Thelonious Monk's "Straight, No Chaser," that have entered the common repertoire of most jazz musicians worldwide and have to some extent become common intellectual property, and other pieces that have not. My research was not broad enough to generalize confidently about this beyond musicians' conceptualizations of Monk's compositions, but I believe it would be a fruitful area for further study.

4. A case could be made that such a balance is characteristic of any music in which the performer and composer are not the same, but there seems to be a difference of significant degree, if not of kind, between the jazz context and, for example, that of Western classical music. While classical musicians strive to put their own interpretive stamp on the pieces they play, there is no sense in which they share authorship with, for example, Beethoven, when playing his music. The extent of their contribution is so small in comparison with jazz as to strain comparison.

CHAPTER 4

1. The single exception to this rule is Steve Lacy, who received unqualified praise from every musician with whom I spoke, from the most iconoclastic avant-gardist to the most pious traditionalist. The reasons for this are manifold, but two stand out. First and foremost, there is the sense that Lacy "earned" his interpretations through a lifetime of dedication. Additionally, although I do not have conclusive evidence to support this position, it is my impression that Lacy's unwavering goodwill and support of his fellow musicians, particularly younger musicians, reinforced positive attitudes about his music within the community.

2. This category of "sound," like "voice," is multidimensional, incorporating both more formal aspects of music making, such as a musician's idiosyncratic approach to melody, harmony, and form, and indexical aspects of the musician's total style, including the particular intermusical relationships he or she foregrounds in his or her playing.

3. For more on Monk's choice of and interpretations of standards, see DeVeaux 1999a.

4. For a description of a similar process in Monk's career with Riverside Records, see Tucker 1999.

5. I use the term "harmonic cluster" here as distinct from both the more common "chords" and "clusters." "Chord" is too generic a term in this instance, because it principally implies consonant, triadic harmony. "Cluster" is too specific, implying the absence of an undergirding triadic frame of reference, and, moreover, the absence of functional harmonic relationships. By "harmonic cluster" I intend to preserve both a sense of the triadic, harmonic, and melodically progressive aspects of these concatenations of pitches, and at the same time underscore

the textural significance of the seconds, which are not reducible to some tertiary extension.

I am in large measure indebted to Roswell Rudd for the foregrounding of the idea of "clusters." He describes drumming as the center of Monk's music, followed by "bass, melody, inner voices, harmony, or changes, if you want. I would rather use Herbie [Nichols's] term, 'clusters.' . . . Clusters come in all kinds of dispositions. . . . Sometimes they're close, sometimes they're spread apart, but I think *cluster* describes it better than *combination* or *voicing* or some other word, any word" (Rudd 1999).

6. This term is somewhat ambiguous, but in this instance, at a minimum, it was used to mean constructing a solo using motives from the melody. More commonly, it is used to refer specifically to the creation of a unified solo through the elaboration of one or a few motives within a solo.

7. In addition to this Vanguard date and a busy touring schedule, during the summer of 1999 Hersch gave a series of Monday night concerts at the Knitting Factory. Each of the four shows featured Hersch in collaboration with one or two progressive musicians, including Marty Erlich, Jane Ira Bloom, Michael Moore, and Gerry Hemmingway, among others.

8. For an informative discussion of the ways framing works in various interpersonal contexts, see Goffman 1974.

9. For more on this subject, see chapter 2.

10. As Ingrid Monson and others have made eminently clear, an analysis of this music necessarily leads to a consideration of race in American consciousness; see Monson 1995.

11. The growing literature on charges of racism and reverse racism in jazz is already too large to adequately summarize here. For the most comprehensive description of a perceived reverse racism, see Sudhalter 1999. Monson (forthcoming) provides a critique of this argument.

12. Hersch's comment is reminiscent of one of Monk's from a 1948 article in *Metronome*: "Chord structure is practically arithmetic anyway. You just have to use common sense" (Simon 1948, 34)

CHAPTER 5

1. I intend this in much the same way that Milan Kundera intended the statement, quoted in the introduction, that "Every novelist's work contains an implicit vision of the history of the novel" (Kundera 1988, iii).

2. I have drawn the term "self-presentation" from Erving Goffman's work. For a detailed explanation of the concept, see *The Presentation of Self in Everyday Life* (Goffman 1959).

3. Joe Lovano is a prime example of a musician who uses "outside" techniques and materials while nonetheless continuing to seem "mainstream."

4. Building on ethnomusicological models, and on literature from cultural theory, anthropology, and literary criticism, a number of writers in historical musicology, the so-called "new" musicology, have also dealt with the ways that music is political at deep levels. Susan McClary, whose work *Feminine Endings* is one of the most prominent works of this "new" musicological literature, describes the sociopolitical aspect of music thus: "Music is always dependent on the conferring of social meaning . . . as ethnomusicologists have long recognized, the study of signification in music cannot be undertaken in isolation from the human contexts that create, transmit, and respond to it" (McClary 1991, 21). Further, she says, "The project of critical musicology (of which feminism would be an important branch) would be to examine the ways in which different musics articulate the priorities and values of various communities. Fortunately, we are not required to reinvent the wheel, for this is, of course, one of the principal activities of ethnomusicology" (26).

5. Of course, my own work is not exempt from this. I am attempting to present a picture of Monk that is broad enough to reveal many, sometimes contradictory, lessons from his example. This is as much conditioned by my own sociocultural and intellectual background and goals as is any other interpretation.

6. Late in the writing of this book John Gennari's *Blowin' Hot and Cool: Jazz and Its Critics* was published. It provides a much more expansive and detailed discussion of Hentoff's and Williams's writing and their place in jazz criticism at large than I can hope to here (Gennari 2006). It almost goes without saying that both writers' work in toto is much more complicated than my discussion of their roles in the canonization of Monk might suggest. In his discussion of Hentoff in the first part of chapter 4, Gennari describes him as, among other things, "an all-purpose heretic" (169). A discussion of Williams, described as "a born pedagogue" and a critic's critic (186, 191), is in the second part of the same chapter.

7. Christopher Small's discussion of the meaning of the words *composer* and *composition* in jazz is interesting in this regard, as it shows how specific and programmatic Hentoff's and Williams's uses of the term were. He writes, "In jazz, as in the great age of classical music, to be a musician is primarily to be a performer, and those who compose regard composition simply as the creation of material for themselves and their colleagues to play. . . . [A composition is usually] a springboard, which may or may not be notated, from which all the musicians may take off into collaborative creation. Many of these 'compositions' . . . are beautiful in themselves, but they reveal, and are meant to reveal, their full character only when the composer and his colleagues have played them" (1987, 316).

8. This point is supported in theory by Christopher Small's work (in which he describes the various genres of African American music as part of a unified

whole—"aspects of the one great and coherent culture"—distinguished more by critics and aficionados than by musicians) and in practice by Ingrid Monson's work (Small 1987, 4; Monson 1996). In *Saying Something* Monson discusses the regularity with which jazz rhythm section players also play gospel, R&B, and rock music. Both Small and Monson note the important continuity of the shuffle groove family across all of these musics, pointing to the relatively subtle differences in accent and the amount of liberty taken with the basic form involved in differentiating the various types of shuffle.

9. The text of HCR 57 is reproduced in *Keeping Time: Readings in Jazz History* (Walser 1999: 332–33).

10. I should say all of *us*, since, as a jazz scholar considering a topic such as this, I am at least implicitly involved in the official canonization of Monk, even as I try to undermine some of the more problematic hegemonies on which that canon has rested.

11. While this level of abstraction is common in music theory, it is by no means the only method of analysis. The work of Benjamin Boretz, Joseph DuBiel, Marion Guck, and Robert Snarrenberg is particularly notable for the ways these writers humanize the study of musical process and reinforce the experiences of listening and performing in their musical analyses.

12. In the past fifteen years there has been a concerted effort among a number of historical musicologists, building conspicuously on the premises of ethnomusicology, poststructuralist and postmodernist literary criticism, and cultural theory, to critique precisely this sort of canon formation. This has led to scholars considering noncanonical works and reconsidering canonical works largely from the perspective of how they become socially meaningful. The best examples of this have often been those informed by feminist theory, notably Susan McClary's *Feminine Endings* (1991) and Craig Monson's *Disembodied Voices* (1995). These works and others like them have affected the discipline of historical musicology substantially, gradually changing the focus from elucidating the canon to understanding the history of music in the West. Still, the Western classical tradition remains the discipline's primary focus, and a history of masterworks remains an important touchstone for the understanding of the whole tradition. In any case, jazz, while important in the development of a historical musicology that is critical of the canon, remains in a difficult position vis-à-vis academic music departments and schools of music, and often progressively minded jazz scholars teach in departments of American studies, history, literature, and so forth.

13. This is a rather complicated proposition, and not one that I can really assess here in the detail it deserves. For more information, see DeVeaux 1995.

14. Jazz recordings often manage to have a longevity not found in most other genres, so record companies often reap profit from back catalogue sales. As a re-

sult, royalties may be an important source of income for some musicians, although they may be a long time in coming. Whether this will be true for recordings made in the 1980s and 1990s remains to be seen.

CHAPTER 6

1. I have chosen to present this and subsequent criticisms of one musician by another anonymously, because no purpose is served by revealing the identity of the speaker.

2. T.S. Monk's description of this event has some qualities of folklore. The specifics of the story change slightly from interview to interview, but the central core remains the same (see Mattingly 1994, 86). In any case, T.S.'s reasoning for taking a contract at Blue Note as described in Richards's interview rings true. It resonates with T.S.'s avowed interest in bringing a pop/rock marketing savvy to jazz and reflects the same sorts of concerns that occupied him with the later *Monk on Monk* project.

3. In *The Lydian Chromatic Concept of Tonal Organization,* George Russell refers to this approach to soloing as "ingoing horizontal melody" construction (Russell 1959, xviii).

4. It is not exactly clear what Monk means by *archival* here, since Monk senior seldom performed with a sextet. The implication is that T.S. Monk sees the activity of arrangement as entirely subsidiary to that of composition.

5. Sickler is in his fifties and has been professionally involved with music, principally as a publisher, since he moved to New York as a young man. He spent a number of years after graduating from the Manhattan School of Music as a working musician, "taking Broadway gigs and all the other stuff you have to do to make it as a struggling musician in New York if you don't know anybody" (Sickler 1999). At some point he became tired of that life and got involved with the music business. He eventually established himself within the jazz community as a successful publisher, concert promoter, and record producer under the auspices of his company, Second Floor Music.

6. The uneasy relationship between art and commerce in the history of jazz is, naturally, a huge topic. For a compelling analysis of its many twists and turns, see Porter 2002.

7. I am referring here to the modern attempts to play the Western classical music of the past in a way that rejects nineteenth-century practices in favor of ones informed by historical investigation of earlier performance practices. This is an internally varied movement, and one that has changed significantly over the course of its history, and thus any generalizations about it will necessarily involve some amount of misrepresentation.

8. In his dissertation "Specters of Jazz," Dale Chapman dedicates an interesting chapter to considering the jazz repertory movement in precisely this light, as

"early music." He argues that there are, in fact, two distinct approaches to jazz repertory, one that he casts as basically a fruitful avenue for further exploration in jazz and the other as something like the rattling death cough of jazz's most significant and enduring spirit. As he sees it, the distinction is represented by, on the one hand, repertory ensembles such as the Mingus Big Band, which is dedicated to exploring the further possibilities for performance suggested by Mingus's work, and, on the other hand, groups such as the Smithsonian Jazz Masterworks Orchestra, which advocate the re-creation of historical recordings, including the originally improvised solos, as precisely as possible. Chapman's distinction is useful in theory, as is his discussion of the consequences of such thinking for the jazz community, but it is not particularly applicable beyond the particular examples he chooses because he neglects to account for the complexity and historical depth of both discourse and practice with regard to "historical authenticity" in jazz. The primary problem is that he never discusses the fact that discourse and practice do not always, or perhaps even generally, match up for repertory jazz. Having neglected to talk with musicians involved in repertory jazz, Chapman never presents a detailed picture of how that one way of playing fits into the larger picture of their musical lives. Moreover, he fails to account for the fact that repertory groups' invocations of authenticity may be marketing strategies. Finally, Chapman reiterates a problem found elsewhere, notoriously in Lydia Goehr's work (as discussed in Solis 2004), that before the repertory movement jazz had no indigenous concept of musical works (Chapman 2003, 141–44). Chapman is right to argue that changing notions of the musical work are significant in the meaning and impact of the repertory movement, but any serious discussion of this must take into account the fact that there was some concept of musical "things" in jazz almost from the very beginning, even if this concept was not the same as that found in the Western classical tradition.

9. For more on this aspect of the HPP movement, see John Butt, *Playing with History: The historical Approach to Musical Performance*, especially chapter 6 (2002, 165–217), and Kay Kaufman Shelemay, "Toward an Ethnomusicology of the Early Music Movement: Thoughts on Bridging Disciplines and Musical Worlds" (2001).

CHAPTER 7

1. In my own fieldwork experience it was uncommon that musicians would describe their own playing with the sorts of stylistic markers critics commonly use, such as "avant-garde," "traditional," or "neoclassical." More commonly, they either simply used an unmarked term, like "jazz," to describe their music, or they substituted a more evocative term like "radical" or "revolutionary." This is supported by Ingrid Monson's ethnographic work, which destabilizes the rigid distinctions these labels attempt to bolster by noting the fluency most jazz musicians have with multiple genres of African American music (1995, 195–99).

2. Mingus was, paradoxically, a notoriously dictatorial leader who let his side-men know, often in cruel terms, the extent of his power as leader. For more on this paradox, see Scott Saul's *Freedom Is, Freedom Ain't* (2003).

3. Leff's idea that Beethoven would not have access to the power centers of classical music today is also very interesting. This is a fairly common discursive strategy used to legitimate aesthetic radicalism in the present through appeals to the past (i.e., Beethoven = Monk = Ornette Coleman = radical innovation). It is predicated on a point of view that equates avant-gardism with earlier innovation by ignoring the relationships between the various kinds of innovation and their cultural milieus. It also allows for a subversive appropriation of the cultural capital of classical music (as distinct from classical music's institutional culture), but nonetheless relies on the salience of that capital for its effect.

CHAPTER 8

1. It is interesting to note here the inadequacy of the term "text" as a shorthand for describing the conceptually prior aspects of a piece of music. What we would think of as the text of a composition—that is, its notation—is not ontologically similar to the notation, the text, of a literary work. There is no musical term that performs the same task.

2. Pianist Fred Hersch, who shares some similar aesthetic grounds with Lacy, emphasized this point as well, as did Bobby Porcelli, despite the significantly different aesthetic terms in which he describes himself. Porcelli is a bebop-oriented alto player of Lacy's generation who has played extensively in Latin jazz contexts with Machito, Mongo Santamaria, Tito Puente, and others. Through-out the 1990s he played in a straight-ahead, hard-bop context with the T.S. Monk sextet. "I pride myself," he told me, "in the fact that I have never learned a tune from sheet music" (Porcelli 1999). Porcelli is a humble man, almost self-effacing in conversation, which made this statement all the more striking.

3. See Ingrid Monson (1995, 398, 403–4).

4. Ingrid Monson, in her work in progress, makes the point that although Jones and others generally correlated political radicalism with the jazz avant-garde, musicians from the hard-bop mainstream were more visibly involved with actual political practice in the 1960s, particularly in the practice of donat-ing their services to civil rights organizations for fundraisers (Monson forth-coming, chapter 6). Interestingly, this point has largely gone unnoticed in other jazz histories.

5. Huyssen provides a summary of modernist aesthetics in *After the Great Di-vide* that, for all its brevity, is a good starting point. Modernist aesthetics are char-acterized by autonomy of the work of art, self-referentiality, experimentalism, the expression of purely individual rather than collective subjectivity, scientistic dis-course, formalism and its concomitant abstraction, and an extreme distancing from entertainment value.

6. Although India is not part of the African diaspora, it has been seen as a kindred nation by African nationalists in the United States since the 1960s, and it has had explicit ties to postcolonial African nations through its status as a nonaligned or third world nation. For a discussion of the significance of this history for jazz musicians in the 1960s, see Ingrid Monson's article "Oh Freedom: George Russell, John Coltrane, and Modal Jazz" (1998, 157–63).

7. For more on the State Department–sponsored tours, see Monson (forthcoming, chapter 3) and Penny Von Eschen (1997).

BIBLIOGRAPHY

WRITTEN WORKS

Agawu, Kofi. 2003. *Representing African Music*. New York and London: Routledge.

Ake, David. 2002. *Jazz Cultures*. Berkeley: University of California Press.

Anderson, Iain. 2002. "Jazz Outside the Marketplace: Free Improvisation and Nonprofit Sponsorship of the Arts, 1965–1980." *American Music* 20, no. 2 (Summer): 131–67.

Anderson, Paul Allen. 2001. *Deep River: Music and Memory in Harlem Renaissance Thought*. Durham, N.C.: Duke University Press.

Arom, Simha. 1991. *African Polyphony and Polyrhythm: Musical Structure and Methodology*. Cambridge: Cambridge University Press.

Asante, Molefi Kete. 1998. *The Afrocentric Idea*, rev. ed. Philadelphia: Temple University Press.

Averill, Gage. 1997. *A Day for the Hunter, A Day for the Prey: Popular Music and Power in Haiti*. Chicago: University of Chicago Press.

Bacon, Paul. 1949. "The High Priest of Be-bop: The Inimitable Mr. Monk." *The Record Changer* 3, no. 4: 9–11.

Baker, Houston A., Jr. 1984. *Blues, Ideology, and Afro-American Literature: A Vernacular Theory*. Chicago: University of Chicago Press.

———. 1987. *Modernism and the Harlem Renaissance*. Chicago: University of Chicago Press.

Bakhtin, M. Mikhail. 1981. *The Dialogic Imagination: Four Essays*. Ed. Michael Holquist, trans. Caryl Emerson and Michael Holquist. Austin: University of Texas Press.

———. 1986. *Speech Games and Other Late Essays*. Ed. Michael Holquist and Caryl Emerson, trans. Vern W. McGee. Austin: University of Texas Press.

Baraka, Imamu Amiri [LeRoi Jones]. 1967. *Black Music*. New York: William Morrow.

———. 2002 [1963]. *Blues People: Negro Music in White America*. New York: Perennial.

Baudrillard, Jean. 1983. *Simulations*. Trans. and ed. Paul Foss, Paul Patton, and Philip Beitchman. New York: Semiotext(e).

Bayles, Martha. 1996. *Hole in Our Soul: The Loss of Beauty and Meaning in American Popular Music*. Chicago: University of Chicago Press.

Berliner, Paul. 1994. *Thinking in Jazz: The Infinite Art of Improvisation*. Chicago Studies in Ethnomusicology, ed. Philip V. Bohlman and Bruno Nettl. Chicago and London: University of Chicago Press.

Birnbaum, Larry. 1996. "Marcus Roberts: Tackling Gershwin." *Down Beat* 63, no. 7 (July): 18ff.

Block, Steven. 1997. " 'Bemsha Swing': The Transformation of a Bebop Classic to Free Jazz." *Music Theory Spectrum* 19, no. 2 (Autumn): 206–31.

Bloom, Harold. 1973. *The Anxiety of Influence: A Theory of Poetry*. Oxford: Oxford University Press.

Bogle, Donald. 1994. *Toms, Coons, Mulattoes, Mammies, and Bucks: An Interpretive History of Blacks in American Films*. New York: Continuum.

Booth, Philip. 1990. "Marcus Roberts: Deep in the Groove." *Down Beat* 57, no. 4 (April): 20–21.

Bourdieu, Pierre. 1977. *Outline of a Theory of Practice*. Trans. Richard Nice. Cambridge and New York: Cambridge University Press.

———. 1984. *Distinction: A Social Critique of the Judgment of Taste*. Trans. Richard Nice. Cambridge, Mass.: Harvard University Press.

Boym, Svetlana. 2001. *The Future of Nostalgia*. New York: Basic Books.

Brown, Frank L. 1958. "Thelonious Monk: More Man Than Myth, Monk Has Emerged from the Shadows." *Down Beat* 25, no. 22 (October): 13–15.

Butt, John. 2002. *Playing with History: The Historical Approach to Musical Performance*. Cambridge: Cambridge University Press.

Chapman, Dale. 2003. "Specters of Jazz: Style, Ideology, and Jazz as Postmodern Practice." PhD diss., University of California, Los Angeles.

Chernoff, John Miller. 1979. *African Rhythm and African Sensibility: Aesthetics and Social Action in African Musical Idioms*. Chicago: University of Chicago Press.

Confino, Alon. 1997. "Collective Memory and Cultural History: Problems of Method." *American Historical Review* 102, no. 5 (December): 1386–1403.

Connerton, Paul. 1989. *How Societies Remember*. New York: Cambridge University Press.

Crouch, Stanley. 1999. Liner notes, *Standard Time, Volume 4: Marsalis Plays Monk*. Columbia 67503.

Davis, Miles, with Quincy Troupe. 1989. *Miles: The Autobiography.* New York: Simon and Schuster.

De Certeau, Michel. 1984. *The Practice of Everyday Life.* Trans. Steven F. Randall. Berkeley: University of California Press.

Derrida, Jacques. 1976. *Of Grammatology.* Trans. Gayatri Chakravorty Spivak. Baltimore, Md.: Johns Hopkins University Press.

DeVeaux, Scott. 1991. "Constructing the Jazz Tradition: Jazz Historiography." *Black American Literature Forum* 25, no. 3: 525–60.

———. 1997. *The Birth of Bebop: A Social and Musical History.* Berkeley: University of California Press.

———. 1999a. " 'Nice Work If You Can Get It': Thelonious Monk and Popular Song." *Black Music Research Journal* 19, no. 2: 169–86.

———. 1999b. "Who Listens to Jazz?" In *Keeping Time: Readings in Jazz History,* ed. Robert Walser. New York: Oxford University Press.

De Wilde, Laurent. 1997. *Monk.* Trans. Jonathan Dickinson. New York: Marlowe and Co.

Dubiel, Joseph. 1992. "Senses of Sensemaking." *Perspectives of New Music* 30, no. 1: 210–21.

Du Bois, W. E. B. 1966 [1935]. *The Black Reconstruction in America, an Essay Toward a History of the Part Which Black Folk Played in the Attempt to Reconstruct Democracy in America, 1860–1880.* New York: Russell and Russell.

———. 1990. *The Souls of Black Folk.* New York: Vintage Books.

Ellison, Ralph. 1952. *Invisible Man.* New York: Random House.

———. 1995. *Shadow and Act.* New York: Vintage Books.

Elworth, Steven B. 1995. "Jazz in Crisis, 1948–1958: Ideology and Representation." In *Jazz among the Discourses,* ed. Krin Gabbard. Durham, N.C.: Duke University Press.

Erikson, Erik. 1980. *Identity and the Life Cycle.* New York: W. W. Norton and Co.

Erlmann, Veit. 1996. *Nightsong: Performance, Power, and Practice in South Africa.* Chicago: University of Chicago Press.

———. 2000. "Communities of Style: Musical Figures of Black Diasporic Identity." In *The African Diaspora: A Musical Perspective,* ed. Ingrid Monson. New York: Garland Press.

Fabre, Geneviève, and Robert O'Meally, eds. 1994. *History and Memory in African-American Culture.* New York: Oxford University Press.

Farrell, Barry. 1964. "The Loneliest Monk." *Time,* February 28, 84–88.

Feather, Leonard. 1994. "Blindfold Test: Thelonious Monk." *Down Beat* 61, no. 2 (February): 78. Originally published in vol. 33, no. 8 (April 1966): 39.

Feurzeig, David. 1997. "Making the Right Mistakes: James P. Johnson, Thelonious Monk, and the Trickster Aesthetic." DMA diss., Cornell University.

Fitterling, Thomas. 1997. *Thelonious Monk: His Life and Music.* Berkeley, Calif.: Berkeley Hills Books.

Floyd, Samuel, Jr. 1990. "Music in the Harlem Renaissance: An Overview." In *Black Music in the Harlem Renaissance: A Collection of Essays*, ed. Samuel Floyd, Jr. New York: Greenwood Press.

———. 1995. *The Power of Black Music: Interpreting its History from Africa to the United States.* New York: Oxford University Press.

———. 1999. "Ring Shout, Signifyin(g), and Jazz Analysis." In *Keeping Time: Readings in Jazz History*, ed. Robert Walser. New York: Oxford University Press.

Ford, Phil. 2002. "Somewhere/Nowhere: Hipness as an Aesthetic." *The Musical Quarterly* 86, no. 1 (Spring): 49–81.

Foucault, Michel. 1972. *The Archaeology of Knowledge and the Discourse on Language.* Trans. A. M. Sheridan Smith. New York: Pantheon Books.

Fox, Richard G. 1985. *Lions of the Punjab: Culture in the Making.* Berkeley: University of California Press.

———. 1997. "Passage from India." In *Between Resistance and Revolution: Cultural Politics and Social Protest*, ed. Richard G. Fox and Orin Starn. New Brunswick, N.J.: Rutgers University Press.

Gabbard, Krin, ed. 1995a. *Jazz among the Discourses.* Durham, N.C.: Duke University Press.

———. 1995b. *Representing Jazz.* Durham, N.C.: Duke University Press.

———. 1995c. "Introduction: The Jazz Canon and Its Consequences." In *Jazz among the Discourses*, ed. Krin Gabbard. Durham, N.C.: Duke University Press.

Gates, Henry Louis, Jr. 1988. *The Signifying Monkey: A Theory of Afro-American Literary Criticism.* New York: Oxford University Press.

Gaunt, Kyra. 1997a. "The Games That Black Girls Play: Music, Body, and Soul." PhD diss., University of Michigan.

———. 1997b. "Translating Double Dutch to Hip-hop: The Musical Vernacular of Black Girls' Play." In *Language, Rhythm, and Sound: Black Popular Cultures into the Twenty-First Century*, ed. Joseph K. Adjaye and Adrianne R. Andrews. Pittsburgh, Penn.: Pittsburgh University Press.

Gendron, Bernard. 1995. " 'Moldy Figs' and Modernists: Jazz at War (1942–1946)." In *Jazz among the Discourses*, ed. Krin Gabbard. Durham and London: Duke University Press.

Gennari, John. 1991. "Jazz Criticism: Its Development and Ideologies." *Black American Literature Forum* 25, no. 3: 449–523.

———. 2006. *Blowin' Hot and Cool: Jazz and Its Critics.* Chicago: University of Chicago Press.

Gillespie, John Birks "Dizzy." 1979. *To Be, Or Not . . . to Bop: Memoirs.* Garden City, N.Y.: Doubleday.

Gilroy, Paul. 1993 *The Black Atlantic: Modernity and Double Consciousness.* Cambridge, Mass.: Harvard University Press.

Gioia, Ted. 1997. *The History of Jazz.* New York: Oxford University Press.

Gitler, Ira. 1957. "Ira Gitler Interviews Thelonious Monk." *Metronome* 74 (March): 19ff.

———. 1964. "Randy Weston: One of jazz's most gifted composer-pianists relates his development and influences." *Down Beat* 31, no. 6 (February), 16ff.

Goffman, Erving. 1959. *The Presentation of Self in Everyday Life.* Garden City, N.Y.: Doubleday and Co.

———. 1974. *Frame Analysis: An Essay on the Organization of Experience.* Cambridge, Mass.: Harvard University Press.

Goldberg, Joe. 1976. "Records: Thelonious Monk, *The Complete Genius.*" *Creem* 8 (November): 59–60.

Gourse, Leslie. 1997. *Straight, No Chaser: The Life and Genius of Thelonious Monk.* New York: Schirmer Books.

Gramsci, Antonio. 1971. *Selections from the Prison Notebooks of Antonio Gramsci.* Ed. and trans. Quentin Hoare and Geoffrey Nowell Smith. New York: International Publishers.

Gridley, Mark C. 2000. *Jazz Styles: History and Analysis.* 7th ed. Englewood Cliffs, N.J.: Prentice Hall.

Griggs, Georgia. 1967. "With Randy Weston in Africa." *Down Beat* 34, no. 14 (July): 16ff.

Guilbault, Jocelyne. 1993. *Zouk: World Music in the West Indies.* Chicago: University of Chicago Press.

Halbwachs, Maurice. 1992. *On Collective Memory.* Ed. and trans. Lewis A. Coser. Chicago: University of Chicago Press.

Hale, Thomas. 1998. *Griots and Griottes: Masters of Words and Music.* Bloomington, Ind.: Indiana University Press.

Hamm, Charles. 1995. *Putting Popular Music in its Place.* Cambridge: Cambridge University Press.

Hawes, Pat. 1995. "Jessica Williams." *Jazz Journal International* 48 (August): 6–8.

Haywood, Mark S. 1994–95. "Rhythmic Readings in Thelonious Monk." *Annual Review of Jazz Studies* 7: 25–45.

Hegel, Georg Wilhelm Friedrich. 1956. *The Philosophy of History.* Trans. J. Sibree. New York: Dover Publications.

Hentoff, Nat. 1956. "Just Call Him Thelonious." *Down Beat* 23, no. 15 (July): 15–16.

———. 1960. "The Private World of Thelonious Monk" *Esquire*, April, 133–37.

Hoefer, George. 1951. "Reviews: Nice Work If You Can Get It/April in Paris." *Down Beat* 18, no. 8 (April): 15.

Hopkins, John, and Bob Houston. 1965. "Archie Shepp: 'We Can't Let the Audience Escape.'" *Melody Maker* 40 (August 7).

Hutton, Patrick. 1993. *History as an Art of Memory.* Hanover, N.H.: University of Vermont Press.

Huyssen, Andreas. 1986. *After the Great Divide: Modernism, Mass Culture, Postmodernism.* Bloomington, Ind.: Indiana University Press.

"Interpretations of Monk Concert Postponed Until the Fall Due to Insufficient Funds: Individual Monkophiles' Assistance Necessary." 1981. Press release held by the Institute for Jazz Studies archive, Rutgers University, Newark, N.J., in the Thelonious Monk 1980–81 file folder.

Ivy, Marilyn. 1995. *Discourses of the Vanishing: Modernity, Phantasm, Japan.* Chicago: University of Chicago Press.

Jackson, Travis. 1998. "Performance and Musical Meaning: Analyzing Jazz on the New York Scene." PhD diss., Columbia University.

———. 2000. "Jazz Performance as Ritual: The Blues Aesthetic and the African Diaspora." In *The African Diaspora: A Musical Perspective,* ed. Ingrid Monson. New York: Garland Press.

James, C. L. R. 1963. *The Black Jacobins: Toussaint L'Overture and the San Domingo Revolution.* 2nd, revised ed. New York: Vintage Books.

Jeske, Lee. 1982. "Caught: Interpretations of a Monk." *Down Beat* 49, no. 2 (February): 57.

Johnson, Martin. 1990. "Three Portraits." *Pulse!,* November, 55ff.

Kammen, Michael. 2000. "Carl Becker Redivivus: Or, Is Everyone Really a Historian?" *History and Theory* 39, no. 2 (May): 230–42.

Keil, Charles. 1966. *Urban Blues.* Chicago: University of Chicago Press.

Kelley, Robin D. G. 1999. "New Monastery: Thelonious Monk and the Jazz Avant-Garde, 1957–1966." *Black Music Research Journal* 19, no. 2: 135–68.

Kernfeld, Barry. 1981. "Adderley, Coltrane, and Davis at the Twilight of Bebop: The Search for Melodic Coherence (1958–59)." PhD diss., Cornell University.

———, ed. 1988. *The New Grove Dictionary of Jazz.* London: Macmillan; New York: Grove's Dictionaries of Music.

———. 1995. *What to Listen for in Jazz.* New Haven, Conn.: Yale University Press.

Koch, Lawrence O. 1983. "Thelonious Monk: Compositional Techniques." *Annual Review of Jazz Studies* 2: 67–80.

Koransky, Jason. 1998. "Now Was the Time: *Down Beat* 63rd Annual Reader's Poll Jazz Album of the Year: T. S. Monk." *Down Beat* 65, no. 12 (December): 26–32.

Kramer, Lawrence. 1990. *Music as Cultural Practice, 1800–1900.* Berkeley: University of California Press.

———. 2001. *Musical Meaning: Toward a Critical History.* Berkeley: University of California Press.

Kundera, Milan. 1988. *The Art of the Novel.* Trans. Linda Asher. New York: Grove Press.

———. 1995. *Testaments Betrayed: An Essay in Nine Parts.* Trans. Linda Asher. New York: Harper Collins Publishers.

Kurzdorfer, James. 1996. "Outrageous Clusters: Dissonant Semitonal Cells in the Music of Thelonious Monk." *Annual Review of Jazz Studies* 8: 181–201.

Lacy, Steve. 1994a. *Findings: My Experience with the Soprano Saxophone.* Paris: CMOP/Outre Mesure.

Lapham, Lewis H. 1964. "Monk: High Priest of Jazz." *Saturday Evening Post* 237 (April 11): 70ff.

Larson, Steven. 1987. "Schenkerian Analysis of Modern Jazz." PhD diss., University of Michigan.

LeGoff, Jacques. 1992. *History and Memory.* Trans. Steven Rendall and Elizabeth Claman. New York: Columbia University Press.

Levin, Mike. 1949. "Reviews: Misterioso/Humph." *Down Beat* 16, no. 11 (June): 14.

Lewis, J. Lowell. 1992. *Ring of Liberation: Deceptive Discourse in Brazilian Capoeira.* Chicago: University of Chicago Press.

Lott, Eric. 1995. "Double V, Double-Time: Bebop's Politics of Style." In *Jazz among the Discourses,* ed. Krin Gabbard. Durham, N.C.: Duke University Press.

Mailer, Norman. 1957. "The White Negro: Superficial Reflections on the Hipster." *Dissent* 4.

Mandel, Howard. 1991. Liner notes, *Thelonious Sphere Monk: Dreaming of the Masters, Volume 2.* DIW/Columbia CK 48962.

———. 1994. "Me and Mr. Jones." *Down Beat* 61, no. 1 (January): 16ff.

Martin, Mel. 1986. "Stan Getz." *Saxophone Journal* 10, no. 4 (Winter): 27–33.

Mattingly, Rick. 1994. "T.S. Monk: The Son Comes Out." *Modern Drummer* 18: 26ff.

Maultsby, Portia. 1996. "Music in African American Culture." In *Mediated Messages and African-American Culture: Contemporary Issues,* ed. Venise T. Berry and Carmen L. Manning-Miller. Thousand Oaks, Calif.: Sage Publications.

McClary, Susan. 1991. *Feminine Endings: Music, Gender, and Sexuality.* Minneapolis, Minn.: University of Minnesota Press.

McKinney, Jack. 1959. "Giants in Jazz: Thelonious Monk." *Metronome* 76, no. 1: 21ff.

Milkowski, Bill. 2000. "One Future—Two Views." *Jazz Times* 30 (March): 30ff.

Monson, Craig. 1995. *Disembodied Voices: Music and Culture in an Early Modern Italian Convent.* Berkeley, Calif.: University of California Press.

Monson, Ingrid. 1994. "Doubleness and Jazz Improvisation: Irony, Parody, and Ethnomusicology." *Critical Inquiry* 20, no. 2: 283–313.

———. 1995. "The Problem with White Hipness: Race, Gender, and Cultural Conceptions in Jazz Historical Discourse." *JAMS* 48, no. 3: 396–422.

———. 1996. *Saying Something: Jazz Improvisation and Interaction.* Chicago Studies in Ethnomusicology, ed. Philip V. Bohlman and Bruno Nettl. Chicago: University of Chicago Press.

————. 1998. "Oh Freedom: George Russell, John Coltrane, and Modal Jazz." In *In the Course of Performance: Studies in the World of Musical Improvisation*, ed. Bruno Nettl and Melinda Russell. Chicago: University of Chicago Press.

————. 1999. "Riffs, Repetition, and Theories of Globalization." *Ethnomusicology* 43, no. 1: 31–65.

————. 2000. *The African Diaspora: A Musical Perspective.* New York: Garland Press.

————. Forthcoming. *Freedom Sounds: Jazz, Civil Rights, and Africa, 1950–67.* Oxford: Oxford University Press.

Morgan, Paula. 1988. "Williams, Martin (Tudor Hansford)." *New Grove Dictionary of Jazz*, ed. Barry Kernfeld. London: Macmillan.

Morrison, Toni. 1972. *The Bluest Eye.* New York: Pocket Books.

Muller, Carol. 1999. *Rituals of Fertility and the Sacrifice of Desire: Nazarite Women's Performance in South Africa.* Chicago: University of Chicago Press.

Murphy, John. 1990. "Jazz Improvisation: The Joy of Influence." *The Black Perspective in Music* 18, nos. 1–2: 7–19.

Nettl, Bruno. 1974. "Thoughts on Improvisation: A Comparative Approach." *The Musical Quarterly* 60, no. 1: 1–19.

————. 1995. *Heartland Excursions: Ethnomusicological Reflections on Schools of Music.* Urbana, Ill.: University of Illinois Press.

Nora, Pierre. 1996–98. *Realms of Memory: Rethinking the French Past.* Trans. Arthur Goldhammer. New York: Columbia University Press.

Owens, Thomas. 1974. "Charles Parker: Techniques of Improvisation." PhD diss., University of California, Los Angeles.

Peretti, Burton. 1995. "Oral Histories of Jazz Musicians: The NEA Transcripts as Texts in Context." In *Jazz among the Discourses*, ed. Krin Gabbard. Durham, N.C.: Duke University Press.

Porter, Eric. 2002. *What Is This Thing Called Jazz? African American Musicians as Artists, Critics, and Activists.* Berkeley: University of California Press.

Porter, Lewis. 1998. *John Coltrane: His Life and Music.* Ann Arbor: University of Michigan Press.

Postif, François. 1963. " 'Round 'bout Sphere." *Jazz Hot* 186 (April): 39.

Potter, Jeff. 1988. "Riley, Ben(jamin A.)" In *The New Grove Dictionary of Jazz*, vol. 2, ed. Barry Kernfeld. London: Macmillan.

Radano, Ronald. 2000. "Hot Fantasies: American Modernism and the Idea of Black Rhythm." In *Music and the Racial Imagination*, ed. Ronald Radano and Philip V. Bohlman. Chicago: University of Chicago Press.

Ramsey, Guthrie, Jr. 1994. "The Art of Bebop: Earl 'Bud' Powell and the Emergence of Modern Jazz." PhD diss., University of Michigan.

————. 2003. *Race Music: Black Cultures From Bebop to Hip-Hop.* Berkeley: University of California Press.

Rasula, Jed. 1995. "The Media of Memory: The Seductive Menace of Records in Jazz History." In *Jazz among the Discourses*, ed. Krin Gabbard. Durham, N.C.: Duke University Press.

Redmond, Eugene. 1976. *Drumvoices: The Mission of African American Poetry: A Critical History*. Garden City, N.Y.: Anchor Press.

Rhyan, John. 1988. "Ore, John." In *The New Grove Dictionary of Jazz*, ed. Barry Kernfeld. London: Macmillan.

Richards, Martin. 1994a. "T.S. Monk Jnr: In the Tradition." *Jazz Journal International* 47, no. 5: 10–11.

———. 1994b. "T.S. Monk Jnr: In the Tradition—Part Two." *Jazz Journal International* 47, no. 7: 16–17.

Roberts, John Storm. 1979. *The Latin Tinge: The Impact of Latin American Music on the United States*. New York: Oxford University Press.

Rosenberg, Emily. 2003. *A Date Which Will Live: Pearl Harbor in American Memory*. Durham, N.C.: Duke University Press.

Russell, George. 1959. *The Lydian Chromatic Concept of Tonal Organization*. New York: Concept Publishing.

Said, Edward. 1978. *Orientalism*. New York: Pantheon Books.

Sales, Grover. 1992. *Jazz: America's Classical Music*. New York: Da Capo Press.

Samet, Bruce. 2000. "Misterioso.edu/essay on the true art." http://www.achilles .net/~howardm/mistedu.html.

Saul, Scott. 2003. *Freedom Is, Freedom Ain't: Jazz and the Making of the Sixties*. Cambridge, Mass.: Harvard University Press.

Sawyer, Keith. 1996. "The Semiotics of Improvisation: The Pragmatics of Musical and Verbal Performance." *Semiotica* 108, nos. 3–4: 269–306.

Schuller, Gunther. 1986. *Musings: The Musical Worlds of Gunther Schuller*. New York: Oxford University Press.

———. 1989. *The Swing Era: The Development of Jazz, 1930–1945*. New York: Oxford University Press.

Seig, Matthew. 1991. *Thelonious Monk: American Composer*. BMG Video.

Shelemay, Kay Kaufman. 2001. "Toward an Ethnomusicology of the Early Music Movement: Thoughts on Bridging Disciplines and Musical Worlds." *Ethnomusicology* 45, no. 1 (Winter): 1–29.

Sheridan, Chris. 2001. *Brilliant Corners: A Bio-Discography of Thelonious Monk*. Westport, Conn.: Greenwood Press.

Simon, George. 1948. "Bop's Dixieland to Monk." *Metronome* 64, no. 4 (April): 20, 34–35.

Small, Christopher. 1987. *Music of the Common Tongue: Survival and Celebration in African American Music*. London: John Calder Press.

Solis, Gabriel. 2002. "Hearing Monk: History, Memory, and the Making of a Jazz Giant." *The Musical Quarterly* 86, no. 1 (Spring): 82–116.

———. 2004. " 'A Unique Chunk of Jazz Reality': Authorship, Musical Work

Concepts, and Thelonious Monk's Live Recordings from the Five Spot, 1958."
Ethnomusicology 48, no. 3 (Fall): 315–47.

Spellman, A. B. 1985. *Four Lives in the Bebop Business.* New York: Limelight Books. First published 1966 by Pantheon Books.

Stein, Stephanie. 1991. "Review: Marcus Roberts, *Alone with Three Giants.*" *Down Beat* 58, no. 4 (April): 32.

Stokes, W. Royal. 1986a. "Thelonious Monk's Moving Classics." *Washington Post,* May 14, C13.

———. 1986b. "Monk Center for the Arts: Closer to Reality." *Jazz Times,* December, 8–9.

Such, David. 1993. *Avant-Garde Jazz Musicians: Performing "Out There."* Iowa City: University of Iowa Press.

Sudhalter, Richard. 1999. *Lost Chords: White Musicians and Their Contribution to Jazz, 1915–1945.* New York: Oxford University Press.

Sugarman, Jane. 1997. *Engendering Song: Singing and Subjectivity at Prespa Albanian Weddings.* Chicago: University of Chicago Press.

Szwed, John. 1998. *Space Is the Place: The Lives and Times of Sun Ra.* New York: Da Capo Press.

———. 2002. *So What: The Life of Miles Davis.* New York: Simon and Schuster.

Taruskin, Richard. 1995. *Text and Act: Essays on Music and Performance.* New York: Oxford University Press.

"Thelonious Sphere Monk Cultural Center." N.d. Press release held by the Institute for Jazz Studies archive, Rutgers University, Newark, N.J., in the Monk Center file folder.

Tomlinson, Gary. 1993. *Music in Renaissance Magic: Toward a History of Others.* Chicago: University of Chicago Press.

———. 1999. *Metaphysical Song: An Essay on Opera.* Princeton, N.J.: Princeton University Press.

Treitler, Leo. 1989. *Music and the Historical Imagination.* Cambridge, Mass.: Harvard University Press.

Trouillot, Michel-Rolph. 1995. *Silencing the Past: Power and the Production of History.* Boston, Mass: Beacon Press.

Troupe, Quincy. 1998. "Remembering Thelonious Monk: When the Music Was Happening He'd Get Up and Do His Little Dance." In *The Jazz Cadence of American Culture,* ed. Robert G. O'Meally. New York: Columbia University Press.

Tucker, Mark. 1999. "Mainstreaming Monk: The Ellington Album." *Black Music Research Journal* 19, no. 2: 227–44.

Tucker, Sherrie. 2000. *Swing Shift: "All-Girl" Bands of the 1940s.* Durham, N.C.: Duke University Press.

Turino, Thomas. 1999. "Signs of Imagination, Identity, and Experience: A Peircian Semiotic Theory for Music." *Ethnomusicology* 43, no. 2: 221–55.

————. 2000. *Nationalists, Cosmopolitans, and Popular Music in Zimbabwe.* Chicago: University of Chicago Press.

Von Eschen, Penny. 1997. " 'Satchmo Blows Up the World': Exploding Cold War Racial Ideology." In *Cold War Constructions: The Political Culture of United States Imperialism, 1945–63,* ed. Christian G. Appy. Amherst: University of Massachusetts Press.

Walser, Robert, ed. 1999. *Keeping Time: Readings in Jazz History.* New York: Oxford University Press.

Waters, Charles H., Jr. 1993. "Anatomy of a Cover: The Story of Duke Ellington's Appearance on the Cover of *Time* Magazine." *Annual Review of Jazz Studies* 6: 1–53.

Waxer, Lise. 2002. *The City of Musical Memory: Salsa, Record Grooves, and Popular Culture in Cali, Columbia.* Middletown, Conn.: Wesleyan University Press.

West, Hollie. 1983. "Wynton Marsalis: Blowing His Own Horn, Speaking His Own Mind." *Jazz Times,* July, 10–11.

Westendorf, Lynette. 1994. "Analyzing Free Jazz." DMA diss., University of Washington.

Wheelock, Gretchen. 1992. *Haydn's Ingenious Jesting with Art: Contexts of Musical Wit and Humor.* New York: Schirmer Books.

Whitehead, Kevin. 1989. "Caught: Classical Jazz at Lincoln Center." *Down Beat* 56, no. 11 (November): 51–52.

————. 1990. "Caught: Classical Jazz at Lincoln Center." *Down Beat* 57, no. 11 (November): 58.

Williams, Martin. 1963. "Thelonious Monk: Arrival without Departure." *Saturday Review,* April 13, 32ff.

————. 1985. Letter to T.S. Monk, Jr., January 2. Held by the Institute for Jazz Studies archive, Rutgers University, Newark, N.J., in the Thelonious Monk 1983–89 file folder.

————. 1986. Letter to Dan Morgenstern, April 1. Held by the Institute for Jazz Studies archive, Rutgers University, Newark, N.J., in the Thelonious Monk 1983–89 file folder.

————. 1992. "What Kind of Composer Was Thelonious Monk?" *Musical Quarterly* 76, no. 3: 433–40.

Williams, Raymond. 1977. *Marxism and Literature.* Oxford: Oxford University Press.

Willner, Hal. 1984. Liner notes, *That's the Way I Feel Now: A Tribute to Thelonious Monk.* A&M Records, SP-6600.

Wilson, John S. 1981. "Jazz: Thelonious Monk Performed by 4 Pianists." *New York Times,* November 5, C15.

Wilson, Olly. 1992. "The Heterogeneous Sound Ideal in African-American Music." In *New Perspectives on Music: Essays in Honor of Eileen Southern,* ed. Josephine Wright with Samuel Floyd, Jr. Warren, Mich.: Harmonie Park Press.

Wittner, Gary, and I. Braus. 1994. "T.S. Monk on T.S. Monk." *Coda Magazine* 255 (May–June).

Zabor, Rafi, and Vic Garbarini. 1999 [1985]. "Wynton vs. Herbie: The Purist and the Crossbreeder Duke It Out." In *Keeping Time: Readings in Jazz History,* ed. Robert Walser. New York: Oxford University Press.

Zak, Albin. 2001. *The Poetics of Rock.* Berkeley: University of California Press.

Zwerin, Charlotte. 1988. *Thelonious Monk: Straight, No Chaser.* Burbank, Calif.: Warner Home Video.

INTERVIEWS BY THE AUTHOR

Drew, Kenny, Jr. 1999. New York, July 16.

Hersch, Fred. 1999. New York, August 10.

Lacy, Steve. 1999a. New York, August 4.

Lovano, Joe. 1999. New York, June 8.

Monk, T.S. 1999. South Orange, N.J., August 13.

Peretti, Burton. 1999. St. Louis, Mo., March 12.

Porcelli, Bobby. 1999. New York, July 13.

Riley, Ben. 1999. St. Louis, Mo., February 25.

Rudd, Roswell. 1999. Accord, N.Y., August 18.

Sickler, Don. 1999. New York, August 5.

Weiss, Michael. 1999. Brooklyn, N.Y., January 5.

Weston, Randy. 1999. New York, August 21.

Williams, Jessica. 1999a. By telephone. October 14.

DISCOGRAPHY

Art Ensemble of Chicago. 1991. *Dreaming of the Masters, Volume 2: Thelonious Sphere Monk.* DIW/Columbia CK 48962.

Davis, Miles. 1987a. *Bags' Groove.* Prestige 7109.

———. 1987b. *'Round About Midnight.* Columbia CK 40610.

Hersch, Fred. 1998. *Thelonious: Fred Hersch Plays Monk.* Nonesuch 79456-2.

Lacy, Steve. 1990. *Reflections: Steve Lacy Plays Thelonious Monk.* New Jazz Records OJCCD 063-2.

———. 1994b. *School Days.* Hat Hut ART CD 6140.

———. 1999b. *Monk's Dream.* Verve France 314 543090-2.

Marsalis, Wynton. 1999. *Standard Time, Volume 4: Marsalis Plays Monk.* Columbia 67503.

Monk, Thelonious. 1959. *The Thelonious Monk Orchestra at Town Hall.* Riverside RLP 12-300.

———. 1971. *The London Collection, Volume Two.* Black Lion BLcd 760116.

———. 1982. *Thelonious Monk.* Prestige OJCCD-010-2.

———. 1986. *The Complete Riverside Recordings.* Riverside RCD 022-2.

———. 1993. *Criss Cross.* Columbia 48823.

———. 1994. *The Complete Blue Note Recordings.* Blue Note D 207178.

Monk, T.S. 1997. *Monk on Monk.* N2KE-10017 Enhanced CD with CD-ROM. New York: N2K Encoded Music.

Perez, Danilo. 1996. *PanaMonk.* Impulse IMPD-190.

Roberts, Marcus. 1991. *Alone with Three Giants.* Novus/RCA 3109-2-N.

Rollins, Sonny. 1957. *Sonny Rollins, Volume 2.* Blue Note B21Y-81558.

Rudd, Roswell. 1983. *Regeneration.* Soul Note 121 054-2.

Shaw, Woody. 1997. *Bemsha Swing.* Blue Note CDP 7243 8 290029 2 8.

Tatum, Art. 1991. *The Complete Solo Masterpieces.* Pablo PACD 4404-2.

Various artists. 1984. *That's the Way I Feel Now: A Tribute to Thelonious Monk.* A&M Records, SP-6600.

Williams, Jessica. 1999b. *In the Key of Monk: Jessica Williams Pays Tribute to Thelonious Monk.* Jazz Focus JFCD029.

INDEX

Page numbers in italics indicate musical examples.

Abdul-Malik, Ahmed, 116, *197*
Abrams, Muhal Richard, 63
Africentrism, 196, 197, 199
Afro-Modernism, 31, 49
Ake, David, 130–31, 152
Allen, Geri, 135–36, 143
Alone with Three Giants (Roberts), 148–50
"America's classical music," 26
Amram, David, 138–39
anti-anti-essentialism, 200
Anxiety of Influence (Bloom), 77–78
"April in Paris" (Duke), 24
Arkestra, 161
art, as discourse, 120
Art Ensemble of Chicago, 160, 169–82
authenticity, 140, 146, 153–54; early music movement and, 35
authorial voice, Monk's, 66, 70
authorship, of musical works, 69–70
avant-garde art, 118–19
avant-gardism, 191–92; jazz and, 194–95
Ayler, Albert, 174, 181
"Azure" (Ellington), 182

Bacon, Paul, 52, 53, 55
"Bags' Groove" (Jackson), 40–41, *42–44*, *44–45*
Baker, Houston, 31
Bakhtin, Mikhail: *Dialogic Imagination*, 5, 78–79; *Speech Genres*, 13
Baraka, Amiri, 161; *Blues People*, 31; "Interpretations of Monk" concert and, 63, 111
Baudrillard, Jean, 7; simulacra, 7
bebop, 22, 113, 118
Beethoven Society of America, 138–39
Bemkey, Andrew, 165–66, 170
Bemsha Swing (Shaw), 135–36
Benitez, Jon, 65
Berliner, Paul: *Thinking in Jazz*, 3, 12, 68, 135
Black Lion (record label), 26
Blakey, Art, 23; as Monk accompanist, 57
Blue Note (record label), 1, 23, 141
"Blue Skies" (Berlin), 149
blues, 152; form of, 69
Bluest Eye (Morrison), masculinity in, 55
body, the: music and, 33

bean music, compared, 84; music of, and traditional jazz, compared, 72, 84; music of, subversion of tonal harmony, 116–17; musical style of, 1; "Nice Work If You Can Get It" and, 24; orchestral pianism and, 45; and Charlie Parker, compared, 166; racism and, 30; rhythm sections and, 35–38, 122–23; solos, approach to endings of, 44–45; on *Time* magazine cover, 2, 25; Town Hall concert, 28; viewed as child by critics, 55; and Anton Webern, compared, 202

Monk, Thelonious, recordings by: *Criss-Cross,* 37; *Genius of Modern Music,* 23; *Monk's Music,* 25, 52, 143; *Solo Monk,* 5, 45; *Thelonious Alone in San Francisco,* 52, 92; *Thelonious Monk,* 57; *Underground,* 26

Monk, Thelonious, works by: "Ask Me Now," 29, 57, 105; "Bemsha Swing," 182; "Blue Monk," 57–59, *58;* "Blues Five Spot," 57; "Bolivar Ba-Lues-Are," 46, 57, 128; "Boo Boo's Birthday," 143; "Bright Mississippi," 65, 92; "Crepuscle with Nellie," 143; "Epistrophy," 129; "Eronel," 37; "Evidence," 117, 129; "Gallop's Gallop," 63, 104; "Humph," 23; "I Mean You," 47–48, 96, *97,* 98, 128, *128;* "In Walked Bud," 59, 149; "Let's Cool One," 24; "Little Rootie Tootie," 28, 39, 143; "Misterioso," 23, 41, 58, 111, 130, 164; "Monk's Mood," 39, 87, 128, 151; "Nutty," 170; "Pannonica," 39; "Reflections," 87–92, *89, 90, 91;* "Rhythm-a-ning," 128; "'Round Midnight," 65, 104–5, 169–82, *172, 173, 175–76, 178, 180–81;* "Ruby, My Dear," 39, 115–17, 142–46, *144, 145;* "Skippy," 24; "Stuffy Turkey," 26; "Thelonious," 23, 151; "Trinkle Tinkle," 59; "Work," 93–94

Monk, T.S., 32, 137–38, 143, 146; and father, relationship with, 137; "Interpretations of Monk" concert and, 111; on Steve Lacy, 191; on sense of time, Monk's, 35–36

Monk on Monk (T.S. Monk), 140–42, 146–48

Monson, Ingrid, 5, 12; ethnography and, 13; *Saying Something,* 3

Morgenstern, Dan, 111–12

Morrison, Toni, 55

Morton, Jelly Roll, 195

movement, physical: as carrier of meaning, 92–93, 94

Murphy, John, 131

music: analysis of, 11, 68, 127–28, 214n11; politics and, 6–7, 114, 196

music, form of: as abstraction, 39; cyclical and linear, 65–66; in improvised performance, 39–46; large-scale, in jazz, 46; narrative and, 45; of song, Monk's approach to, 47–49

music, quotations of: by Dizzy Gillespie, in "Ool-Ya-Koo," 52; by Roscoe Mitchell, in "'Round Midnight," 177; by Monk, in "Bags' Groove," 41; by Monk, in "Blue Monk," 57–59, *58;* by Monk, in "Rhythm-a-ning," 59; by Monk, in "Trinkle Tinkle," 59

musical reference. *See* intermusicality

musicking, 12

musicology, 68, 208n4

neo-bop, 156

neo-clacissism, in jazz, 125

new criticism, 119

new musicology, 12, 68, 213n4

New Orleans jazz, 113

New Thing, 160

New York Times, 64, 153

Newborn, Phineas, 164

"Nice Work If You Can Get It" (Gershwin), 24

Nora, Pierre, 8–9

O'Meally, Robert, 9

orality, 2

Ore, John, 37

Overton, Hall, 143, 147

Pablo Records, 125

PanaMonk (Perez), 86–87

Parker, Charlie, 1, 22, 118

tension and release, as basis of musical
    form, 39
Thelonious Monk competition, 138
Thelonious Monk Institute of Jazz, 114,
    138–40
Thigpen, Ed, 60
time: flow of, phenomenology of, 31,
    45–46; importance of, in jazz, 32; mu-
    sical interaction and, 32–33
Tin Pan Alley, standards of, 74
Tomlinson, Gary, 12
Tonic (nightclub), 165
Tovey, Donald, 3
tribute albums, 86–87, 141–42, 182
tribute concerts, 63
Trouillot, Michel-Rolph, 31, 79–80
Tucker, Mark, 207n2
Tucker, Sherrie, 7

University of Southern California, 138

Vaché, Warren, 125
Vinnegar, Leroy, 60
vocality, in jazz instrumental technique, 176
voice, as quality in jazz performance, 63,
    70, 71, 136

Waldron, Mal, 63
Watts, Jeff "Tain," 87
Weiss, Michael, 9–10, 75–77
West, Danny Quebec, 23
Weston, Randy, 185, 196–99, 200–
    201; "Brooklyn: African Village,"
    197; *Portraits of Thelonous Monk*,
    198
Williams, Jessica, 101–4; and Fred Hersch,
    compared, 103; influence and, 103–4;
    and Sonny Rollins, 105
Williams, Martin, 111, 119, 121–22, 143,
    213n6; canonization and, 126
Williams, Mel, 70
Williams, Willie, 141
Willner, Hal, 203; *That's the Way I Feel
    Now,* 203–4
Wolff, Francis, 1
World Saxophone Quartet, 11

"You'd Be So Nice To Come Home To"
    (Porter), 182
"Young Lions," 123
Yusef, Malik, 202

Zak, Albin, 207–8n3

Text:	11.5/13.5 Adobe Garamond
Display:	Perpetua, Adobe Garamond
Compositor:	Binghamton Valley Composition
Printer and binder:	Maple-Vail Manufacturing Group